NEOLIBERALISM AND THE POLITICAL ECONOMY OF TOURISM

Tourism has become increasingly shaped by neoliberal policies, yet the consequences of this neoliberalisation are relatively under-explored. This book provides a wide-ranging inquiry into the particular manifestations of different variants of neoliberalism, highlighting its uneven geographical development and the changing dynamics of neoliberal policies in order to explain and evaluate the effects of neoliberal processes on tourism.

Covering a variety of different aspects of neoliberalism and tourism, the chapters investigate how different types of tourism are used as part of more general neoliberalisation agendas, how neoliberalism differs according to the geographic context, the importance of discourse in shaping neoliberal practices and the different approaches of putting the neoliberal ideology into practice. Aiming to initiate debates about the connections between neoliberalism and tourism and advance further research avenues, this book makes a timely contribution which discusses the relationships between markets, nation-states and societies from a social science perspective. Neoliberalism is considered as a political-economic ideology, as variants of the global neoliberal project, as discourse and practices through which neoliberalism is enacted.

Jan Mosedale is Senior Lecturer and Senior Research Fellow at the Institute of Tourism and Leisure of the University of Applied Sciences HTW Chur, Switzerland.

Current Developments in the Geographies of Leisure and Tourism

Series Editors:

Jan Mosedale, University of Applied Sciences HTW Chur, Switzerland and **Caroline Scarles**, University of Surrey, UK in association with the Geographies of Leisure and Tourism Research Group of the Royal Geographical Society (with the Institute of British Geographers).

Tourism and leisure exist within an inherently dynamic, fluid and complex world and are therefore inherently interdisciplinary. Recognising the role of tourism and leisure in advancing debates within the social sciences, this book series is open to contributions from cognate social science disciplines that inform geographical thought about tourism and leisure. Produced in association with the Geographies of Leisure and Tourism Research Group of the Royal Geographical Society (with the Institute of British Geographers), this series highlights and promotes cutting-edge developments and research in this field. Contributions are of a high international standard and provide theoretically-informed empirical content to facilitate the development of new research agendas in the field of tourism and leisure research. In general, the series seeks to promote academic contributions that advance contemporary debates that challenge and stimulate further discussion and research both within the fields of tourism and leisure and the wider realms of the social sciences.

Neoliberalism and the Political Economy of Tourism

Edited by
JAN MOSEDALE

Routledge
Taylor & Francis Group

LONDON AND NEW YORK

First published 2016
by Routledge
2 Park Square, Milton Park, Abingdon, Oxon OX14 4RN

and by Routledge
605 Third Avenue, New York, NY 10017

First issued in paperback 2021

Routledge is an imprint of the Taylor & Francis Group, an informa business

Publisher's Note
The publisher has gone to great lengths to ensure the quality of this reprint but points out that some imperfections in the original copies may be apparent.

British Library Cataloguing in Publication Data
A catalogue record for this book is available from the British Library

Library of Congress Cataloging-in-Publication Data
Names: Mosedale, Jan, editor of compilation.
Title: Neoliberalism and the political economy of tourism / edited by
    Jan Mosedale.
Description: Farnham, Surrey, UK ; Burlington, VT : Ashgate, 2016. |
    Series: Current developments in the geographies of leisure and
    tourism | Includes bibliographical references and index.
Identifiers: LCCN 2015041464 (print) | LCCN 2015049354 (ebook) |
    ISBN 9781472465016 (hardback) | ISBN 9781472465023 (ebook) |
    ISBN 9781472465030 (epub)
Subjects: LCSH: Tourism. | Neoliberalism.
Classification: LCC G155.A1 N423 2016 (print) | LCC G155.A1 (ebook) |
    DDC 338.4/791—dc23
LC record available at http://lccn.loc.gov/2015041464

Typeset in Times New Roman
by Apex CoVantage, LLC

ISBN 13: 978-1-03-224254-5 (pbk)
ISBN 13: 978-1-4724-6501-6 (hbk)

DOI: 10.4324/9781315597782

Contents

Contributors

C. Michael Hall is a Professor in the Department of Management, Marketing and Entrepreneurship, University of Canterbury, New Zealand and a Visiting Professor in Linneaus University, Kalmar, Sweden. A docent in the Department of Geography, University of Oulu, Finland and co-editor of *Current Issues in Tourism*, he has published widely on tourism, regional development and environmental change. Current research includes comparative studies of World Heritage in Germany, Israel, Mauritius and Sweden and farnarkling in Finland.

Kevin Hannam is Professor of Tourism Mobilities at Leeds Metropolitan University, UK and Visiting Senior Research Fellow at the University of Johannesburg, South Africa. With John Urry and Mimi Sheller he is a founding co-editor of the journal *Mobilities*. He is the co-author of the books *Understanding Tourism* (Sage, 2010), *Tourism and India* (Routledge, 2010) and co-editor of *Moral Encounters in Tourism* (Ashgate, 2014) as well as *The Routledge Handbook of Mobilities* (Routledge, 2014).

Dimitri Ioannides is Professor of Human Geography in the Department of Tourism Studies and Geography at Mid-Sweden University and Senior Fellow at Missouri State University, USA. His research interests include, among others, tourism and sustainable development, the equity dimension of sustainability, and particular the rights of low-level workers in the tourism sector. He has published articles and book chapters relating to the economic geography of tourism. He is series editor for *New Directions in Tourism Analysis* (Ashgate).

Lynn Minnaert is Assistant Professor at the Preston Robert Tisch Center for Hospitality and Tourism at New York University, USA. Her main research interest is social inclusion in tourism (social tourism) and events (the Olympic Games and business events). Lynn has published widely on social tourism and has conducted research in this field in different countries (UK, Belgium, Kazakhstan, Brazil) and with different target groups (disadvantaged families, teenage mothers, women affected by domestic violence).

Jan Mosedale is Senior Lecturer and Senior Research Fellow at the Institute of Tourism and Leisure of the University of Applied Sciences HTW Chur, Switzerland. He is editor of *Political Economy of Tourism: A Critical Perspective* (Routledge, 2011) and series editor of *Current Developments in the Geographies* *of Leisure and Tourism* (Ashgate). Jan is currently Chair of the Geographies of Leisure and Tourism Research Group with the Royal Geographical Society, UK.

Dzingai K. Nyahunzvi is at the Tourism and Hospitality Management Department, Midlands State University, Zimbabwe. He has completed his PhD at the University of Otago, New Zealand on the conservation and development implications of Kruger National Park's commercialization process. He has written on corporate social responsibility, the 2010 FIFA World Cup and tourism livelihoods in Zimbabwe.

Francis Offeh is a Tourism Development Expert and Senior Lecturer at City of London College, UK where he is also course leader of Hospitality Management. He has completed his PhD at the University of Sunderland with a thesis on the commodification of heritage tourism in the Ashanti Kingdom, Ghana.

Evangelia Petridou is a doctoral candidate in Political Science at Mid-Sweden University, Sweden. She received a master in Public Administration (MPA) from Missouri State University. Her research interests include theories of the policy process, political entrepreneurship, and urban governance. Her latest article appeared in the *Policy Studies Journal* and together with Inga Aflaki and Lee Miles she is the co-editor of *Entrepreneurship in Polis: Understanding Political Entrepreneurship* (Ashgate, 2015).

Markus Pillmayer was a research fellow at the Chair of Cultural Geography of the Catholic University of Eichstätt-Ingolstadt, Germany and now works among other things as a lecturer at the Faculty of Tourism of the University of Applied Sciences Munich, Germany. He holds a PhD in Geography and is an expert for internationalization matters, especially in terms of the Arab region. His research interests also include intercultural communications, destination development, tourism policy and especially tourism lobbying.

Maharaj Vijay Reddy is a Principal Lecturer in Tourism at the Bournemouth University, UK. His expertise lies in the fields of sustainable consumption and production, green strategy, CSR, disasters and oceans. He has completed challenging research projects supported by international and national agencies, for example on the Indian and Pacific Ocean coasts following the 2004 Asian and 2011 Japanese tsunamis. Vijay's consultancies resulted in the inscription of natural and cultural properties on the UNESCO List. He has been invited by policy organizations including UN Secretariat, UNEP, UNWTO and UNESCO to comment on sustainability issues.

Nicolai Scherle is Professor of Tourism Management and Intercultural Communication at the Business and Information Technology School Iserlohn, Germany. His research interests in tourism mainly focus on entrepreneurship, intercultural communication and tourism media. Furthermore, he is Fellow of the Royal Geographical Society and serves as a consultant of the Centre of Expertise for Intercultural Communication (FORAREA).

Michael C. Shone is a Lecturer in Tourism and Recreation at Lincoln University, New Zealand. His research interests are centred on tourism public policy and planning, and the role of the public sector in regional tourism development. He is particularly interested in the way in which local government utilizes the tourism sector to promote rural community development objectives, and the way in which this public sector intervention is manifested at the community level. His additional research interests include tourism geographies, destination management and community tourism impacts.

Michael Wearing is a Senior Lecturer in the School of Social Sciences, Faculty of Arts and Social Sciences, University of New South Wales, Sydney, Australia. He completed a PhD in sociology from UNSW whilst a scholar at their Social Policy Research Centre in the 1980s and has gone on to teach and publish in the areas of social policy, sociology and political sociology while employed at Sydney University and the UNSW. He is the author of several books and over 50 refereed publications in the areas of socio-cultural aspects of tourism, community services, social welfare and social policy. His current research interests are in the environment and ecotourism, the politics of welfare rhetoric, change in human service organizations and comparative social policy.

Stephen Wearing is Associate Professor at the University of Technology, Sydney (UTS), Australia. His research is in the area of leisure and tourism studies, with a PhD focused on sustainable forms of tourism. He has taught at a variety of universities in his career, including Wageningen, the Netherlands and Newcastle and Macquarie Universities, Australia. In 2008 he received an Australian National Teaching Award. He is co-author of *International Volunteer Tourism: Integrating Travellers and Communities* (CABI, 2013) and *Social Psychology and Theories of Consumer Culture: A Political Economy Perspective* (Routledge, 2013).

Sandra Wilson is a former student of the Department of Management, University of Canterbury, New Zealand. She had previously attended the University of Otago.

Acknowledgements

The idea for this edited collection has its origins in several sessions organized by the Geographies of Leisure and Tourism Research Group (GLTRG) of the Royal Geographical Society with IBG. It is therefore only appropriate that it has been published in the *Current Developments in the Geographies of Leisure and Tourism* book series, produced in association between the GLTRG and Ashgate. I would like to thank Katy Crossan of Ashgate for her enthusiasm and patience.

Of course, such a book entirely depends on the work and interest of its contributors. I am immensely grateful to them for engaging with the project throughout. Their work show the various implications neoliberal projects, discourses and practices have on tourism and should provide a solid platform for launching further research into the political economy of tourism.

Finally, I am grateful to colleagues at the University of Sunderland, UK and the University of Applied Sciences HTW Chur, Switzerland for stimulating debates and their support and encouragement.

Chapter 1

Neoliberalism and the Political Economy of Tourism: Projects, Discourses and Practices

Jan Mosedale

Tourism has become increasingly shaped by neoliberal policies, yet the consequences of this neoliberalization have received relatively little specific attention in the literature. Only few contributions to the tourism literature have analysed the role of tourism within neoliberal change and vice versa. In particular, the neoliberalization of nature has received recent and concerted interest from tourism scholars such as Duffy (2008, 2013 and, 2014), Rytteri and Puhakka (2012) and Keul (2014). Other contributions have focussed on particular nation states (Desforges, 2000; Tamborini, 2005; Yüksel et al., 2005), regions and communities and the neoliberal change in their institutional structures (Shone and Memon 2008; Mair, 2006), policies or specific types of tourism such as medical tourism (Ormond, 2013) or agritourism (Timms, 2006), as well as wider international policy (Wood, 2009) and, more specifically, its link to international aid (Schilcher, 2007; Lacey and Ilcan, 2015).

This edited collection brings together different perspectives of neoliberalism and tourism in order to illustrate, explain and evaluate the effects of different variants of neoliberalism and thus to provide a solid basis for further, more specific analyses of the effects of the wider neoliberal project on tourism. Drawing on concepts from political economy and regulation theory, this chapter will introduce neoliberalism as a continuous and evolving process that results in local variations or projects of the wider neoliberal ideology, underpinned by neoliberal discourse and practices. At the same time, it will attempt to position neoliberalism within contemporary debates in the social sciences drawing on examples within a tourism context.

How did Neoliberalism Develop?

There is no set start date for the idea of neoliberalism. It emerged from a number of different starting points with the aim of bringing a revised classical liberalism to the fore and rebranding it as 'neoliberalism' (Springer, 2010). Discussions began in the late 1930s to situate neoliberalism as an alternative to Keynesianism and Friedrich von Hayek's *Road to Serfdom* (1944) positioned him as the main protagonist in the expansion of the neoliberal idea. In 1947, the Mont Pèlerin Society was created and is now widely accredited as having been the first neoliberal think tank. Not satisfied with merely identifying an alternative to the current relationship between states and markets (Keynesianism), they purposefully engaged in a programme of discourse-building within their international networks and wider dissemination in order to position neoliberalism as a desirable and inevitable project to fix the problems of the Fordist/Keynesian regulatory system (Plehwe, 2009). Over time, the idea of a neoliberal project spread not just geographically but also across society and eventually succeeded in becoming the dominant political-economic discourse.

The rise of neoliberalism came with the financial crisis of the 1970s, when Keynesianism – the intervention of the state in the market or even substitution of the market (as in state ownership of key sectors, such as public transport) in order to maintain the welfare of its population – was no longer viewed as a suitable mode of regulation due to the severity of the crisis. It was generally felt that governments did not have the necessary acumen and knowledge to predict market changes and that it was best for governments not to intervene but to provide the necessary environment for the functioning of free markets. Neoliberal theory posits that " ... human well-being can best be advanced by liberating individual entrepreneurial freedoms and skills within an institutional framework characterized by strong property rights, free markets, and free trade' (Harvey, 2005: 2).

In what way does neoliberalism differ from liberalism? Castree (2010) identifies three key differences. First, neoliberalism revives classical liberalism, after the interlude of the Fordist-Keynesian system, and has been rebranded to distinguish it from liberalism and the crisis of accumulation, which lead to the great depression. Second, neoliberalism interprets individual freedoms as economic freedoms. Following liberal thought, individual property rights are paramount: "private property is the embodiment of individual liberty ... and market freedoms are indivisible components of the basic liberties of the person" (Gray, 1995: 61, cited in Hardin, 2014: 202). Yet neoliberalism does not stop there but extends market rationality to all social action with individuals expected to engage with markets and become individual entrepreneurs: "human well-being can best be advanced by liberating individual entrepreneurial freedoms and skills ... The role of the state is to create and preserve an institutional framework appropriate to such practices" (Harvey, 2005: p 2). Individuals should use their agency to acquire the necessary capital (intellectual, social, human and cultural) in order to be able to negotiate and engage in free markets and thus become *homo economicus* (Fitzsimons, 2000). Potential structural disadvantages that may hinder the development of social capital are largely discounted and left to charitable organizations to address.

Third, neoliberalism also differs from liberalism as it has been strategically pursued as an "epistemological project of the neoliberal thought collective" (Hardin, 2014: 214), gained impetus beyond 'first world' countries as it is being disseminated by global institutions such as the International Monetary Fund and the World Bank via structural adjustment programmes (Schilcher, 2007; Lacey and Ilcan, 2015).

Although the previous paragraphs suggests a linear trajectory and a common goal, "the zigzagging prehistories of neoliberalism serve as timely reminders of the contradictory, contingent and *constructed* nature of the neoliberal present, its produced and contextually embedded form, and its inescapable impurity" (Peck, 2008: 4, emphasis original). Chile was among the first states to implement neoliberal policies when General Pinochet took power in 1973 and former students of Milton Friedman at the University of Chicago were given positions in government and – in collaboration with the International Monetary Fund – engaged in structural reforms geared at incorporating neoliberal economic policies. In the UK, Margaret Thatcher took office in May 1979 and implemented her own brand of neoliberalism largely by privatizing profitable national entities such as British Aerospace and Cable & Wireless to reduce state borrowing. Later, the Thatcher government justified extensive privatization campaigns with the increased efficiency and productivity of private enterprise with the aim to increase the competitiveness of these newly private firms in the wider European and global market (Seymour, 2012). In the US, Ronald Reagan introduced a supply-side oriented Program for Economic Recovery, upon taking office in 1981, aimed at cutting taxes and reducing the deficit and spending in order to guarantee monetary and fiscal stability to ensure continued economic growth (Steger and Roy, 2010). Later, more moderate interpretations of neoliberalism, were introduced in social-democratic states such as Canada (Keil, 2002), New Zealand (Larner, 1997) and Germany (Brenner, 2000) and existing neoliberal projects in the UK (Tony Blair's Third Way) and the US (Bill Clinton) were adjusted in response to the socio-political effects of the actions of the previous governments (Brenner and Theodore, 2002).

Theorizing Neoliberalism

Neoliberal ideology is the belief in the principle of unregulated markets as the optimal strategy for economic development and growth. This involves the adoption of policies to reduce state involvement in order to allow the extension of market forces (for example competition and commodification) to all aspects of economic activity and indeed throughout society – for example via the erosion of elected governance, privatization of assets and services culminating in a general shift away from Keynesian social policies (Brenner and Theodore, 2002). Neoliberalism has restructured and rescaled the relationships between institutions, governance and markets (Peck and Tickell, 2002) in order to disembedd capital and its accumulation from state-led constraints (Harvey, 2005).

Neoliberalism has its origins in classical liberal economic theories (such as of Adam Smith) and its focus on individual freedoms and thus limited involvement of the nation state. Neoliberalism as a neoclassical economic theory thought to revive, an adapted version of liberal capitalism (prominent as political economic system from the mid-1800s to the World War I) and thus to oppose the 'Fordist-Keynesian' combination of regime of accumulation and mode of regulation.

The rationale behind this was that the state a) is too easily influenced by special interest groups (for example labour unions) and b) does not have the necessary market information in order to take necessary decisions. Neoliberalism opposes the previous regime of accumulation and mode of regulation (the welfare state) and thus changes the relationship between markets, the state and society. The main characteristics of neoliberalism according to Castree (2010) are the privatization of assets, increased commercialization of the public sector (the implementation of market proxies), the creation of new markets for services previously not subject to free market principles, deregulation, reregulation, the implementation of flanking mechanisms to counteract the effects of neoliberalism and a focus on self-sufficient individuals. These characteristics will now be discussed in a tourism context.

Privatization of National Assets

The first priority of the new neoliberal policies of Thatcher's first-wave neoliberalism was the privatization of public utilities and public services in order to reduce public spending and to increase efficiencies and thus competitiveness. The reinforcement of private property rights and the elimination of public ownership is a strong theme in neoliberal theory so that markets may regulate themselves without government intervention. State ownership is the ultimate government intervention and therefore an anathema to neoliberal thought.

The privatization of former national assets such as transport and, in some cases, hotel infrastructure probably had the largest impact on tourism. The transportation sector was one of the first industrial sectors to be privatized (in particular air, but also train and bus transport). Nowadays public transport is rarely in public ownership and, more often than not, is at least operated by private enterprise. Other examples of privatization include the selling of hotel infrastructure, as has only recently occurred in India, where the state government of Karnataka sold 18 tourism properties under a Renovate, Operate, Manage and Transfer scheme (Venkatesh, 2014), or the increasing privatization of park infrastructure (see Chapter 9 by Nyahunzvi).

However, certain types of tourism have also benefited from the privatization of other sectors. For example, the privatization of health care has led to medical tourism, as medical tourists exploit political-economic differences (i.e. different regulatory contexts) between countries for their personal well-being. "Health-care is becoming less enshrined as a public good and instead increasingly reimagined as a tradable commodity via international, regional and bilateral trade agreements … and through the involvement of transnational agencies and companies" (Ormond, 2011: 248). This is a growing market with new entrants to the tourism sector: " … hundreds of medical tourism companies have become travel agents, brokering and facilitating medical travel … " (Connell, 2011: 260). Medical tourism has become a profitable niche market for many developing countries and "a way of outsourcing healthcare for Western countries with escalating waiting lists and costs" (Smith, 2012: 2). Medical tourism therefore eases the pressure on public health care systems battling continual budget cuts and puts the onus on the individual to fund his/her treatment. While medical tourism has benefitted from the privatization of health care in some countries, it exacerbates the negative effects of neoliberalism as medical tourism may increase inequalities in terms of access to health care, as well as its cost and quality (Connell, 2011; Smith, 2012) in both source markets and the medical tourism destinations.

Commercialization of the Public Sector

Those public sectors that have not (yet) been privatized have to function (at least internally) according to market principles. For example, the cost of environmental conservation has to be recouped and protected areas must run cost efficiently. The UK Department for Environment, Food & Rural Affairs states that "protected natural areas can yield returns many times higher than the costs of their protection" (DEFRA, 2011: 4 cited in Sullivan, 2013: 198). Under neoliberal economic regimes, protected areas are expected to top up the government support via new innovative funding concepts, which position protected areas within a market context. Protected areas therefore engage in a number of different activities in order to gain sufficient funds to be able to achieve their aim of conservation. Yet, paradoxically, these funding activities may be in conflict with that same aim, as protected areas commodify nature by providing tourism activities, extracting natural resources or by bioprospecting. "[Protected area] financial sustainability requires that funds are managed and administered in a way that promotes cost efficiency and management effectiveness" (Emerton et al., 2006: 15). Consequently, commercialization involves charging market-based fees for these goods and services provided.

Nyahunzvi (Chapter 9) analyses the effects of such commercialization in Kruger National Park, South Africa and concurs with Fletcher's statement (2012: 296–7) "the market-based mechanisms upon which [protected areas] usually rely to generate income from *in situ* resources and thereby incentivize their conservation ... commonly force into opposition the very conservation and development goals they purportedly seek to reconcile ... ". Nyahunzvi further problematizes the resulting distribution of capital from the commercialization activities and the power relationship between the park organization and local villages.

A further example of the use of market proxies demonstrates the trajectory from commercialization towards the creation of new markets: the ecosystem services concept follows an accounting approach to measure socio-environmental relations and thus places monetary values on services that ecosystems deliver to society (Sullivan, 2013). These services include ecological and physical services that benefit human society, such as storing carbon in soils, vegetation and water bodies, filtering grey water for human consumption and also cultural functions, such as the use and commodification of nature for purposes of recreation and tourism. This use of market proxies – full cost accounting and the economic valuation of ecosystem services in order to provide an argument for their protection – is the first step towards the creation of markets for the commodification and exchange of nature in ways previously not imaginable.

Creation of Markets

As the neoliberal ideology views unrestrained markets as the best organization of exchange, this form of organization is to be expanded into all spheres of society. Following this argumentation, externalities are increasingly being sold in markets or at least valued according to market principles. For example, carbon credit schemes allow an international trade in carbon emissions between nations or companies with a credit deficit and those with a credit surplus. As much of the international tourist flows is dependent on modes of transport that emit greenhouse gases (Gössling et al., 2007), the EU has set a cap on greenhouse gases emitted by companies in 2005 and has introduced an EU trading system (ETS). This cap and trade system also limits emissions for airlines operating in the EU and in member states of the European Free Trade Association. Although the pricing of emissions may act as a 'rationing mechanism' and thus help to avoid anthropocentric change (Holden, 2009), the creation of markets to trade surplus credits may result in new political-economic power relationships (especially between industrialized and developing countries) in an international trading regime (Markussen and Svendsen, 2005).

Deregulation

The initial neoliberal strategies were devised to destruct the Keynesian organizational form of state institutions and to roll-back the nation-state and its interventions in markets so as to allow rational actors free choice to maximize their interests (Brenner and Theodore, 2002; Peck and Tickell, 2002). Deregulation as a strategy allows unconstrained competition and the self-regulation of markets and a reduction of government expenditure, which may thus attract inward investment. Unregulated markets are regarded as being the most efficient way to achieve economic development and growth. Government interventions are inefficient, costly and therefore withdrawn. The political economy of air transport is a good example of discussions surrounding opening markets to international competition and state regulation with the rationale of national interests such as economic stability, health and safety and risk of terrorism (Duval and Macilree, 2011). After World War II, international air transport was regulated via multilateral and bilateral agreements and domestic air transport was strictly regulated.

The deregulation of the US domestic airline sector in the late 1970s has become a symbol of the shift towards neoliberal policies and has been called "the beginning of a tectonic shift in global economic policy" (Goetz and Vowles, 2009: 251). The US Airline Deregulation Act came into effect in 1978 with the view to open the domestic market to competition and to eliminate the control exerted by the Civil Aeronautics Board, a federal agency, over fares and access to routes (Goetz and Vowles, 2009). Yet the effects of this deregulation on smaller and peripheral communities had to be curbed by further government intervention (see the next point on reregulation), the introduction of the 'Essential Air Services Programme' also in 1978 to guarantee the continued air service to smaller communities which were no longer profitable but of social importance.

In the EU, a 'third package' of liberalization measures was introduced in 1993 which allowed free entry of EU carriers to routes within Europe and no constraints on fares, frequency or capacity (Reynolds-Feighan, 1995). These deregulation policies have led to the development of route networks between airlines either via mergers & acquisitions, franchising or code sharing in order to benefit from economies of scope (Papatheodorou, 2002). There is more variation in the deregulation of the international compared to domestic air transport sectors, as the extent of deregulation in bilateral agreements is dependent on individual national policies. Yet so-called open skies agreements with the right to unlimited market access for airlines are now largely the norm (Duval and Macilree, 2011).

Reregulation

After the first phase of roll-back neoliberalism (de-regulation), institutional arrangements were restructured and new forms of state organization, modes of governance and regulation were rolled-out and 'normalized' (Peck and Tickell, 2002). These roll-out strategies served to produce a new network of institutional and regulatory relations, which were conducive to stabilizing the neoliberal trajectory and seemingly soften its effects. This institutional restructuring, the re-negotiation and transfer of responsibilities, led to new forms of governance in a different relational network of state, para-statal and non-state regulatory organizations across space (Mosedale, 2014; Mosedale and Albrecht, 2011). The state as a singular regulatory institution (if this was ever an accurate description) was transformed to a network consisting of different forms of governance crossing various geographical scales: "the state exists in new and more complex relations – including partnership and multi-level governance – with other tiers of state regulation and with other bodies" (Shaw and Williams 2004: 47). Neoliberal reregulation has restructured the relations between capital, institutions and society (Mosedale and Albrecht, 2011): 'Tourism is a diverse and at times chaotic policy arena ... [with] numerous policy strands at a variety of geographical scales ... ' (Church et al., 2000: 330). Following this shift towards multi-level and multi-actor governance, the nation-state still retains an important, albeit different position: it plays 'a central role in mediating the mechanics, ethos and outcomes of this [collaborative governance] process' (Church et al., 2000: 332). At a subnational level, Shone (Chapter 4) highlights the challenges for new regulatory constellations under a neoliberal regime in his analysis of regional tourism development in a New Zealand case study. In particular, the differentiation of roles of local government in tourism development remains a challenge at a regional level.

Flanking Mechanisms to Counter De- and Reregulation

While the nation-state is rolled back under neoliberalism (de-regulation) and new institutions are rolled out (reregulation) with reduced involvement in providing necessary services for its citizens, other actors need to assume some of the roles formerly held by government institutions. Governments have transferred much social responsibility to non-state actors grouped together in the social economy or big society. Under neoliberalism, governments are " ... integrating the free market with a theory of social solidarity based on the conservative communitarian principles of order, hierarchy and voluntarism" (Corbett and Walker, 2013: 455) in order to reproduce the neoliberal project. Not-for-profit organizations and, more or less formal, community groups are providing social services following non-market logics and, on the surface at least, seem to provide an alternative to market or state provision of social services (Amin et al., 2003). Yet in many cases, these social economy projects have been set up because the state has withdrawn funding for public social services and private enterprises have not entered the market place or are not providing the appropriate service at the right price. The neoliberal social economy discourse (Graefe, 2006a) emphasizes the responsibility of individuals and communities to be self-sufficient and not to rely on government support when faced with difficulties (such as unemployment, debts, serious illness etc.). While social economies (Amin et al., 2003) and communal alternative economic practices (Mosedale, 2012) are in themselves to be encouraged for a number of reasons, keywords such as social innovation, social entrepreneurship and social enterprise have become subsumed within a neoliberal discourse (Graefe, 2006b) used to further reproduce the neoliberal project.

   In the context of tourism, the most prominent example of flanking mechanism are social tourism initiatives, designed to offer support to disadvantaged sectors of society. Yet, "social tourism in Europe seems to represent an awkward mix of social liberalism and the concerns for propping up an important sector of the European economy (the mainstream tourism industry)" (Diekman and McCabe, 2011: 427). The approach taken towards social tourism and the actors involved (commercial – non-commercial, state – private organizations) vary greatly over time and space (Minnaert et al., 2012). Minnaert (Chapter 8) offers a detailed analysis of the changing discourse of social tourism and demonstrates the implications of neoliberal discourse on the practices and structures of social tourism in Europe. Part of the changing discourse is the neoliberal shift from social to individual responsibility.

Focus on 'Self-sufficient' Individuals and Communities

On a more abstract level, neoliberalism de- and re-regulation has resulted in state withdrawal from certain responsibilities and the dismantling of the welfare state. This comes with a shift in focus towards individual responsibility and the subsumation of risk (in terms of future development of markets) by the individual rather than the state or corporation (for example private pension plans). From a neoliberal viewpoint, individuals are rational actors who need to negotiate and engage in free markets. Structural inequalities are generally not considered in neoliberal discourse, as any redistributive measures to support disadvantaged groups or individuals are deemed to be contributing to a dependency culture. Minnaert (Chapter 8) analyses the shift towards this neoliberal view of the structure-agency spectrum in the context of social tourism.

Neoliberalism as Projects, Discourse and Practices

Neoliberalism is an "amorphous political-economic phenomenon" (Peck, 2004: 394), yet it can be analysed as distinct neoliberal projects, discourses and practices. These constitute what is generally referred to as neoliberalism and their analysis may shed light onto the workings of neoliberalism.

Projects

Neoliberalism as a global project aims to institutionalize a new regulation regime – based on the primacy of the market – to displace, defuse, or resolve the crisis of accumulation under the preceding Fordist-Keynesian era (Harvey, 2005). While the term 'neoliberalism' suggests a monolithic conception of the economic world order, it has involved a variety of concurrent projects following a general script for the neoliberal project. The transition to neoliberalism has not been consistent across space, as path-dependency and place-specific characteristics have resulted in unevenly realized strategies and effects (Peck, 2004): "The capitalist world stumbled towards neoliberalization … through a series of gyrations and chaotic experiments … " (Harvey, 2005: 13). This messy evolution of 'the neoliberal idea' has resulted in a cornucopia of neoliberalisms prompting Barnett (2005: 9) to declare, "There is no such thing as neoliberalism" and Castree (2006: 2), in a similar way, the "thing called 'neoliberalism' … can be held responsible for anything". It is argued that the label of 'neoliberalism' obscures the complex and varied processes of neoliberal experiments (Larner, 2003). Hence, it is necessary to pay attention to "the *different variants* of neoliberalism, to the *hybrid nature* of contemporary policies and programmes or [and] to the *multiple and contradictory aspects* of neoliberal spaces, techniques, and subjects" (Larner, 2003: 509, original emphasis). Neoliberalism must be recognized as being spatiotemporally specific, embedded in a particular geographic, political, social and economic context and therefore multiple, complex and varied. At the same time, one has to view theses neoliberal variants as part of wider global discourses. Neoliberalism is embedded in local, regional and national contexts but is also affected by the wider global neoliberal project. Brenner and Theodore (2002: 351) call this "actually existing neoliberalism". The term 'neoliberalization' is therefore used to denote processes within the wider neoliberal political-economic ideology that lead to neoliberal variants or projects in different locations.

In their contributions to this volume, Ioannides and Petridou (Chapter 2), Hannam and Reddy (Chapter 6), Shone (Chapter 4), Scherle and Pillmayer (Chapter 5) explore the extent that the ideals of neoliberalism are manifested locally. These case studies of US urban tourism, ecotourism development in India, the creation of special economic zones in Jordan and a changing regional governance in New Zealand demonstrate the varied nature of neoliberal projects due to path-dependence in a space-time context.

Of particular interest is the case study of Jordan, as Scherle and Pillmayer (Chapter 5), analyse Jordan's moderate transformation from rent-seeking (a different political-economic organization from western, industrial countries) towards neoliberalism, in specific reference to the creation of a special economic zone in Aqaba to boost tourism investment and development. This transformation process is dependent on the geo-political position of Jordan as interface between US and Middle East interests and its position within the international network of tourist and capital flows.

The neoliberal project has implications at a national and subnational scale. Hannam and Reddy (Chapter 6) demonstrate the role that tourism development, as part of a wider liberalization and deregulation of the state, may play in transforming urban and rural landscapes and the associated livelihoods in India. In their analysis of the development of a new multi-sports stadium in Dunedin, New Zealand, for the Rugby World Cup in 2011, Hall and Wilson (Chapter 3) reveal the complex relationship between de-regulation and re-regulation at different levels of the state. On the one hand, the state has withdrawn from the regulation and investment in public sports and sporting events and those opened up the market to private entrepreneurship. On the other hand, local governments often support and subsidize private enterprise in developing multi-use infrastructure associated with major sporting events in order to attract tourists and suitable residents for continued urban growth and comparable competitiveness.

Not only are the neoliberal projects place- and time-specific, but economic actors may also react differently to neoliberal transformations, which in turn shapes the articulation of "actually existing neoliberalism". For instance, in an analysis of the network structures of low cost carriers in Asia, Europe, and North America, Graham (2009) demonstrates that low cost carriers follow different spatial strategies to exploit the deregulation of the airline industry.

Discourse

A different approach to analysing neoliberal processes is to focus on discourses surrounding the neoliberal projects. There are different understandings of discourse in the academic literature depending on the particular field of humanities or social sciences involved. In the context of this chapter, discourse is used more broadly than language, as a term that denotes the social construction of reality via its representation (following Foucault, 1972, 1977). Discourse, thus, bestows meaning to reality and re-produces identities, values, norms and social relations. This is not to lessen the importance of the material in favour of its representation (see, for instance, Mosedale (2011) for a brief discussion of the discourse – material debate in tourism), but to include its representation, which in turn materializes in practices and actions: "The ways we think and talk about a subject influence and reflect the ways we act in relation to that subject" (Karlberg, 2005: 1). Meanings, identities, values, norms and social relations and their imaginaries are expressed discursively (Fairclough, 2001) but are also enacted and thus connect the immaterial and the material.

'Discourses, sensuous bodies, machines, objects, animals and places are choreographed *together* and build heterogeneous cultural orders that have the capacity to act, to have effects and affects' (Haldrup and Larsen, 2010: 60, emphasis in the original). 'Realities' are therefore are therefore mutually constituted of a number of different elements such as objects, discourse, practices, feelings, aesthetics, political economic structures etc.

How discourses are formed, gain dominance and lead to the formation of formal or informal social structures that control/govern our societies is of interest to critical scholars. The discursive formations around the narratives of a free market economy, competition, continued economic growth and the past failures of regulation (big government) sustains and justifies the larger neoliberal project and hinders the development of alternatives (Peck, 2004). " … [N]eoliberalism is … a mutable, inconsistent, and variegated process that circulates through the discourses it constructs, justifies, and defends. … What is at stake is an understanding of neoliberalism that is duly aware of both 'structure' and 'agency', thus capturing the discursive production of neoliberalism." (Springer, 2012: 135). The neoliberal ideology is not only re-produced via a set of discursive elements (language in text and spoken and other practices of representation such as pictures, videos, art, performances etc.), it is also regulating alternative discourses in order to remain the dominant political discourse and create the social norms that determine which discourses are deemed acceptable in society. Margaret Thatcher's often cited sound bite referring to the inevitability of her economic reforms: "There is no alternative", is such an attempt at stifling counter-political economic imaginaries and practices. It is the continuous selection of accepted discourses and the exclusion of inacceptable discourses, which leads to the social regulation of discourses. Therefore, discourse is political, as it determines and regulates the possibility of some options, actions, practices and imaginaries over others (Gee, 1999). The success of neoliberalism can be attributed to its diffusion across national, international and transnational institutions thus firmly embedding the accompanying discourse within these institutions.

Although still underrepresented, discourse is gathering pace in tourism scholarship since the seminal paper by Thurot and Thurot (1983) on the discourse of tourism marketing and the edited volume on discourse and tourism by Jaworski and

Pritchard (2005) was a timely milestone as it offered a basis for further contributions on the discursive construction and representation of tourist spaces (Hovardas and Stamou, 2006), experiences (Norton, 1996; Stamou and Paraskevopoulos, 2003), identities (Yan and Santos, 2009; Calkin, 2014) and performances (Hall-Lew and Lew, 2014). Especially the body of work on the sociolinguistics of discourse and tourism by Thurlow and Jaworski (for example Jaworski and Thurlow, 2004, 2010 and Thurlow and Jaworski, 2010, 2011) has done much to theorize the relationship between tourism and discourse. Yet, discourse analysis is rarely used to analyse political-economic transformations and their effect on tourism. Notable exceptions are two analyses of political speeches by Deng Xiaoping (considered leader of the People's Republic of China from 1978 to, 1992) from 1978 to 1979 (Xiao, 2006) and speeches given by the Cambodian Prime Minister Hun Sen from 1999 to 2008 (Chheang, 2009). Of course, the analysis of neoliberal discourse should not be limited to official speeches given by heads of state, as discourses are heterogeneous and reproduced by various actors and in different modes (not limited to speeches). As Fairclough (2012: 9) states, "there are no social events or practices without representations, construals, conceptualizations or theories of these events and practices".

Social events are embedded in sets of, sometimes differing, discourses that are employed to make sense of these events. Yet these discourse do not merely describe the meanings of social events, in themselves they generate meanings and are thus constitutive (Philo, 2011). In a study of the neoliberal discourse in labour markets, public-private job-training programmes, Ayers and Carlone (2007) analyse how neoliberal discourse were manifested and employed to further the neoliberal project. In particular, learning was reduced to those skills that would produce individual entrepreneurs and the social relationship between employees and employers was represented as short-term with much of the responsibility lying with the individual (*homo economicus*). Minnaert (Chapter 8) demonstrates this neoliberal focus on individual agency in her analysis of the changing discourse of social tourism being a distributive measure to becoming an economic regeneration measure and thus supporting the accumulation of capital in new niche markets.

Practices

As discussed in the previous section on discourse, representations may materialize in practices and actions. A methodological focus on practices (as outlined in a different context in Mosedale, 2012) can therefore be helpful in analysing how neoliberalism is enacted, (re)produced and potentially transformed into everyday practices by individuals or institutions. Practices provide ' ... ways of knowing the world through action, but also form – through action – the materiality of the world through the creation, reproduction and unfolding of material social relations' (Smith and Stenning, 2006: 192–3). Analysing practices then allows for the interpretation of wider socio-economic processes (Jones and Murphy, 2010) and can inform our understanding of neoliberalism as constituted of multitudes of practices, social structures, materials and meanings.

The process of neoliberalization requires the continuous management of relationships between the market, the nation-state and society in line with the ideologies of the neoliberal ideology and the supporting economic discourse. Although neoliberalism is an abstract concept, and it is something that is translated into individual and institutional practices. Through practices, neoliberalism is realized in particular places. Actors are not just passive subjects of the neoliberal phenomenon, they engage in, shape, (re)produce and counter neoliberalism via everyday practices. These are shaped by the characteristics of the neoliberal ideology and by discourse: "Both structure and agency meet and become visible in practices" (Mosedale, 2012: 166). A focus on practices allows an examination of contextually situated social processes where agents and structures co-constitute one another (Jones and Murphy, 2010).

Offeh and Hannam (Chapter 9) demonstrate, in a case study of the Ashanti Kingdom in Ghana, how neoliberalism has been 'enacted on the ground' and how it has shaped the market and production practices of cloth weavers, which produce heritage souvenirs. They introduce the concept of institutional commodification (Wank, 1999: 29) " ... the transformation of institutionalised social relations of control over ... resources" in relation to the power exerted by international and national governments in the production and sale of craft heritage souvenirs.

Non-neoliberal Imaginaries

Practices in response to the neoliberalization of societies will also include practices to contest or counter neoliberalism, which help to create future imaginaries. Neoliberalism, as the current regime of accumulation and mode of regulation in many countries, is suffering from a prolonged economic crisis since 2008. The litmus test of the neoliberal ideological discourse will be how long it will withstand the increasing contestation levelled against it. As Leitner et al. (2007: viii) argue, the rise of neoliberalism was based on the contestation of the Fordist/Keynesian regime of accumulation/mode of regulation and "[n] eoliberalism ... will surely itself sooner or later be replaced by something else". It is therefore important to analyse the current attempts at reworking, supplanting and discounting neoliberalism. Even within a wider neoliberal structure, there remain alternative possibilities to engage in different types of social practices that do not follow the marketization and commodification of all aspects of social life, but instead promote the inclusion of social values into the economic domain (see for example Higgins-Desboilles (2011) or Morgan et al. (2012) for the tourism academy). Mosedale (2012) provides examples of alternative economic practices such as home exchange, voluntourism and wwoofing (see also Mosedale, 2009) which follow alternative market or non-market opportunities for exchange. In this volume, Wearing and Wearing (Chapter 10) use the example of ecotourism to advocate for a decommodification of tourism, including a focus on social justice, in particular a fair (re)distribution of capital, the recognition of cultural identity in order to counter institutional commodification (see Chapter 9). Such non-neoliberal imaginaries (Leitner et al., 2007) based on a different set of moral grounding (Butcher, 2005) are necessary in order to discuss a future political economic system after neoliberalism.

The aim of this book is to provide a starting point for the analysis of neoliberalism and tourism. As an introductory chapter, this chapter has taken a broad approach and provided a theoretical discussion of the concept and discussed neoliberalism as a particular political-economic ideology, as distinct projects or variants of this global project, as discourse surrounding the relationship between the economy and nation-states and as practices through which neoliberalism is being enacted. Although these have been discussed in separate sections in order to make sense of the processes of neoliberalization, in reality (and as the chapters in this volume will demonstrate), neoliberalization cannot be easily be separated into these neat categories. Neoliberal projects consist of place- and time-specific practices and local as well as global discourses, which provide and prevent particular development paths. This book can only make a small contribution to start unravelling the intricacies of neoliberalism. Further theoretically informed empirical studies are necessary to a) understand how neoliberal projects are created and rationalized by institutions and actors, b) analyse the discursive formations of neoliberalism, its contestations and alternatives and c) examine practices to understand how actors, institutions and communities interpret and respond to neoliberalism.

References

Amin, A., Cameron, A. and Hudson, R. (2003). *Placing the Social Economy.* London: Routledge.

Ayers, D.F. and Carlone, D. (2007). Manifestations of neoliberal discourses within a local job-training program. *International Journal of Lifelong Education,* 26(4), 461–79.

Barnett, C. (2005). The consolations of 'neoliberalism'. *Geoforum,* 36(1), 7–12.

Brenner, N. (2000). Building 'euro-regions' locational politics and the political geography of neoliberalism in post-unification Germany. *European Urban and Regional Studies,* 7(4), 319–45.

Brenner, N. and Theodore, N. (2002). Cities and the geographies of "actually existing neoliberalism". *Antipode,* 34(3), 349–79.

Butcher, J. (2005). *The Moralisation of Tourism: Sun, Sand ... and Saving the World?* London: Routledge.

Calkin, S. (2014). Mind the 'gap year': A critical discourse analysis of volunteer tourism promotional material. *Global Discourse,* 4(1), 30–43.

Castree, N. (2006). From neoliberalism to neoliberalisation: Consolations, confusions, and necessary illusion. *Environment and Planning A*, 38(1), 1–6.

Castree, N. (2010). Neoliberalism and the biophysical environment 1: What 'neoliberalism' is, and what difference nature makes to it. *Geography Compass*, 4(12), 1725–33.

Chheang, V. (2009). Hun Sen's talks and Cambodia's tourism development: The discourse of power. *Ritsumeikan Journal of Asia Pacific Studies*, 25, 85–105.

Church, A., Ball, R. and Bull, C. (2000). Public policy engagement with British tourism: The national, local and the European Union. *Tourism Geographies*, 2(3), 312–36.

Connell, J. (2011). A new inequality? Privatisation, urban bias, migration and medical tourism. *Asia Pacific Viewpoint*, 52(3), 260–71.

Corbett, S. and Walker, A. (2013). The big society: Rediscovery of 'the social' or rhetorical fig-leaf for neo-liberalism? *Critical Social Policy*, 33(3), 451–72.

DEFRA (2011). *The Natural Choice: Securing the Value of Nature*. London: UK Government.

Desforges, L. (2000). State tourism institutions and neo-liberal development: A case study of Peru. *Tourism Geographies*, 2(2), 177–92.

Diekmann, A. and McCabe, S. (2011). Systems of social tourism in the European Union: A critical review. *Current Issues in Tourism*, 14(5), 417–30.

Duffy, R. (2008). Neoliberalising nature: Global networks and ecotourism development in Madagascar. *Journal of Sustainable Tourism*, 16(3), 327–44.

Duffy, R. (2013). The international political economy of tourism and the neoliberalisation of nature: Challenges posed by selling close interactions with animals. *Review of International Political Economy*, 20(3), 605–26.

Duffy, R. (2014). Interactive elephants: Nature, tourism and neoliberalism. *Annals of Tourism Research* 44, 88–101.

Duval, D.T. and Macilree, J. (2011). The political economy of trade in international air transport services. In J. Mosedale (ed.) *Political Economy and Tourism: A Critical Perspective*. London: Routledge, 225–42.

Emerton, L., Bishop, J. and Thomas, L. (2006). *Sustainable Financing of Protected Areas: A Global Review of Challenges and Options* (Best Practice Protected Area Guidelines Series No. 13). IUCN.

Fairclough, N. (2001). The dialectics of discourse. *Textus*, 14(2), 231–42.

Fairclough, N. (2012). Critical discourse analysis. In J.P. Gee and M. Handford (eds) *The Routledge Handbook of Discourse Analysis*. London: Routledge, pp. 9–20.

Fitzsimons, P. (2000). *Neoliberalism and Social Capital: Re-Inventing Community*. Paper given at the Annual Conference of the American Education Research Association, New Orleans.

Fletcher, R. (2012). Using the master's tools? Neoliberal conservation and the evasion of inequality. *Development and Change*, 43(1), 295–317.

Foucault, M. (1972). *The Archaeology of Knowledge*. London: Tavistock.

Foucault, M. (1977). *Discipline and Punish: The Birth of the Prison*. London: Allen Lane.

Gee, J.P. (1999). *An Introduction to Discourse Analysis: Theory and Method*. London: Routledge.

Goetz, A.R. and Vowles, T.M. (2009). The good, the bad, and the ugly: 30 years of US airline deregulation. *Journal of Transport Geography*, 17(4), 251–63.

Gössling, S., Broderick, J., Upham, P., Ceron, J.P., Dubois, G., Peeters, P. and Strasdas, W. (2007). Voluntary carbon offsetting schemes for aviation: Efficiency, credibility and sustainable tourism. *Journal of Sustainable Tourism*, 15(3), 223–48.

Graefe, P. (2006a). Social economy policies as flanking for neoliberalism: Transnational policy solutions, emergent contradictions, local alternatives. *Policy and Society*, 25(3), 69–86.

Graefe, P. (2006b). The social economy and the American model relating new social policy directions to the old. *Global Social Policy*, 6(2), 197–219.

Graham, M. (2009). Different models in different spaces or liberalized optimizations? Competitive strategies among low-cost carriers. *Journal of Transport Geography*, 17(4), 306–16.

Gray, J. (1995) *Liberalism*. Minneapolis, MN: University of Minnesota Press.

Haldrup, M. and Larsen, J. (2010). *Tourism, Performance and the Everyday: Consuming the Orient*. London: Routledge.

Hall-Lew, L.A. and Lew, A.A. (2014). Speaking heritage: language, identity, and tourism. In C.M. Hall, A.A. Lew and A.M. Williams (eds) *The Wiley-Blackwell Companion to Tourism*. Oxford: Wiley-Blackwell, 336–48.

Hardin, C. (2014). Finding the 'neo' in neoliberalism. *Cultural Studies*, 28(2), 199–221.

Harvey, D. (2005). *A Brief History of Neoliberalism*. Oxford: Oxford University Press.

Hayek, F.A. (1944). *Road to Serfdom*. Chicago, IL: University of Chicago Press.

Higgins-Desbiolles, F. (2011). Resisting the hegemony of the market: Reclaiming the social capacities of tourism. In S. McCabe, L. Minnaert and A. Diekmann (eds) *Social Tourism in Europe: Theory and Practice*. Bristol: Channel View Publications, 53–68.

Holden, A. (2009). The environment-tourism nexus: Influence of market ethics. *Annals of Tourism Research*, 36(3), 373–89.

Hovardas, T. and Stamou, G.P. (2006). Structural and narrative reconstruction of representations of "environment", "nature" and "ecotourism". *Society and Natural Resources*, 19(3), 225–37.

Jaworski, A. and Pritchard, A. (eds) (2005). *Discourse, Communication and Tourism*. Clevedon: Channel View Publications.

Jaworski, A. and Thurlow, C. (2004). Language, tourism and globalization: Mapping new international identities. In S.H. Ng, C.N. Candlin and C-Y. Chiu (eds) *Language Matters: Communication, Identity, and Culture*. Hong Kong: City University of Hong Kong Press, 297–321.

Jaworski, A. and Thurlow, C. (2010). Language and the globalizing habitus of tourism: Toward a sociolinguistics of fleeting relationships. In N. Coupland (ed.) *The Handbook of Language and Globalization.* Oxford: Wiley-Blackwell, 255–86.

Jones, A. and Murphy, J.T. (2010). Theorizing practice in economic geography: Foundations, challenges, and possibilities. *Progress in Human Geography,* 35(3), 366–92.

Karlberg, M. (2005). The power of discourse and the discourse of power: Pursuing peace through discourse intervention. *International Journal of Peace Studies,* 10(1), 1–25.

Keil, R. (2002). "Common-sense" neoliberalism: Progressive conservative urbanism in Toronto, Canada. *Antipode,* 34(3), 578–601.

Keul, A. (2014). Tourism neoliberalism and the swamp as enterprise. *Area,* 46(3), 235–41.

Lacey, A. and Ilcan, S. (2015). Tourism for development and the new global aid regime. *Global Social Policy,* 15(1), 40–60.

Larner, W. (1997). "A means to an end": Neoliberalism and state processes in New Zealand. *Studies in Political Economy,* 52.

Larner, W. (2003). Neoliberalism? *Environment and Planning D: Society and Space,* 21(5), 509–12.

Leitner, H., Peck, J. and Sheppard, E.S. (2007). *Contesting Neoliberalism: Urban Frontiers.* New York and London: Guilford Press.

Leitner, H., Sheppard, E.S., Sziarto, K. and Maringanti, A. (2007). Contesting urban futures: Decentering neoliberalism. In H. Leitner, J. Peck and E.S. Sheppard (eds). *Contesting Neoliberalism: Urban Frontiers.* New York and London: Guilford Press, 1–25.

Mair, H. (2006). Global restructuring and local responses: Investigating rural tourism policy in two Canadian communities. *Current Issues in Tourism,* 9(1), 1–45.

Markussen, P. and Svendsen, G.T. (2005). Industry lobbying and the political economy of GHG trade in the European Union. *Energy Policy,* 33(2), 245–55.

Minnaert, L., Diekmann, A. and McCabe, S. (2012). Defining social tourism and its historical context. In S. McCabe, L. Minnaert and A. Diekmann (eds) *Social Tourism in Europe: Theory and Practice.* Bristol: Channel View Publications, 18–30.

Morgan, N., Ateljevic, I. and Pritchard, A. (2012). *The Critical Turn in Tourism Studies: Creating an Academy of Hope.* London and New York: Routledge.

Mosedale, J. (2009). Wwoofing in NZ as alternative mobility and lifestyle. *Pacific News,* 32: 25–7.

Mosedale, J. (2011). Thinking outside the box: Alternative political economies in tourism. *Political Economy of Tourism: A Critical Perspective.* Routledge, pp. 93–108.

Mosedale, J. (2012). Diverse economies and alternative economic practices in tourism. In N. Morgan, I. Ateljevic and A. Pritchard (eds) *The Critical Turn in Tourism Studies: Creating an Academy of Hope.* London and New York: Routledge, pp. 194–207.

Mosedale, J. (2014). Political economy of tourism: Regulation theory, institutions and governance networks. In C.M. Hall, A.A. Lew and A.M. Williams (eds) *The Wiley-Blackwell Companion to Tourism.* Oxford: Wiley-Blackwell.

Mosedale, J.T. and Albrecht, J. (2011). Tourism regulation and relational geography: The global, local and everything in between. In J.T. Mosedale (ed.) *Political Economy of Tourism: A Critical Perspective.* London and New York: Routledge, pp. 243–55.

Norton, A. (1996). Experiencing nature: The reproduction of environmental discourse through safari tourism in East Africa. *Geoforum,* 27(3), 355–73.

Ormond, M. (2011). Shifting subjects of health-care: Placing 'medical tourism' in the context of Malaysian domestic health-care reform. *Asia Pacific Viewpoint,* 52(3), 247–59.

Ormond, M. (2013). *Neoliberal Governance and International Medical Travel in Malaysia.* London: Routledge.

Papatheodorou, A. (2002). Civil aviation regimes and leisure tourism in Europe. *Journal of Air Transport Management,* 8(6), 381–8.

Peck, J. (2004). Geography and public policy: Constructions of neoliberalism. *Progress in Human Geography,* 28(3), 392–405.

Peck, J. (2008). Remaking laissez-faire. *Progress in Human Geography,* 32(1), 3–43.

Peck, J. and Tickell, A. (2002). Neoliberalizing space. *Antipode,* 34(3), 380–404.

Philo, C. (2011). Discursive life. In V.J. Del Casino, M. Thomas, P. Cloke and R. Panelli (eds) *A Companion to Social Geography.* John Wiley & Sons. 362–84.

Plehwe, D. (2009). The origins of the neoliberal economic development discourse. In P. Mirowski and D. Plehwe (eds) *The Road from Mont Pèlerin: The Making of the Neoliberal Thought Collective.* Cambridge, MA: Harvard University Press, 238–79.

Reynolds-Feighan, A.J. (1995). European and American approaches to air transport liberalisation: Some implications for small communities. *Transportation Research Part A: Policy and Practice,* 29(6), 467–83.

Rytteri, T. and Puhakka, R. (2012). The art of neoliberalizing park management: Commodification, politics and hotel construction in Pallasyllästunturi National Park, Finland. *Geografiska Annaler B* 94(3), 255–68.

Schilcher, D. (2007). Growth versus equity: The continuum of pro-poor tourism and neoliberal governance. *Current Issues in Tourism* 10(2–3), 166–93.

Seymour, R. (2012). A short history of privatisation in the UK: 1979–2012. *The Guardian.* Online. Available at: http://www.theguardian.com/commentisfree/2012/mar/29/short-history-of-privatisation (Accessed 28 February 2015).

Shaw, G. and Williams, A.M. (2004). *Tourism and Tourism Spaces.* London: Sage.

Shone, M.C. and Memon, P.A. (2008). Tourism, public policy and regional development: A turn from neo-liberalism to the new regionalism. *Local Economy,* 23(4), 290–304.

Smith, A. and Stenning, A. (2006). Beyond household economies: Articulations and spaces of economic practice in postsocialism. *Progress in Human Geography*, 30(2), 190–213.

Smith, K. (2012). The problematization of medical tourism: A critique of neoliberalism. *Developing World Bioethics*, 12(1), 1–8.

Springer, S. (2010). Neoliberalism and geography: Expansions, variegations, formations. *Geography Compass*, 4(8), 1025–38.

Springer, S. (2012). Neoliberalism as discourse: Between Foucauldian political economy and Marxian poststructuralism. *Critical Discourse Studies*, 9(2), 133–47.

Stamou, A.G. and Paraskevopoulos, S. (2003). Ecotourism experiences in visitors' books of a Greek reserve: A critical discourse analysis perspective. *Sociologia Ruralis*, 43(1), 34–55.

Steger, M.B. and Roy, R.K. (2010). *Neoliberalism: A Very Short Introduction*. Oxford: Oxford University Press.

Sullivan, S. (2013). Banking nature? The spectacular financialisation of environmental conservation. *Antipode*, 45(1), 198–217.

Tamborini, C.R. (2005). *The 'Reinvented' State in Emerging Industries: A Comparison of Tourism in Peru and Chile*. PhD thesis at the University of Texas.

Thurlow, C. and Jaworski, A. (2010). *Tourism Discourse: Language and Global Mobility*. Basingstoke: Palgrave Macmillan.

Thurlow, C., and Jaworski, A. (2011). Tourism discourse: Languages and banal globalization. *Applied Linguistics Review*, 2, 285–312.

Thurot, J.M. and Thurot, G. (1983). The ideology of class and tourism confronting the discourse of advertising. *Annals of Tourism Research*, 10(1), 175–89.

Timms, B. (2006). Caribbean agriculture–tourism linkages in a neoliberal world: Problems and prospects for St Lucia. *International Development Planning Review*, 28(1), 35–56.

Venkatesh, M. (2014). Govt notifies 18 tourism properties for privatisation. *The New Indian Express*, Online. Available at: http://www.newindianexpress.com/states/karnataka/2014/11/22/Govt-Notifies-18-Tourism-Properties-for-Privatisation/article2535413.ece (Accessed 28 February 2015).

Wank, D. (1999). *Commodifying Communism: Business, Trust and Politics in a Chinese City*. Cambridge: Cambridge University Press.

Wood, R.E. (2009). Tourism and international policy: Neoliberalism and beyond. In: T. Jamal and M. Robinson (eds) *The SAGE Handbook of Tourism Studies*. SAGE, 596–614.

Xiao, H. (2006). The discourse of power: Deng Xiaoping and tourism development in China. *Tourism Management*, 27(5), 803–14.

Yan, G. and Santos, C.A. (2009). "CHINA, FOREVER": Tourism discourse and self-orientalism. *Annals of Tourism Research*, 36(2), 295–315.

Yüksel, F., Bramwell, B. and Yüksel, A. (2005). Centralized and decentralized tourism governance in Turkey. *Annals of Tourism Research*, 32(4), 859–86.

Chapter 2

Contingent Neoliberalism and Urban Tourism in the United States

Dimitri Ioannides and Evangelia Petridou

Academic debates regarding tourism's ascendancy as key for urban transformation and revival in a post-industrial era have become increasingly popular for the better part of the last two decades (Judd, 1995; Hoffman et al., 2004; Judd, 2004; Judd, 2006; Gladstone and Préau, 2008; Ioannides and Timothy, 2010). Nevertheless, the extant scholarship on urban tourism barely examines this phenomenon in tandem with the "critique of neoliberalism" (Hall and Page, 2012: 16; see other chapters in this volume), which currently preoccupies many human geographers. Highlighting this point, Hall and Page indicate just a handful of studies like Clancy's (1998) examination of neoliberalism's inter-linkages to tourism's development context. Hall (2006) himself discusses how urban entrepreneurialism's marriage to neoliberalism ideologically validates "place-competitive re-imaging strategies including the hosting of sports mega-events" (ibid.: 64).

Though Hall's (2006) discussion on the inter-linkages of visitor-oriented mega events to urban neoliberalism falls within the realm of a broader political economy approach in tourism geography as advocated by Britton (1991) (see also Debbage and Ioannides, 2012; Bianchi, 2012; Mosedale, 2011), recent writings on urban tourism exhibit limited explicit awareness of social scientists' strides relating to neoliberalism's contingent nature (Brenner and Theodore, 2002; Keil, 2002; Jessop, 2002; Peck and Tickell, 2002; Wilson, 2004; Hackworth, 2007; Sternberg, 2012). If anything, most observers discussing tourism's phenomenal growth within cities only implicitly tie this to a generic form of neoliberal ideology, failing to account for the "contextual embeddedness of neoliberal restructuring projects insofar as they have been produced within national, regional, and local contexts defined by the legacies of inherited institutional frameworks, policy regimes, regulatory practices, and political struggles" (Brenner and Theodore, 2002: 351).

This chapter focuses on urban tourism's evolution in the US since the beginning of the neoliberal era. Upfront, we remind the reader that over the last quarter century or so the transformation of cities – especially their central parts – into standardized tourism enclaves (Judd, 2004) has occurred in phases mirroring the shift from "proto" to "roll-back" and eventually "roll-out" neoliberalism as postulated by Peck and Tickell (2002). Thus, the late 1970s and 80s witnessed indiscriminate investments in mega-projects such as dockland redevelopments, convention centres, festival market halls, and sports stadia whereby the public sector assumed the role of facilitator (e.g., by establishing public-private partnerships), thus circumventing traditional regulatory instruments and citizen participation. During the period of roll-out neoliberalism in the 1990s, the private sector's role in the redevelopment process became far clearer while the public sector entered its revanchist period (Smith, 1998; MacLeod, 2002). The latter effectively amounted to efforts in New York's Times Square to enhance the quality of life of residents and visitors by disciplining the elements perceived as harmful to the city's new image (i.e., the homeless, immigrants, and unwanted land uses like red light districts).

The story does not end here. Rather, over the last 15 years or so we have witnessed a period marked by initiatives (sometimes emerging at the grassroots) to revitalize and commodify run-down neighbourhoods and industrial districts beyond the standardized centre city tourist bubbles (Lloyd, 2002; Judd, 2004). We caution that this movement to develop so-called "neo-bohemias", which links to Richard Florida's (2002) "creative class" concept, continues to rest within neoliberalism's boundaries since it happens within the realm of the *de facto* competition between cities, persists on placing the burden of revitalization on non-state actors, and continues to operate in a manner that excludes undesirable persons and land uses.

At this juncture, we emphasize two points: first, though we agree with neoliberalism's hypothesized evolution since the 70s, the process, which has influenced tourism development in US cities, cannot be neatly compartmentalized in clear stages as the aforementioned discussion may suggest. After all, social processes tend to be messy with phases overlapping. Second, to meet the challenges of devolution imposed in a neoliberal regime, various local governments react in widely divergent ways (Elander, 2002). History and geography matter, meaning neoliberalism is marked by a high degree of contingency as it plays out in various localities. For instance, cities' political priorities are reflected in their institutional structure, which will be different in places that make catering to private businesses their main concern compared to those that prioritize social justice. "Urban policy choice is thus embedded in a structural framework that allows or facilitates some choices more than others (Pierre, 2011: 17). Further, even cities with identical priorities employ different strategies to achieve them since the neoliberal project is moulded by local (place-bound) idiosyncrasies.

This chapter begins with a brief description of urban redevelopment and tourism's ascendancy in US cities since the beginning of the neoliberal era in the late 1970s. After reminding the reader of the effects of the transition from roll-back to roll-out neoliberalism we focus on a relatively new phenomenon that is gathering steam in many metropolitan areas around the country; namely the appearance of neo-bohemian neighbourhoods. We see these places as ones where the concept of contingent neoliberalism is becoming most evident.

Setting the Scene

Back in the 1980s it had become strikingly evident that numerous cities throughout the US had experienced the amalgamated result of post-Second World War sociopolitical forces, including the 1949 "Urban Renewal" Act (Title 1 of the 1949 Housing Act), the 1956 Federal Highway Act, the Civil Rights Movement of the 1960s, widespread decline of manufacturing, and the gradual erosion of federal funding for cities (Beauregard, 1998). These factors had precipitated, albeit to varying degrees, the mass exodus, first of white middle class residents and increasingly their jobs to the suburbs, leaving behind within the inner cities entire swathes of boarded up commercial districts, abandoned housing stock and pockets of ultra-low income neighbourhoods, and decaying infrastructure. This loss of people and jobs eroded the inner cities' tax base hurling these places into a downward economic spiral.

Within the inner part of the "average American city" of the 1980s the likely land uses lingering on were certain governmental services (e.g., municipal offices, the State welfare office, or the Department of Motor Vehicles), thrift stores, soup kitchens, buildings converted into SROs (single room occupancy) or boarding houses. Occasionally, a museum or a theatre, most likely in a state of disrepair, reflected the vestiges of a bygone era. In many respects, unless one had an important reason for being downtown (like renewing one's driving license) there was little reason to visit.

Nowadays, if one were to revisit one or more of the aforementioned "average American cities", one would encounter a remarkably transformed setting. The vacant commercial spaces have likely transformed into niche-oriented clothing boutiques, specialized bookstores, an independent movie theatre, jazz bars, restaurants (from fast food joints to expensive gourmet level establishments), coffee houses, or a microbrewery. New benches and street lamps, planter boxes, red brick sidewalks, bicycle lanes and parking racks, not to mention various types of traffic calming create an inviting streetscape. All of these services and amenities have served to resuscitate these once-barren urbanscapes by drawing new residents as well as numerous visitors many of whom come in from the highly predictable suburbs (Beauregard, 1998).

To explain the remarkable transformation of US cities, Hackworth (2007) adopts David Harvey's "spatial fix" as a "useful schema for understanding the connection between political restructuring and physical landscape change" (ibid.: 79). Hackworth contends that the spatial fix for generating economic growth and new jobs in the aftermath of the Great Depression and World War II until the 1970s was "centrifugal" (ibid.: 80), mirrored by widespread suburbanization and the growth of the Sunbelt, arising through government-sponsored programs favouring enhanced homeownership, highways, and the automobile. This spatial fix was undoubtedly anti-urban, resulting in wide-scale inner-city decline throughout the country (Gillette, 2010). Yet, by the mid-1970s, this particular spatial fix could not deal with the problems arising from the 1973 oil crisis, the massive downturn in the fortunes of the manufacturing sector, and the erosion of federal funding. Hackworth asserts that:

> Investors scrambled to find more productive outlets for their capital. It is little surprise that this period prompted a tremendous switch of capital to the secondary circuit, of which the commercial built environment is one significant part. As industrial decline had been in place for several decades prior to 1973, it made little sense to swim upstream, as it were, by reinvesting in the American industrial infrastructure. The most profitable returns were to be made in the commercial property market. With the commercial real estate growth in the suburbs (shopping malls) beginning to taper off by the 1970s, the blighted downtown suddenly became an attractive investment possibility. A switch from the industrial infrastructure of the primary circuit to the downtown commercial real estate of the secondary circuit ensued with vigor. The older urban cores of the industrial Northeast were the first to experience the state assisted return of capital in the form of festival marketplaces and, later, office complexes. Boston's Faneuil Hall, Baltimore's Harborplace, and New York's South Street Seaport are early examples of the capital switch 'back to the city'. (2007: 152)

The reorientation of the spatial fix was in itself inextricably linked to neoliberalism's ascent in its proto and roll-back guise (Peck and Tickell, 2002; see introductory chapter in this volume) that began already in the mid-1970s and gathered steam during the Reagan years, transforming the American CBD into a landscape, among others, for visitors but also new residents and businesses. Criley (quoted in Hackworth, 2007: 151) explains the CBD was especially suited in its role as "circus", a space of visitor consumption, making up for the decline and eventual loss of production of "bread", a hallmark of urban economic growth during the earlier industrial age (Judd, 1995; Clark et al., 2002).

Tourism's Take-off

A key problem associated with neoliberalism's entrenchment in its roll-back phase was the massive loss in federal funds for economically depressed urban areas. This caused local authorities throughout the US to struggle to provide basic services (Smith, 2002) resulting in intense place wars whereby communities compete to lure new business investment, households, and visitors through lucrative incentives (e.g., generous tax breaks and the relaxation of regulations) (Kotler et al., 1993; Ioannides and Timothy, 2010).

Neil Smith (2002; 427) aptly labels such incentives – the mantra of urban redevelopment efforts throughout the country since neoliberalism's early phases – "geobribes" to footloose private capital. Often, inner city areas came under the auspices of so-called urban development corporations (UDCs), which were essentially public-private partnerships with complete planning and development rights within their designated area. Within UDC-administered jurisdictions, existing planning and zoning regulations were legally overridden while active involvement of citizens in the planning process was discouraged. Additionally, it was common for UDCs to exercise power of eminent domain (compulsory purchase). The overriding aim was to facilitate the private sector's ability to redevelop these areas, many of which were blighted, leading to further investment whilst also causing trickle-down economic growth (Fainstein, 2010).

During this time, mega tourism projects became an active ingredient of urban redevelopment especially within central parts of larger cities (Fainstein et al., 2004). Even smaller cities were inspired to recreate parts of their urban fabric into visitor spaces by adapting, albeit on a smaller scale, elements that had worked in their larger counterparts (Ioannides and Timothy, 2010). The popularity of visitor-oriented projects for inner city redevelopment stemmed from the realization that spaces once used for industrial production, warehousing, markets, railway stations, or port facilities could easily be recycled into places of consumption. Much of this historical building stock possessed an architectural quality lacking in the banal suburban residential and commercial districts where most Americans now choose to live, go to school, work, shop, and entertain themselves. According to Beauregard (1998), since the point of origin of most contemporary visitors to urban areas are the suburbs, these people are often enticed by powerful feelings of nostalgia for the inner city neighbourhoods and buildings their grandparents or parents left behind some decades ago (Turner and Rosentraub, 2002).

Several reasons lie behind tourism's popularity as an urban redevelopment tool in the neoliberal era. First, while many US communities continue active smokestack-chasing by portraying themselves as business friendly, such efforts burden local residents since the generous financial incentives offered are commonly derived from taxpayers' contributions (Clark et al., 2002). Visitor-oriented strategies, by contrast, are often funded by the state and not the local community (perhaps matched by contributions from the private sector) while entry barriers and job-creation costs in tourism tend to be substantially lower than other economic sectors (Ioannides, 2003). Additionally, when a city develops a visitor attraction, the key rationale is not only to draw tourists but also to boost the city's image thus enhancing liveability for present residents, drawing new inhabitants, and attracting other potential investors (Turner and Rosentraub, 2002). This is the very reason many city leaders throughout the country shun a detailed feasibility analysis when projects like a ballpark are proposed (Judd, 1995). To them, the fact their city can find itself on the tourist map is enough to justify such projects regardless of cost (Ioannides, 2003).

Urban Tourism in the Revanchist Era

By the 1990s, numerous urban areas throughout the US had become spaces for visitors. Within these islands engulfed by "a sea of decay" (Judd, 1999:36) threats to the quality of the visitors' experience were and still are curtailed and/ or eliminated through the use of security personnel and enhanced policing as well as closed-circuit surveillance systems, better lighting, and turnstiles. Effectively, these became what Judd (2004) terms "tourist bubbles," highly regulated enclavic spaces geared entirely to the well-being of their users as long as the latter are not undesirable (Fainstein et al., 2004). Within these areas the homeless, the poor, or protesters have no place.

These tourist bubbles mirror the rise of the revanchist city (Smith, 2002), essentially amounting to the area's control "through a range of architectural forms and institutional practices so that the enhancement of city's image is not compromised by the visible presence of those very marginalized groups" (MacLeod, 2002: 602). Peck and Tickell (2002) warn, however, that this form of the neoliberal project hardly signifies the demise of the pro-economic growth agenda, demonstrating instead that rather than being a passive observer, the public sector's role has shifted and, in fact, been reanimated.

The trademarks of the public sector's new role include programs initiated by the Clinton administration to reform welfare (Smith, 2002), variations of which were adopted by municipalities throughout the country. Notably, New York City "implemented the nation's largest and most successful workfare program. In exchange for welfare benefits, our 35,000 workfare participants help maintain streets, parks, and city buildings and gain experience in more than 20 city agencies" (Giuliani, 2000: 162). According to Giuliani, this step was part of a package of measures "to implement the largest and widest-ranging privatization program of any city in the country" (ibid.: 161) because he saw this as the only way for New York to be reinstalled as the world's preeminent metropolis. Variations of this theme were seen in other cities including Chicago and Indianapolis (Daley, 2000; Goldsmith, 2000).

Both visitors and residents need to feel comfortable in the areas they frequent. Arguing that the best way to induce safety is to halt crime before it begins many communities installed "zero tolerance" programs (Smith, 2001: 69). These include the Chicago Alternative Policing Strategy (CAPS), introduced in 1993 to create "safer streets for everyone" (Daley, 2000: 144) and *Police Strategy No. 5*, Mayor Rudolph Giuliani's effort to demonstrate no tolerance in New York City for crime nor other threatening activities in public spaces. Smith (2001) sees these programs as nothing more than social cleansing strategies. "Zero tolerance policing has encouraged race and class profiling that places a premium on street arrests of suspects while minimizing concerns about evidence" (ibid.: 71). Elsewhere, Smith (1998: 3) has argued that:

> Rather than indict capitalists for capital flight, landlords for abandoning buildings, or public leaders for a narrow retrenchment to class and race self-interest, Giuliani led to the clamor for a different kind of revenge. He identified homeless people, panhandlers, prostitutes, squeegee cleaners, squatters, graffiti

artists ... unruly youth as the major enemies of public order and decency, the culprits of urban decline generating widespread fear.

Ironically, enhanced regulation of public spaces in the name of protecting citizens' right to the city aided cities like New York in their gentrification efforts and, particularly, their aim to make entire areas welcoming for tourists and middle-income residents. Certainly the transformation over the last two decades of Times Square and areas surrounding it, much of it attributed to the efforts of the Disney Corporation, would not have been as effective if the red-light district and various activities and people seen by the Giuliani administration as having no place there had not been forced out. Of course, as this area and others including parts of Harlem (see Hoffman, 2004) were reclaimed for visitors this meant the homeless, the poor, the unlicensed street vendors, the gypsy taxi-cabs and anyone else threatening these sanitized spaces were shoved aside, ending-up in other less fashionable districts.

On a troubling note, it is evident such revanchist behaviour on the part of city administrations shown no signs of abatement. During 2011, New York police officers undertook as many as 700,000 searches of persons suspected of engaging in an illegal activity. This was done under the policy known as "stop, question, and frisk" (Kastenbaum, 2012), which gives the right to any officer to apprehend and search any person perceived to be up to no good. Proponents of the law say it works as a deterrent to crime, citing a phenomenal lowering in the city's murder rate over the last two decades. Opponents maintain this revanchist activity amounts to nothing more than racial profiling since most of the people are apprehended are African Americans and Hispanics.

Neo-Bohemias: Expressing Neoliberalism's New Phase?

More than a decade into the new century, the effects of "roll-out" neoliberalism within US cities are firmly set while, simultaneously, strategies associated with the earlier "roll-back" neoliberalism persevere. To be sure, the recent worldwide economic crisis have stalled many large-scale programs aimed at enhancing visitor spending but undoubtedly the transformation of cities into spaces of tourism consumption will continue into the foreseeable future.

Few would argue that downtown areas of cities like Cleveland or Pittsburgh have not taken a turn for the better if the measures for gauging this improvement are declining vacancy rates and the expansion of retailing, entertainment, and residential activities. The introduction of public safety measures within these spaces leads users (visitors or residents) to feel far less threatened than in the past. Additionally, the visitors and residents are subject to highly regulated environments in terms of the sights and facilities on offer (shops and services, many displaying well-known global corporate symbols) or signature architectural marvels, while the types of land uses and the activities the users of these spaces engage in are enveloped in an aura of predictability. This is precisely the message both public officials and private capital managing these enclosures wish to project.

On the surface, the proliferation of downtown tourist bubbles in so many metropolitan areas paints a depressing picture that in the neoliberal age, places are becoming increasingly alike despite striving to project their competitive uniqueness. However, according to Fainstein et al. (2004), the fact that not all urban touristic enclaves have met with the same level of success (some like Flint Michigan have notably proven major flops) (Hackworth, 2007) highlights the importance of contingency, implying that predictions of cities becoming carbon copies of each others are vastly exaggerated (Ioannides and Timothy, 2010). We should stress that although the *type* of neoliberal governance driving urban redevelopment throughout the country fundamentally has the singular aim to "'re-entrepreneurialize' cities physically and socially" (Wilson, 2004: 771) this hardly signifies a "one-size-fits-all" approach playing out in an identical fashion in every single locality. Rather, one has to account for the fact that "in the world of evolving places, we see a patchwork of wildly varying neoliberal governances that often barely resemble each other" (Wilson, 2004: 772).

To illustrate this point, Wilson compares the way neoliberal governance plays out in Indianapolis and Chicago. His argument is that although a neoliberal agenda drives governance in both cities, in Chicago emphasis is on becoming a global city by encouraging, for example, the high tech sector whereas in Indianapolis a far less ambitious aim, driven by local developers, is to convert the downtown into a gleaming attraction through a process that "associates capital accumulation with real-estate" (ibid.: 774). Wilson maintains that while in both cities mechanisms are in place to "discipline [their] physical, cultural, and social 'infrastructure" (ibid.), both the growth engines as well as the expected outcomes differ.

Contingency's significance is also reflected in Harlem's recent revival as a visitor hot spot in New York. According to Hoffman (2004) this cannot only be attributed to forces of global capital been imposed from above. Rather, a complex layer of internal dynamics, including the area's unique rich cultural heritage, underpins this revival. To be sure, Harlem has been infiltrated by global symbols of capitalism (e.g., Disney and AOL Time Warner) displaying revanchist activities aimed at dampening its notoriety as a crime-ridden ghetto. However, it also strongly reflects elements of its rich African-American heritage that have been incorporated in the total tourism product, setting it aside from other sterile enclaves.

Reversing his earlier opinion concerning the dominance of tourism enclaves as direct outgrowths of urban restructuring, Judd (2004) asserts that "despite the effects of globalization, cities vary significantly from one another, and they are not necessarily converging" (ibid.: 24). Referring to Boston, one of the oldest North American cities, Judd argues that despite the clear existence of enclaves like Faneuil Hall and Copley Plaza, more and more visitors delight in venturing beyond these areas, spending time in commercial, residential, and mixed-use neighbourhoods, rubbing shoulders with the locals.

The growing phenomenon of visitors seeking escape from the tourist bubbles is not confined to famous historic districts and/or upper middle class zones of only a handful of cities. Instead, more and more individuals visit gritty areas such as "transitional neighbourhoods or zones where people are on the margins of urban society" (Judd, 2004: 30). Districts like Chicago's Wicker Park and Kansas City's Westport retain elements of their past industrial heritage and, as such, are not naturally touristic (Ioannides and Timothy, 2010). However, these neo-bohemias (Clark et al., 2002; Lloyd, 2002) emit a feeling of far greater originality than the predictable downtown bubbles, precisely because they retain much of their original (albeit refurbished) urban fabric and, importantly, because the visitor mingles with locals representing various ages, socioeconomic levels, and ethnicities living, working, and playing.

Drawing visitors to these areas, which the American Planning Association labels "great neighborhoods" (Hinshaw, 2008: 8), is their image of uniqueness in that they commonly offer a rich mix of architectural types, an unforgettable character, and may be transit-oriented and pedestrian-friendly. There is also a preponderance of independently-owned businesses and not the clichéd national and international chain operations. Sometimes, the forces shaping the transformation of such neighbourhoods are distinctly bottom-up (at least during the early stages), differing substantially from those underpinning the stereotypical inner-city tourist bubble. They could, for instance, involve actors such as long-term residents wanting to improve their quality of life but also members of the "creative class" (Florida, 2002) including software designers, artists, and musicians. Often, these individuals become vocal advocates for the future of their neighbourhoods, which despite their anachronism deriving, for example, from their industrial heritage offer elements enabling the production and consumption of cultural amenities.

However, it is naïve to maintain that only bottom-up forces shape what goes on in these neo-bohemias. What we see in these places is the significance of contingency in the way a particular city's neoliberal, redevelopment governance structure – including instruments like historic preservation and tax incentives – plays out as affected by local circumstances (stakeholders, history, political motives, etc.). In the case of Chicago, for instance, the redevelopment of neo-bohemias such as Wicker Park or Pilsen was actively supported by the city's underlying aim to boost gentrification with an eye on becoming globally competitive (Sternberg, 2012). Attracting members of the creative class, for instance, to these areas was an explicit goal of strengthening the city's pursuit of becoming a centre of culture and high tech activities (Wilson, 2004).

We believe the noticeable trend in North American cities over the last decade whereby neo-bohemian neighbourhoods beyond the standardized tourist bubbles have begun attracting the attention of visitors marks a new approach in the neoliberal project, albeit one that does not replace but occurs concurrently with elements commonly associated with roll-back and roll-out neoliberalism. However, unlike, straightforward "roll-back" and "roll-out" neoliberalism, which are noticeable in the sterilized mega projects of rehabilitated downtowns, we recognize that in neo-bohemias the forces of transformation are far more opaque. In many cases, local forces (bottom-up) are apparent and yet these are not operating in a vacuum; rather they are dictated by and respond to a city's neoliberal regime – regardless of what the citywide eventual desired outcome may be – as this becomes embedded within different parts of the metropolitan area.

This can be clarified further as follows. First, neo-bohemian projects, despite their creative nature, operate within a neoliberal framework because their objectives remain anchored in economic growth and development. However, the quest to attract businesses has probably shifted to a quest to attract culture-consuming individuals and visitors. Second, neo-bohemian projects are more localized in focus. The emphasis is on a neighbourhood, not the city at large; on the locally owned art gallery instead of a mega-museum, and on everyday experiences instead of staged escapism. The further devolution to the micro-local has the potential to make local contingencies even more evident. For example, although both Wicker Park and New York City's DUMBO (Down Under the Manhattan Bridge Overpass) neighbourhood are places of consumption, they are two very different neighbourhoods historically, demographically, politically, and economically. This attention to the micro-local can serve as a metaphor understanding local contingencies, especially if juxtaposed to the earlier, more monolithic stage of investing in tourist bubbles.

Arguably, the proliferation of such neighbourhoods, many of which are lauded as success stories, causes tensions. To begin with, their popularity ensures these places regularly attract the attention of global capital, which seeks to derive a share of the economic spoils by locating a facility in their midst. However, it is not unusual for this capital to encounter varying levels of resistance, obviously depending on these neighbourhoods' bargaining power. Even in those cases where they are permitted to set up a facility in a neo-bohemian neighbourhood, it is common for brand name chains to be subject to a strict set of regulations, often imposed to limit their visibility and their ability to compete unfairly with lesser-known independent operators (Hinshaw, 2008). The bottom line, which the agents controlling these neighbourhoods recognize, is that if a chain company wishes to start up an operation in their midst it must comply to the local regulatory regime. In this way, we could argue that the forces of globalization, represented by the interests of the brand name chain, become contingent on local forces to a far greater extent than what is witnessed in conventional tourism bubbles.

Concurrently, however, the very success of so many neo-bohemias nationwide means that despite their obvious resistance to standardized representations of global capital we are beginning to encounter increasing predictability in their offerings. This predictability is mirrored through the expected assemblage of Ethiopian, Thai, and Indian restaurants, boutique hotels and bed and breakfasts, microbreweries, independently-owned coffee houses and ice-cream parlours, as well as artists' studios and cinemas specializing in foreign movies. Meanwhile, the visitors to these areas who are initially drawn by their need to escape the drab standardization of the tourist bubbles (Judd, 2004) themselves become more standardized and conventional lending to a feeling that ultimately, these neo-bohemian environs may not be impervious to forces of growing homogeneity.

Further, Judd (2004) adds that even within these non-enclavic spaces, visitors and residents are subject to a barrage of regulations. The more popular they become as destinations, the more likely they are to encounter instruments of the revanchist city because, ultimately, public officials and private interests want to ensure removal of threatening elements to the users' experience. Such measures, ironically, likely ensure the very grittiness that initially served to put these places on the visitor map is eventually swept aside. On a broader front, they demonstrate that even though the emergence of such neo-bohemias may be contingent on local bottom-up forces, these areas operate increasingly within the confines of the neoliberal agenda. What is more, the nature of these experiences necessitates the imposition of various inherent inequities. For example, the members of the creative class who live and work within the neo-bohemian areas and the visitors who frequent these districts depend on an army of lowly paid workers performing various functions of social reproduction. Despite the need for these workers' services the gentrification of the neo-Bohemian neighbourhoods and the rising cost of housing that goes with it mean that they also have no place within these areas once their shift is over. Just like the people who are kept out as a direct result of revanchist practices, these workers end up being outsiders.

Conclusions

The adoption of visitor-oriented projects as a means of revitalizing ailing cities has been a key strategy in the U.S. since the inception of the neoliberal era. In this essay we have highlighted how by the beginning of the 21st century, downtown tourist enclaves represented the outcome of a blended form of neoliberalism, combining both characteristics of its original roll-back form with those of its roll-out successor (Peck and Tickell, 2002). Particular places within American cities had, in effect, been transformed into fairly standardized visitor attractions through a form of governance, which (a) paid homage to incentive-driven private sector involvement while (b) local governments themselves adopted an increasingly revanchist role, aimed primarily at disciplining any elements (persons and activities) seen as threats to these areas' attraction.

To the casual observer the high level of predictability found in so many of these so-called tourist bubbles (Judd, 2004) generates the belief that neoliberalism is enforced everywhere in a non-malleable top-down manner, not allowing for local contingencies. However, it has been our main aim to demonstrate that this is, in fact, far from the case. We contend that, in reality, a multitude of varying forces shape the neoliberal approach as it becomes enmeshed within the local level. As Wilson (2004: 771) maintains neoliberal governances are "anything but a 'top-down' brute and desensitized imposition on cities" and can be "best conceptualized as a series of differentiated, keenly negotiating, procedural, and space mobilizing constructions".

Although we acknowledge that a handful of other observers have already remarked on neoliberalism' contingent nature our principal argument is that the best places to observe this contingency in action are the so-called neo-bohemian neighbourhoods (Lloyd, 2002) that have been emerging in more and more cities over the last few years. Places like Wicker Park in Chicago are transforming into popular points of visitor consumption while also attracting new residents precisely because they display elements of uniqueness setting them aside from the more predictable enclaves. In other words, these places draw more and more visitors who are becoming disillusioned with the standardization of the bubble (Judd, 2004).

Nevertheless, despite the fact some of these neo-bohemias may have begun as bottom-up initiatives and even though they may display a lot of elements of uniqueness in terms, for example, of the built environment or the locally owned businesses in their midst, we are aware that in many instances their transformation still operates within the realm of a city's neoliberal governance structure albeit one that is definitely shaped by local historical and geographical circumstances. Thus, we conclude that neo-bohemian neighbourhoods as places of visitor consumption have emerged as the perfect metaphor of neoliberalism's highly contingent nature.

References

Beauregard, R.A. (1998). Tourism and economic development policy in US urban areas. In D. Ioannides and K.G. Debbage (eds) *The Economic Geography of the Tourist Industry: A Supply Side Analysis*. London: Routledge, 220–34.

Bianchi, R.V. (2012). A radical departure: A critique of the critical turn in Tourism Studies. In J. Wilson (ed.) *The Routledge Handbook of Tourism Geographies*. London: Routledge, 46–54.

Brenner, N. and Theodore, N. (2002). Preface: From the "new localism" to the spaces of neoliberalism. *Antipode*, 34(3), 341–7.

Britton, S.G. (1991). Tourism, capital, and place: Towards a critical geography of tourism. *Environment and Planning D: Society and Space*, 9(3), 451–78.

Clancy, M. (1998). Commodity chains, services and development: Theory and preliminary evidence from the tourism industry. *Review of International Political Economy*, 5(1), 122–48.

Clark, T.N., Lloyd, R., Wong, K., and Jain, P. (2002). Amenities drive urban growth. *Journal of Urban Affairs*, 24(5), 493–515.

Daley, R.M. (2000). The Chicago Alternative Policing Strategy (CAPS). In P.J. Andrisani, S. Hakim, and E. Leeds (eds) *Making Government Work: Lessons from America's Governors and Mayors*. New York: Rowman & Littlefield, 145–60.

Debbage, K.G. and Ioannides, D. (2012). The economy of tourism spaces: A multiplicity of "critical turns". In J. Wilson (ed.) *The Routledge Handbook of Tourism Geographies*. London: Routledge, 149–56.

Elander, I. (2002). Partnerships in urban governance. *International Social Science Journal*, 54(172), 191–204.

Fainstein, S.S. (2010). *The Just City*. Cornell: Cornell University Press.

Fainstein, S.S., Hoffman, L.M., and Judd, D.R. (2004). Introduction. In L.M. Hoffman, S.S. Fainstein and D.R. Judd (eds) *Cities and Visitors: Regulating People, Markets, and City Space*. Oxford: Blackwell, 1–19.

Florida, R. (2002). *The Rise of the Creative Class and How it's Transforming Work, Leisure, Community and Everyday Life*. New York: Basic Books.

Gillette, H. Jr. (2010). Is this the neoliberal moment? *Journal of Urban History*, 36(3), 393–7.

Giuliani, R.W. (2000). Reforming New York City: A new chapter in reinventing government. In P.J. Andrisani, S. Hakim, and E. Leeds (eds) *Making Government Work: Lessons from America's Governors and Mayors*. New York: Rowman & Littlefield, 161–6.

Gladstone, D. and Préau, J. (2008). Gentrification in tourist cities: Evidence from New Orleans before and after Hurricane Katrina. *Housing Policy Debate*, 19(1), 137–75.

Goldsmith, S. (2000). City services in the competitive marketplaces. In P.J. Andrisani, S. Hakim, and E. Leeds (eds) *Making Government Work: Lessons from America's Governors and Mayors*. New York: Rowman & Littlefield, 173–83.

Hackworth, J. (2007). *The Neoliberal City: Governance, Ideology, and Development in American Urbanism*. Ithaca, NY: Cornell University Press.

Hall, C.M. (2006). Urban entrepreneurship, corporate interests and sports mega-events: The thin policies of competitiveness within the hard outcomes of neoliberalism. *Sociological Review*, 52(s2), 59–70.

Hall, C.M. (2007). Tourism and regional competitiveness. In J. Tribe and D. Airey (eds) *Advances in Tourism Research: New Directions, Challenges and Applications*. Oxford: Elsevier, 217–30.

Hall, C.M. and Page, S.J. (2012). From the geography of tourism to geographies of tourism. In J. Wilson (ed.) *The Routledge Handbook of Tourism Geographies*. London: Routledge, 9–25.

Hinshaw, M. (2008). Great neighborhoods. *Planning*, 74(1), 6–11.

Hoffman, L.M., Fainstein, S.S., and Judd, D.R. (2004). *Cities and Visitors: Regulating People, Markets, and City Space*. Oxford: Blackwell Publishing.

Hoffman, L.M. (2004). Revalorizing the inner city: Tourism and regulation in Harlem. In L. Hoffman, SS. Fainstain and D.R. Judd (eds) *Cities and Visitors: Regulating People, Markets, and City Space*. Oxford: Blackwell, 91–112.

Ioannides, D. (2003). The economics of tourism in host communities. In S. Singh, D.J. Timothy and R.K. Dowling (eds) *Tourism in Destination Communities*. Wallingford: CABI, 37–54.

Ioannides, D. and Debbage, K.G. (eds) (1998). *The Economic Geography of the Tourist Industry: A Supply Side Analysis*. London: Routledge.

Ioannides, D. and Timothy, D.J. (2010). *Tourism in the USA: A Spatial and Social Synthesis*. London: Routledge.

Jessop, B. (2002). Liberalism, neoliberalism, and urban governance: A state-theoretical perspective. *Antipode*, 34(3), 452–72.

Judd, D.R. (1995). Promoting tourism in US cities. *Tourism Management*, 16(3), 175–87.

Judd, D.R. (1999). Constructing the tourist bubble. In D.R. Judd and S.S. Fainstein (eds) *The Tourist City*. New Haven, CT: Yale University Press, 35–53.

Judd, D.R. (2004). Visitors and the spatial ecology of the city. In L. Hoffman, SS. Fainstain and D.R. Judd (eds) *Cities and Visitors: Regulating People, Markets, and City Space*. Oxford: Blackwell, 23–38.

Judd, D.R. (2006). Commentary: Tracing the commodity chain of global tourism. *Tourism Geographies*, 8(3), 323–36.

Kastenbaum, S. (2012). NYPD's "stop, question and frisk" policy is racial profiling, critics say. *CNN Online* 3 April 2012. Available at http://inamerica. blogs.cnn.com/2012/04/03/nypds-stop-question-and-frisk-policy-is-racial-profilingcritics-say/?hpt=hp_c2 [6 April 2012].

Keil, R. (2002). "Common-sense" neoliberalism: Progressive conservative urbanism in Toronto, Canada. *Antipode*, 34(3), 578–601.

Kotler, P., Haider, D.H, and Rein, I. (1993). *Marketing Places. Attracting Investment, Industry, and Tourism to Cities, States, and Nations*. New York: The Free Press.

Lloyd, R. (2002). Neo-bohemia: Art and neighborhood redevelopment in Chicago. *Journal of Urban Affairs*, 24(5), 517–32.

MacLeod, G. (2002). From urban entrepreneurialism to a "revanchist city"? On the spatial injustices of Glasgow's Renaissance. *Antipode*, 34(3), 602–24.

Mosedale, J. (ed.) (2011). *Political Economy of Tourism: A Critical Perspective*. London: Routledge.

Peck, J. and Tickell, A. (2002). Neoliberalizing space. *Antipode*, 34(3), 380–404.

Pierre, J. (2011). *The Politics of Urban Governance*. Basingstoke: Palgrave MacMillan.

Smith, N. (1998). Giuliani time: The revanchist 1990s. *Social Text 57*, 16(4), 1–20.

Smith, N. (2001). Global social cleansing: Postliberal revanchism and the export of zero tolerance. *Social Justice*, 28(3), 68–74.

Smith, N. (2002). New globalism, new urbanism: Gentrification as global urban strategy. *Antipode*, 34(3), 427–50.

Sternberg, C.A. (2012). *The Dynamics of Contingency: Neoliberal Redevelopment Governance in Chicago and Buenos Aires*. PhD Dissertation submitted at University of Illinois at Urbana-Champaign.

Turner, R.S. and Rosentraub, M.S. (2002). Tourism, sports and centrality of cities. *Journal of Urban Affairs*, 24(5), 487–92.

Wilson, D. (2004). Toward a contingent urban neoliberalism. *Urban Geography*, 25(8). 771–83.

Chapter 3

Mega-events as Neoliberal Projects: 'Realistic if we want Dunedin to Prosper' or 'the Biggest Civic Disgrace ... in Living Memory'?

C. Michael Hall and Sandra Wilson

Neoliberalism has, as Harvey (2005: 3) observed, 'become hegemonic as a mode of discourse'. However, neoliberalism is not just an abstract discourse that occurs "out there". It affects policy decisions that have real impact on their targets. Shifting the way in which the role of the state in relation to the market and what constitutes "public good" and "welfare" is understood has concrete consequences. This chapter defines neoliberalism after Harvey (2005: 2) as 'a theory of political practices that proposes that human well-being can best be advanced by liberating entrepreneurial freedom and skills within an institutional framework characterized by strong private property rights, free markets and free trade.' Although this 'neoliberal hegemony, both in its pomp and in its crisis, has had global implications' (Hall et al., 2013: 10), the effects of the neoliberal project are experienced and evidenced in practices, processes and events that 'exists in articulation with actors, institutions, and agendas' (Castree, 2006: 2) at a local scale.

The local state has been a particular focus of changed understandings of what constitutes the appropriate roles of the state with respect to social and economic development policy. Many areas of social provision, including that of community-based leisure and sport, have been redefined with respect as to who should deliver services and how they should be paid for. What was once regarded as a public good has become a private good as the local state focuses on "core responsibilities". This means that state activity in sport has been subject to deregulation and in some cases re-regulation, corporatization, privatization and the withdrawal of the state, while simultaneously, the provision and subsidy of sporting events by the local state for private commercial benefit has substantially increased and become subject to a profound marketization (e.g. Hall, 2006, 2012; Horne and Manzenreiter, 2006; Schimmel, 2006; Smith and Himmelfarb, 2007; Sam and Scherer, 2008; Hutton, 2008; Andrews and Silk, 2012). Nevertheless, neoliberalism cannot be just understood as the reduction of state function and power, rather it is the 'rolling back' and restructuring of 'a particular kind of state' (Peck and Tickell, 2007: 28–9):

Only rhetorically does neoliberalism mean 'less state'; in reality, it entails a thoroughgoing reorganization of governmental systems and state-economy relations. Tendentially, and more and more evidently as neoliberalism has been extended and deepened, this program involves the roll-out of new state forms, new modes of regulation, new regime of governance, with the aim of consolidating and managing both marketization and its consequences (Peck and Tickell, 2007: 33).

This chapter discusses such issues in relation to the public funding and provision of stadia for the hosting of the 2011 Rugby World Cup (RWC) in New Zealand in 2011 and subsequent events. Although substantial debates as to stadia development for the event have occurred at a number of locations in the country, the focus of the present chapter is primarily on stadia development in Dunedin. The chapter extends the authors' previous work (Hall and Wilson, 2011), which tracked the initial stadium proposal, through to the post event aftermath. The example is also significant as they reinforce the way in which popular sporting culture and national and regional identities can be utilized to reinforce neoliberal agendas. However, as will be discussed, such examples only serves to continue the 'suspension of disbelief' that so often seems to categorize local state consideration of the funding and support of event related stadia development (Hall and Wilson, 2011).

The Hosting of Mega Sports Events

Hallmark or mega-events have become integral to many local and national development strategies (Roche, 1992; Hall, 1992, 2006, 2012). Historically, mega-events were utilized as part of urban regeneration and development strategies. This reinforces the need not to see them in an isolated sports context but frame them as entwined with theoretical understandings of the causes of place change and the role of state intervention in urban development and redevelopment. From this perspective the desire to host and, even more importantly, build for mega-events can be understood within the context of a shift from the use of events to encourage urban regeneration in the Keynesian welfare state, which enacted urban policy to internalize economic crisis and used events to "improve" locations, to a neoliberal "transformational" approach that understood the need to support for mega-events within the context of market failure, rather than economic structures (see Lipton and Fuller (2009) for a discussion of this shift in the context of housing). In the former, mega-events were hosted primarily to help solve internal spatial issues; in the latter, they are hosted to help solve external issues of competitiveness. Neoliberal restructuring is therefore invariably a destructively creative process, in which the dismantling of the Keynesian state and social institutions are accompanied by the roll-out of new institutional and discursive practices (Lee et al., 2010).

The reasons why governments and the private sector are usually positive towards the hosting of such events lie in the perceived economic benefits, place reimaging, marketing opportunities and therefore place competitiveness. Indeed, the role of the perceived media benefits of hosting events is often crucial for publically justifying the investment of state funds into event related stadia and infrastructure development. Such an approach is also part of the "new urban entrepreneurialism" (Harvey, 1989) in which city governments move away from service delivery roles to envision and promote economic growth and competitiveness, thereby creating the conditions for capital accumulation and investment (Hall, 2006).

Although mega-events are usually run by specifically established organizations, stadia costs are usually underwritten by a combination of the local and national state (usually in that order), sometimes with some corporate support. Nevertheless, the local state internalizes many of the costs of stadium and infrastructure construction and risks of the market process upon subsequent retention of the event infrastructure, i.e. ensuring long-term use and maintenance. It does this on the belief that such investment will create favourable conditions for investment, and with the understanding that stadia will return on their investment via their subsequent use and that new developments invested in as a result of the new found attractiveness of the city will return local taxes that will help recoup actual spend and therefore fund new entrepreneurial and municipal initiatives (Lipton and Fuller, 2009).

In business terminology, mega-events are therefore a form of 'loss-leader' that will otherwise generate benefits for the host economy (Hall and Wilson, 2011). Although it is important to recognize that the loss, in the form of public debt, is usually borne by the state and hence taxpayer with the direct benefits being accrued by the private sector as part of a strategy of providing a 'public good': with the term often being used within the neoliberal lexicon without any trace of irony. However, such an approach is also regarded as appropriate when countries are treated like a business in public discourse. For example, in New Zealand the phrase "NZ Inc" is widely used by right wing politicians and senior members of the business community with respect to the need for engaging in what is argued as "internationally competitive behaviour" (Wood, 2011). Of course, even though citizens may be described as shareholders in such an artifice they have little say in the selection of members of the board.

The hosting of mega-events implies, as Peck and Tickell (2003) suggest, that neoliberalism as practice involves the contradictory process of market functionality and expansion depending on interventionist regulatory institutions. Such a paradox with respect to such events is also reflected in the academic sphere because while their role with respect to regional competitiveness increases, so also does the literature that questions their long-term contribution to economic development and employment generation (e.g. Hall, 1992, 2004, 2006; Roche, 1992; Crompton and McKay, 1994; Crompton, 1995; Noll and Zimbalist, 1997; Andranovich, 2002; Whitson and Horne, 2006; Andrews and Silk, 2012). State evaluation of the link between increased expenditure and global recognition and long-term development is uncommon. In addition, mega-events frequently have significant social consequences in terms of their contribution to community disruption, and changes in the property and rental market (Jones, 2001). However, these are often positioned as the inevitable and even desirable outcomes of mega-event related revitalization and promotion of urban locations.

Harvey (2005) outlined four features of the neoliberal state in practice. First, its *activist role* in creating a 'good business climate' and behaving 'as a competitive entity in global politics' (Harvey, 2005: 79), which reflects the desire of the neoliberal state to host mega-events as part of the promotion of urban and national competitiveness. Second, the *dependence on authoritarianism* by using coercive legislation and policing in market enforcement; which is highlighted in the development of special legislation and regulation to ensure the development and running of events. In the case of mega-events, many normal policy and planning practices are abandoned. For example, event sponsors typically require bans on competing products in stadia or official event venues, or even in the surrounds of event venues in what is otherwise ostensibly public space. Third, the *regulation of finance* to reduce chronic financial instability. Although this is more related to national economic management this is also potentially linked to the hosting of mega-events as a means of economic stimulation. Fourth, the *reconstruction of social solidarity* in order to ease the social anomie caused by neoliberal reform. This approach is linked to the use of mega-events to appeal to national and, in some cases, local sentiment and ideology.

In New Zealand the improvement of sports stadia along with changes in legislation were central to the hosting agreements of the successful 2011 RWC bid that was made by the New Zealand Rugby Union (NZRU) with the full political and financial support of the New Zealand government. Yet very little of the costs of such developments were borne by NZRU, and relatively little by the national government. Instead, the majority was borne by the local state via loans, increased local taxes or opportunity costs. Leading to regional development trajectories in some cases that are increasingly bound to hosting events. The development of stadia and the new legal framework for hosting events therefore became the basis of bidding for or hosting other events. In the New Zealand case, this includes the Cricket World Cup 2015, the 2015 FIFA under-20 World Cup, and the Rugby tour of the British and Irish Lions in 2017. The next section discusses the 2011 RWC before specifically discussing the proposed stadia development in Dunedin.

The 2011 Rugby World Cup (RWC, 2011)

Rugby is an important element of New Zealand's identity (Laidlaw, 1999), although rugby only turned professional in 1995. Since that time rugby throughout the world has seen the development of new and the commoditization of old senior domestic and international competitions in conjunction with global media interests, most notably those of News Corporation, and the construction of sports venues in which rugby is the dominant code (Higham and Hall, 2003).

In November 2005, the governing body for international rugby the International Rugby Board (IRB) accepted New Zealand has bid to host the RWC 2011. In a reflection of Harvey's (2005) notion of the reconstruction of social solidarity, New Zealand's bid was built around the theme that the tournament would be hosted in a 'Stadium of Four Million' (Ministry of Business, Innovation and Enterprise (MBIE), 2012a) and that it would be an 'ALL RUGBY" experience for all involved' (IRB, 2008).

As is often the case with mega-events, the success of the bid was lauded as a 'victory' of place competitiveness and strategy. The national rugby team is an important element of branding New Zealand with the hosting of the RWC positioned as significant for the reaffirmation of the country as the 'homeland' of rugby (Ministry for Culture and Heritage, 2007). However, in a country in which rugby has historically been closely related to identity, the event was also utilized for political purposes to describe how society and governance should operate. For example, the then Minister for the Community and Voluntary Sector, Hon Winnie Laban, linked RWC to the value of the market and public-private partnerships in ensuring an "inclusive" society, if not economy.

A good example of how the State, the market, and civil society can work well together was seen when the New Zealand Rugby Union won the hosting rights for the Rugby World Cup. A sporting association—the New Zealand Rugby Union—with solid business links with sponsors and support from the Government, in the form of the Prime Minister, carried the day. We have learnt in the past that the market by itself does not build a good society, and the State cannot, either. We need the State, the market, and civil society working well together in order to build the economic and social development of our nation and to build a strong, inclusive nation. (Laban, 2005: 317)

The then Minister for Sport and Recreation, Hon Trevor Mallard, noted that the bid had received cross party support and suggested

Hosting the Rugby World Cup will be positive, not only for New Zealand rugby but also because the tournament will deliver significant economic benefits and tourism spin-offs. It is estimated that it will attract around 60,000 extra visitors to New Zealand, will generate an extra $400 million for the economy, and result in an extra tax take exceeding $90 million ... In addition to the extra visitors we expect to visit New Zealand, television-viewing numbers for the last world cup were 3.4 billion. That will be a fantastic opportunity to showcase New Zealand. (Mallard, 2005: 302)

The economic impact and promotional benefits of the RWC was the primary justification given by government to financially support the hosting of the event. The IRB promotes the Rugby World Cup as the third largest global sporting event behind the Olympics and the FIFA World Cup (Deloitte, 2006). In 2006, the NZRU commissioned economic consultants Horwath Asia Pacific Limited to assess the economic impact of hosting the 2011 RWC (Deloitte, 2006). Based on the precedents set at the 2003 Rugby World Cup in Australia and allowing for growth, the Horwath Report estimated that the 2011 RWC would generate more than NZ$1.15 billion in total economic activity, contributing $507m to New Zealand's GDP. This would result in $476m of total direct additional expenditure within New Zealand ($262m of this going to the Auckland economy) and provide the New Zealand government an additional $112m in tax revenue (Rugby New Zealand, 2006). Horwath Asia Pacific Limited estimated the RWC 2011 would attract approximately 66,000 international supporters, 2,500 international media and 2,500 corporate guests (Deloitte, 2006). Using International Visitor Survey (IVS) data the MBIE (2012b) report on the tourism impact of the RWC concluded that out of the total 785,600 visitors who came to New Zealand during the RWC time period, 133,200 of these came for the RWC. They also found that international RWC visitors spent a total of $387 million. RWC visitors spent on average $3,400 each compared to $2,400 for non-RWC visitors over the same time period. The net increase in visitor expenditure attributable to the RWC was estimated at approximately $280 million. However, it is important to note that 'For total RWC visitor expenditure the margin of error (radius of a 95 percent confidence interval) is 20%' (MBIE, 2012b: 24).

The RWC is administered by Rugby World Cup Limited, a subsidiary of the International Rugby Board (IRB), and is the primary source of revenue for the funding of global rugby development with 95 per cent of all money distributed by the IRB coming from World Cup revenue. As part of the bid requirements and subsequent Host Union Agreement with the New Zealand Rugby Union, a government-underwritten provision to deliver a minimum guarantee to the IRB was provided although the tournament was organized by Rugby New Zealand Limited (RNZ, 2011) a joint company of the NZRU and the New Zealand government. Any profits from the 2011 RWC would have been shared on a 50/50 basis between the NZRU and the New Zealand Government, while losses would be met by a one-third/two-third split between the NZRU and the New Zealand Government respectively (IRB, 2008). The tournament was celebrated as 'Truly amazing success' by NZRU chairman Mike Eagle (Rattue, 2012) with a financial loss of $31.3 million.

The commercial structure for the tournament meant that the IRB retained the broadcasting, sponsorship and merchandising rights, and limited the NZRU's revenue stream to ticket sales. There were 48 matches in 12 venues with an average attendance of over 30,000 people. The fact that the revenue stream for RWC 2011 was determined by ticket sales clearly placed pressure on those cities that sought to bid to host games to provide as large a venue as possible in order to be selected. As Martin Snedden, Chief Executive of RNZ 2011 noted in commenting on the allocation of quarterfinal matches, "The tension is between the 'stadium of four million' people and the financial model". According to Snedden, the tournament was estimated to cost $310 million to run, with ticket sales forecast to return $280 million, resulting in a $30 million loss, similar to Rugby New Zealand's forecast.

The commercial interests of the IRB and its corporate partners were paramount in the hosting of the event and the development of new legislative frameworks. A new law regarding the hosting of major events was brought in as part of the preparation for hosting the 2011 Rugby World Cup. Under the *Major Events Management Act 2007* the Minister of Economic Development after consultation with the Commerce Minister and the Sports Minister, can declare 'that an event is a major event'. Under Part 2, Section 7 of the Act

(3) The Economic Development Minister may only make a recommendation if—
(a) an event organiser has applied for an event to be declared to be a major event under this Act; and
(b) the event activities will take place, at least in part, in New Zealand; and
(c) the Minister is satisfied that the event organiser has the capacity and the intention to—
(i) successfully and professionally stage and manage the event; and
(ii) use all practicable measures available under the existing law to prevent unauthorised commercial exploitation of the major event and to protect its intellectual property and other legal rights (including, for example, registering relevant trade marks).
(4) Before making a recommendation, the Economic Development Minister must take into account whether the event will—
(a) attract a large number of international participants or spectators and therefore generate significant tourism opportunities for New Zealand:
(b) significantly raise New Zealand's international profile:
(c) require a high level of professional management and co-ordination:
(d) attract significant sponsorship and international media coverage:
(e) attract large numbers of New Zealanders as participants or spectators:
(f) offer substantial sporting, cultural, social, economic, or other benefits for New Zealand or New Zealanders. (Major Events Management Act, 2007)

The Act explicitly seeks to protect major events from ambush marketing in time and space. The 'protection period need not be limited to the period when major event activities are to occur, but cannot end later than 30 days after the completion or termination of all major event activities' (*Major Events Management Act 2007*, sec. 9(2)). The spatial implications of such state-sponsored corporate protection are remarkable with the Act providing for 'declaration of clean zones, clean transport routes, and clean periods' not only within event facilities but also in 'proximate areas'; 'areas that are otherwise necessary to enable the major event activity to occur', and 'a clean transport route' with a spatial boundary that can extend up to 5km from a clean zone along a motorway, state highway or railway line. Such conditions are extremely significant given the extent to which they extend outside of the immediate space of the event and enter to what is otherwise public space.

According to the IRB (2010) which endorsed the Act,

> New Zealand is the first country in the world where non-event specific ambush
> marketing legislation has been introduced and this is a huge step forward in
> bringing major events to this country. This legislation (as it relates to RWC,
> 2011) ensures that the exclusive rights of association granted to RWC 2011's
> commercial family are protected, thereby ensuring that sponsors will continue
> to acquire or renew rights in relation to future tournaments which all goes back
> into funding the game of Rugby globally. (IRB, 2010)

Although such clean space is a hallmark of many major events in terms of stadia,
the extent to which a country changed its laws in order to accommodate the
corporate dimension of major events reflects the suspension of normal policy and
planning practices in the belief that this will enhance the economic returns from
hosting such an event, and attracting more in the future.

In addition to specific legislation to protect the commercial interests of the
IRB and sponsors there were also major redevelopments of stadia in Christchurch,
Auckland and Dunedin as well as in a number of smaller regional centres in
preparation for the RWC 2011. Following a regional council rejection of the
development of a new waterfront stadium, the existing Eden Park stadium,
situated in Auckland, underwent a $240.5m redevelopment, with stands being
expanded to increase the maximum capacity of the stadium. Of this, the New
Zealand Government funded $190m and the NZRU $10m (Hall and Wilson,
2011). The AMI stadium in Christchurch was also redeveloped at an estimated
cost of $60m (Hall and Wilson, 2011), although no matches were held there as
a result of earthquake damage. Dunedin, eventually hosted four games, partly
because of Christchurch's loss of games.

The new Dunedin Stadium, now known as the Forsyth Barr Stadium, is a multi-
purpose roofed facility situated on the fringe of the centre of Dunedin and is located
adjacent to the University of Otago and the Otago Polytechnic. Logan Park, another
sporting venue, is across the road from the site. Although designed as a multi-purpose
venue capable of hosting a range of cultural and sporting events it cannot host cricket
because it has a rectangular sport field. At the time of writing, the pitch is a mix of
grass and synthetic fibres although this is under review because of maintenance costs.
The stadium can hold up to 36,000 people in concert format, and just under 31,000
people in a football format (see http://www.forsythbarrstadium.co.nz/). However, as
discussed below, the stadium is controversial with its development embedded in the
contemporary neoliberal project.

The Dunedin Stadium Development

Dunedin is located on the south-eastern coast of the South Island in New Zealand
and is the main centre of the Otago region. The city has a population of just over
110,000 and the wider region almost 200,000. New Zealand's successful bid for
the RWC catalysed action in Dunedin regarding the future of their existing major

sports stadium, Carisbrook. However, Carisbrook was increasingly seen as having inadequate facilities to host international sporting fixtures, including top tier rugby tests, for which the city might bid. Therefore for Dunedin to be considered as a venue for as many RWC 2011 games as possible Carisbrook required either significant upgrading or replacement (Carisbrook Stadium Trust n.d. a).

In March 2004, the Dunedin City Council established the Carisbrook Working Party to investigate options for the stadium's future. After preliminary research, it was suggested that an independent trust be established to manage the project and take ownership of Carisbrook. This led to the establishment of the Carisbrook Stadium Trust (CST) in August 2006, the Chairman of which was Malcolm Farry, prominent Dunedin businessman (Critic, 2007) and chair of the Otago Highlanders rugby franchise (Kilgallon, 2012). The CST (n.d. b) proposed the development of a new multi-purpose stadium rather than upgrading Carisbrook, as this was the only 'long-term solution'. Initial responses from the Dunedin City Council (DCC) focussed on the $188m cost of the new stadium and the possible location, with land acquisition seemingly problematic (Critic, 2007). There were options presented that would have cost considerably less to develop. Redevelopment of Carisbrook was expected to cost between $29.3m and $69m and a new stadium without a roof was expected to cost approximately $131m (CST, 2007a). However, by October 2006 the Preliminary Feasibility Report presented by the CST suggested that the new covered multi-purpose stadium was feasible and warranted further investigation. Following the presentation of the February 2007 Master and Feasibility Report to the DCC the vote was made to progress with the 'preferred' multi-purpose stadium option in association with the Otago University (CST n.d. b), which eventually provided an indirect contribution of $10 million into the project, mainly in the form of land (Kilgannon, 2012).

Malcolm Farry, also a part-time lecturer at the University, stated that the Stadium would 'future-proof' the University ensuring it continued to grow and remain competitive (Critic, 2007). Strong links between the CST and the University were also evidenced by the membership of John Ward, then Pro-Chancellor of the University, as a trustee. The CST also claimed that having a 'world-class' stadium on campus would attract or retain 500–1,000 students a year in Dunedin. The then Vice-Chancellor, David Skegg (2007), estimated that it had a total economic impact of $63,000 per student on the Dunedin economy, thus the CST suggested that the Stadium would provide an additional $30m-60m a year to the Dunedin economy from the University (CST, 2007a; Skegg, 2007). The involvement of the University in the stadium development was controversial. A former Dunedin City Councillor, Leah McBey, questioned its involvement; suggesting students have the right to ask why it would pay for the stadium instead of cutting fees (McBey, 2007), while Sam (2007) noted that perhaps the city and the University would be better to create a trust to distribute scholarships to entice students to Dunedin as a less costly alternative.

The CST (2007a) closely linked the building of a new stadium and the hosting of RWC 2011 to Dunedin's urban regeneration and reimaging strategies (DCC, 2005; Hall, 2007), and focussed on its role in harbourside regeneration as well the international media exposure that a mega-event being held in Dunedin, such as the RWC 2011, would bring (CST n.d. c). They also suggested it would attract new residents to Dunedin as well as increasing tourism and attracting new business developments (CST n.d. c).

Interest groups lead the debate on the stadium: the Dunedin Ratepayer and Household Association (DRHA) and the related Stop the Stadium who opposed the stadium development on financial grounds and 'Our Stadium' who were advocates of the CST and the new stadium. The DHRA criticized the new stadium as being unnecessary, unwanted, and unaffordable and dubbed it "Farry's Folly" (Rudd, 2007). Spokesman Syd Adie stating 'People like the idea of a stadium but they don't want to pay for it on their rates' (One News, 2007). In 2005, both the DCC and the ORC were presented with a petition from DHRA with 6,025 names calling for a binding ratepayer's referendum to be held before public money was committed (Loughrey, 2006). Protests were also held demanding ratepayer money not to be used to fund the proposed stadium (MacKnight and Lewis, 2007), as well as questioning the information provided by the CST, the viability of the new stadium, and the economic benefit (Rudd, 2007; MacKnight and Lewis, 2007). However, such opposition to the new stadium proposal prompted supporters of the project to rally.

Our Stadium was a supporters club intent on 'mobilising positive public opinion' for the Dunedin Stadium project (MacKnight and Porteous, 2007: 1) that was also regarded as a "development partner and stakeholder" by the CST. It was headed by businessman and former Dunedin mayor Sir Clifford Skeggs and backed by a group of businesspersons, media representatives and sportspeople (Loughrey, 2007). Dunedin City Councillor Lee Vandervis described them as 'a rich old boys' club' (Loughrey, 2007: 1) implying that they were influential due to their corporate relationships and wealth within Dunedin. Skeggs stated 'Big projects often get captured by a noisy minority who claim to speak for everybody. They don't. Our job is to unite the positive people in the region and their voices will make the local authorities decision to say YES a much easier task' (Our Stadium n.d.). The growth coalition characteristics of Our Stadium are well illustrated by Skeggs' comment 'The reality is if you don't have a stadium, you don't have a future in Dunedin' (MacKnight and Porteous, 2007: 2).

Our Stadium and the CST promoted the Stadium as providing employment during and after construction (Our Stadium n.d.; Loughrey, 2007) and was given 'significant contributions of cash and service' towards their activities, which Sir Clifford Skeggs said totalled more than $20,000. When asked about the effect on ratepayers of having to pay for the stadium, especially those of limited means, Skeggs said he is sympathetic 'But we've got to be realistic if we want Dunedin to prosper' (Loughrey, 2007: 1).

Public opinion surveys undertaken to judge support for the new stadium showed mixed results depending on who the survey was conducted for and methods used (Hall and Wilson, 2011). Debate was focussed on whether the Stadium would be able to be built for $188m (Newstalk ZB, 2006) and who pays. However, the CST (2007b) assured the DCC that they would not go over the $188m budget they proposed. In the end, the DCC underwrote the project and contributed funds, directly or indirectly to the balance of $162.7 million, with the final cost of the stadium being $206.4 million to build plus interest of $18 million, a total of $224.4 million (PWC, 2012).

There were also questions as to whether Dunedin's citizens would be able to support and benefit from events held at the new stadium given that existing capacity was often not being filled (Rudd, 2006). Horwath HTL (2007) stated that Dunedin's relatively low income levels, small population and the low population in the surrounding regions may impact on the area's ability to support events. The hosting of rugby events in New Zealand is increasingly competitive; New Zealand has more test capable grounds than the number of test matches that are hosted in any one year, with the city's possible competitive advantage and its ability to attract events reliant on developments at other New Zealand stadia (Horwath HTL, 2007). Horwath HTL (2007) prepared the financial feasibility projections for the CST with the optimistic scenario showing the stadium making $536,000 average per year from 2011–2025, and the pessimistic scenario suggesting an $108,000 average per year. The CST also suggested that the stadium would benefit the region by $24m annually (Otago Daily Times, 2008).

However, by 2012 the stadium had come to be described by Russell Garbutt, formerly of Stop the Stadium as 'Perhaps the biggest civic disgrace perpetrated upon ratepayers in living memory' (Kilgannon, 2012). In contrast, Malcolm Farry argued 'We're excited and delighted we were able to achieve something of lasting value to this community ... It delighted the majority of people; we're disappointed at the remnants of those who were against it still trying to make their point. Surely it's time to give it up and relish and embrace the stadium?' (Kilgannon, 2012).

In the year after it was opened, only two major non-rugby events were held: an Elton John concert, and the 150th birthday celebrations of *Otago Daily Times* publishers Allied Press. Neither paid a stadium hire fee (Kilgannon, 2012). In 2012 rather than the expected profit council-owned stadium management company Dunedin Venues Management Limited's (DVML) predicted a $2.4m loss and stated it could not cover the cost of debt-servicing on stadium loans (Kilgannon, 2012). In 2013, concerts by Paul Simon and Aerosmith were held although relatively poor crowds raised questions about the stadium's future viability for concert promoters, while the DCC made a loss on the sale of the Carisbrook Stadium (Morris, 2013) after previously bailing out Otago Rugby (Kilgannon, 2012). In August 2013, the number of unemployed in Otago had reached its highest level since 1991 (Mackenzie, 2013).

With a new stadium planned for construction in Christchurch, a city with a much larger population, Dunedin is also anticipating its 'point of difference' in hosting events will disappear, as the *Otago Daily Times* (2013) editorial stated, 'Why come to Dunedin'? However, the development of a new stadium in post-earthquake Christchurch should come with the same caution that the DCC and those in favour of the new Dunedin Stadium did not embrace. As DCC councillor Lee Vandervis, who was voted off council between 2007 and 2010, stated:

'Absolutely they didn't understand, but if they had wanted to understand, the information was available ... but it was spread all over different places and they were never encouraged to look ... [but] if you google "stadiums plus economic impact", all the information you need is right there' (Kilgannon, 2012).

The Neoliberal Discourse of Competitiveness and Stadia Development

There is little positive evidence for the medium to long-term economic effects of sports event led economic regeneration strategies (Coalter, 2000). The pro-stadium discourse of the CST and Our Stadium highlights the competitive neoliberal imperatives of stadia development and the hosting of mega-events (Malecki, 2004). As Harvey's (1989: 12) review of urban entrepreneurialism identified: 'Many of the innovations and investments designed to make particular cities more attractive as cultural and consumer centres have quickly been imitated elsewhere, thus rendering any competitive advantage within a system of cities ephemeral ... Local coalitions have no option, given the coercive laws of competition, except to keep ahead of the game'

The fusion of urban entrepreneurialism with the neoliberal agenda has provided the ideological justification for place competitive reimaging strategies including the hosting of mega-events and stadia development (Peck and Tickell, 2002). In Dunedin, as elsewhere, neoliberal discourse has served to structure ideas about and the objectives set for community development, definitions of the public good, and being a "good citizen" (Bristow, 2005; Hall, 2006). The desire to host sports mega-events and the requirements of having to develop new or upgraded sports facilities and city infrastructure as part of a belief in place competitiveness has meant that cities face the possibility of having to provide larger subsidies and finance projects that deliver fewer public benefits (Hall, 2006). Even Kotler et al. (1993: 15) who provide the standard business studies text on place marketing acknowledges that the increasing place competition for investment has the marks of a 'zero-sum game or worse, a negative-sum game, in that the winner ultimately becomes the loser.' Indeed, all this begs the question of how entrepreneurial is regional or urban entrepreneurialism? (Hall and Wilson, 2011). However, disputing the benefits of a sport stadium is difficult, especially within the taken-for-granted context that sport and mega-events are good for you and the neoliberal logic that the public funding of private benefits will be good for the community as a whole (Hall, 2004, 2006).

As noted at the start of the chapter the hegemonic discourse of neoliberalism is not just global, it is also located at various scales including the local and the national. The discourses surrounding the new stadium proposal do not occur in an abstract space, they affect the construction and representation of place as well as the definition of urban policy winner and losers. They also represent the role of interests in shaping policy (Bristow, 2005). Undoubtedly, there is a genuine local desire to arrest the increasing economic, political and sporting peripherality of what was once New Zealand's leading industrial centre (Hall and Wilson, 2011). Stadia development as a form of regional development is essentially a zero-sum game in the long-term. Yet such is the strength of neoliberal discourses of competitiveness that alternative strategies are often not fully examined. Unfortunately, the inherent attractiveness of the neoliberal contest for regional competitiveness combined with the symbolic importance of having a stadium with the capacity to host major rugby internationals is not only a powerful discourse but also has the support of a significant coalition of interests (Hall and Wilson, 2011). However, as this chapter has suggested, a strategy based on stadia development in a peripheral city for which a successful competitive economic identity seems increasingly linked to its capacity in attracting events is highly problematic.

References

Andranovich, G., Burbank, M.J. and Heying, C.H. (2002). Olympic cities: Lessons learned from mega-event politics. *Journal of Urban Affairs*, 23(2), 113–31.
Andrews, D.L. and Silk, M.L. (2012). *Sport and Neoliberalism: Politics, Consumption and Culture*. Philadelphia, PA: Temple University Press.
Bristow, G. (2005). Everyone's a "winner": Problematising the discourse of regional competitiveness. *Journal of Economic Geography*, 5(3), 285–304.
Castree, N. (2006). Commentary: From neoliberalism to neoliberalisation: Consolations, confusions, and necessary illusions. *Environment and Planning A*, 38(1), 1–6.
Carisbrook Stadium Trust (CST) (2007a). *The New Dunedin Multipurpose Stadium: Concept Design*. Online. Available at: http://www.carisbrook.org. nz/pdfs/Concept_Design_Report/Concept_Design_Report.pd (Accessed 17 May 2008).
Carisbrook Stadium Trust (CST) (2007b). *Carisbrook Opportunity, Dunedin, Master Plan and Feasibility Report: 19 February 2007*. Online. Available at: http://www.carisbrook.org.nz/pdfs/Masterplan_Feasibility/Section_01.pdf.
Carisbrook Stadium Trust (CST) (n.d.a). *Why we need a new stadium*. Online. Available at: http://www.ourstadium.co.nz/why.html (Accessed 10 May 2008).
Carisbrook Stadium Trust (CST) (n.d. b). *History*. Retrieved 10 May, 2008, from http://www.carisbrook.org.nz/pages/history.html (Accessed 10 May 2008).
Carisbrook Stadium Trust (CST) (n.d. c). *Economic Benefits*. Online. Available at: http://www.carisbrook.org.nz/pages/economic.html (Accessed 15 May 2008).
Coalter, F., Allison, M. and Taylor, J. (2000). *The Role of Sport in Regenerating Deprived Urban Areas*. Edinburgh: Centre for Leisure Research, University of Edinburgh.
Critic (2007). State of play. *Critic*, 16 April.
Crompton, J. (1995). Economic impact analysis of sports facilities and events: Eleven sources of misapplication. *Journal of Sport Management*, 9(1), 14–35.

Crompton, J. and McKay, S. (1994). Measuring the economic impact of festivals and events: Some myths, misapplications and ethical dilemmas. *Festival Management and Event Tourism*, 2(1), 33–43.

Deloitte (2006). *Economic Benefits of Jade Stadium Development: October 2006*. Retrieved 17 May, 2008, from http://www.ccc.govt.nz/HaveYourSay/StevensStreetJadeStadium/Appendix%207%20-%20Economic%20Benefits.pdf.

Dunedin City Council (2005). *Vision for Dunedin Harbourside Out For Consultation*. Dunedin: DCC.

Hall, C.M. (1992). *Hallmark Tourist Events: Impacts, Management, and Planning*. London: Belhaven Press.

Hall, C.M. (2004). Sports tourism and urban regeneration. In B. Ritchie and D. Adair (eds) *Sports Tourism: Interrelationships, Impacts and Issues*. Clevedon: Channel View Publications, 192–205.

Hall, C.M. (2006). Urban entrepreneurship, corporate interests and sports mega-events: The thin policies of competitiveness within the hard outcomes of neoliberalism. *The Sociological Review*, 54(s2), 59–70.

Hall, C.M. (2007). Competing from the periphery: Regional contexts for doing business in Dunedin. In K. Inkson, V. Browning and J. Kirkwood (eds) *Working on the Edge: A Portrait of Business in Dunedin*. Dunedin: Otago University Press.

Hall, C.M. (2012). The political analysis and political economy of events. In S. Page and J. Connell (eds) *The Routledge Handbook of Events*. London: Routledge, 186–201.

Hall, C.M. and Wilson, S. (2011). Neoliberal urban entrepreneurial agendas, Dunedin Stadium and the Rugby World Cup: Or "If you don't have a stadium, you don't have a future". In D. Dredge and J. Jenkins (eds) *Stories of Practice: Tourism Policy and Planning*. Farnham: Ashgate, 133–52.

Hall, S., Massey, D. and Rustin, M. (2013). After neoliberalism: Analysing the present. *Soundings*, 53(1), 8–22.

Harvey, D. (1989). From managerialism to entrepreneurialism: The transformation of urban governance in late capitalism. *Geografiska Annaler, Series B, Human Geography*, 71(1), 3–17.

Harvey, D. (2005). *A Brief History of Neoliberalism*. Oxford: Oxford University Press.

Higham, J. and Hall, C.M. (2003). Editorial: Sports tourism in Australia and New Zealand: Responding to a dynamic interface. *Journal of Sport Tourism*, 8(3), 131–43.

Horne, J. and Manzenreiter, W. (2006). An introduction to the sociology of sports mega-events. *The Sociological Review*, 54(s2), 1–24.

Horwath HTL (2007). *New Carisbrook Stadium Development: Financial Feasibility Study and Economic Impact Assessment*. Retrieved 15 May, 2008, from http://www.carisbrook.org.nz/pdfs/Masterplan_Feasibility/Appendices/Howart_HTL_Report.pdf.

Hutton, T. (2008). *The New Economy of the Inner City: Restructuring, Regeneration and Dislocation in the 21st Century Metropolis.* London: Routledge.

International Rugby Board (IRB) (2008). RWC 2011 and RNZ 2011 Fact Sheet: Rugby World Cup 2011 and Rugby New Zealand 2011 Ltd, Retrieved 15 August 2008 from http://www.rugbyworldcup.com/destinationnewzealand/aboutrnz/factsheet.html.

International Rugby Board (2010). *RWCL Endorses Major Events Management Act*, 25 March. Online. Available at: http://www.rugbyworldcup.com/destinationnewzealand/news/newsid=2036702.html (accessed August 2011).

Jones, C. (2001). Mega-events and host-region impacts: Determining the true worth of the 1999 Rugby World Cup. *The International Journal of Tourism Research*, 3(3), 241–51.

Kilgallon, S. (2012). Dunedin's House of Blame, *Stuff Business*, 3 June. Online. Available at: http://www.stuff.co.nz/business/7035623/Dunedins-House-of-Blame (accessed 1 April 2013).

Kotler, P., Haider, D., and Rein, I. (1993). *Marketing Places: Attracting Investment, Industry, and Tourism to Cities, States, and Nations.* New York: Free Press.

Laban, W. Hon. (2005). Address in Reply, 22 September 2005, Debate resumed from 17 November, New Zealand Parliament, Hansard, 628: 317.

Laidlaw, C. (1999). *Rights of Passage: Beyond the New Zealand Identity Crisis.* Hodder Moa Beckett: Auckland.

Lupton, R. and Fuller, C. (2009). Mixed communities: A new approach to spatially concentrated poverty in England. *International Journal of Urban and Regional Research*, 33(4), 1014–28.

Loughrey, D. (2006). Not all councillors respond favourably: Some support plans, others hostile. *Otago Daily Times*, 12 August: 42.

Loughrey, D. (2007). Ground-breaking permanent roof, University link cemented, $188 million price tag. *Otago Daily Times*, 23 February: 1.

Mackenzie, D. (2013). Govt doing plenty: Joyce. *Otago Daily Times*, Auguest 9.

MacKnight, L. and Lewis, J. (2007). Stadium groups polls apart: Not our money, protesters say. *Otago Daily Times*, 24 May: 1.

MacKnight, L. and Porteous, D. (2007). Majority of annual plan submissions against stadium. *Otago Daily Times*, 18 May: 1.

Major Events Management Act 2007, Public Act 2007 No 35, Date of assent 28 August 2007.

Malecki, E. (2004). Jockeying for position: What it means and why it matters to regional development policy when places compete. *Regional Studies*, 38(9),1101–20.

Mallard, T. Hon. (2005), Questions for Oral Answer — Questions to Ministers, Questions to Members. New Zealand Parliament, Hansard, 628, 302.

McBey, L. (2007). When councillors feel the need to ask public to trust them. *Otago Daily Times*, 21 February, 19.

Ministry of Business, Innovation and Enterprise (MBIE) (2012). *The Stadium of Four Million*, Wellington: MBIE.

Ministry for Culture and Heritage (2007). *The 1987 Rugby World Cup*. Retrieved 15 May, 2008, from http://www.nzhistory.net.nz/culture/the-1987-rugby-world-cup.

Morris, C. (2013). No Carisbrook inquiry, auditor says. *Otago Daily Times*, 28 May.

Newstalk ZB (2006). *Doubts Over Costing for New Stadium*. Retrieved 21 May, 2008, from http://www.newstalkzb.co.nz/newsdetail1.asp?storyID=101345.

Noll, R., and Zimbalist, A. (eds) (1997). *Sports, Jobs and Taxes: The Economic Impact of Sports Teams and Stadiums*. Washington, DC: Brookings Institution.

Otago Daily Times (2008). How the Dunedin stadium debate has unfolded, *Otago Daily Times*, 16 February, 5.

One News (2007). *Limited Support for new Carisbrook*. Online. Available at: http://tvnz.co.nz/view/page/411317/1150025 (accessed 21 May 2008).

Our Stadium (n.d.). *Our Stadium*. Online. Available at: http://www.ourstadium.co.nz/ (accessed 17 May 2008).

Otago Daily Times (2013). Editorial: Bribes for big cities. *Otago Daily Times*, 5 July.

Peck, J. and Tickell, A. (2002). Neoliberalizing space. *Antipode*, 34(3), 380–403.

Peck, J. and Tickell, A. (2003). Making global rules: Globalisation or neoliberalisation? In J. Peck and H. Yeung (eds) *Remaking the Global Economy*. London: Sage, 163–81.

Peck, J. and Tickell, A. (2007) Conceptualizing neoliberalism, thinking Thatcherism. In H. Leitner, J. Peck and E. Sheppard (eds) *Contesting Neoliberalism: Urban Frontiers*. New York: The Guilford Press, 26–50.

PWC (Price Waterhouse Coopers) (2012). *Report on Review of Forsyth Barr Stadium Costs for Dunedin City Council*. Dunedin: PWC and DCC.

Rattue, C. (2012). Rugby: Lower than expected loss for World Cup. *The New Zealand Herald*, 30 May.

Roche, M. (1992). Mega-events and micro-modernization: On the sociology of the new urban tourism. *The British Journal of Sociology*, 43(4), 563–600.

Rudd, A. (2007). Ratepayers slam 'Farry's Folly'. *Otago Daily Times*, 14 April, 1.

Rugby New Zealand (2006). *2011 Rugby World Cup Bigger and Better*. Media release, 15 September.

Sam, M. (2007). Stadium benefits misrepresented. *Otago Daily Times*, 30 May, 15.

Sam, M.P. and Scherer, J. (2008). Stand up and be counted. *International Review for the Sociology of Sport*, 43(1), 53–70.

Schimmel, K.S. (2006). Deep play: Sports mega-events and urban social conditions in the USA. *Sociological Review*, 54(s2), 160–74.

Skegg, D. (2007). Question is not what it will cost, but what is it worth? *Otago Daily Times*, 26 February, 17.

Smith, C.J. and Himmelfarb, K.M.G. (2007). Restructuring Beijing's social space: Observations on the Olympic Games in 2008. *Eurasian Geography and Economics*, 48(5), 543–54.

Whitson, D. and Horne, J. (2006). Underestimated costs and overestimated benefits? Comparing the outcomes of sports mega-events in Canada and Japan. *Sociological Review*, 54(s2), 71–89.

Wood, B. (2011). The dislocation of agriculture and food: A network analysis of interlocking directorates in New Zealand's corporate economy. *Kotuitui: New Zealand Journal of Social Sciences Online*, 6(1–2), 100–12.

Chapter 4

The Changing Role of the State: Neoliberalism and Regional Tourism Development in New Zealand

Michael C. Shone

In New Zealand the past 25 years has seen a radical restructuring of local–central relations, with a significant outcome of this restructuring being a dramatic shift in the roles and responsibilities of local government within their constituencies. This restructuring has been informed largely by a changing public policy landscape, in which the historical social democratic pattern of Keynesian welfarism was supplanted in 1984 by a policy framework influenced by the principles of economic neoliberalism. In adopting a neoliberal policy framework, New Zealand mirrored the international rejection of Keynesianism occurring across the West at this time (Brohman, 1996; Shone and Memon, 2008; Telfer, 2002). New Zealand, however, went further and faster than any other country in its restructuring programme; both "out-Thatchering Thatcher" in its embrace of market neoliberalism and significantly revamping its governance structures (Haggerty, 2007: 223).

In New Zealand, the economies of regional areas were faced with the effects of the reform process with more immediacy and greater acuity than their larger urban counterparts. The declining profitability of the agricultural sector was the principal contributor to this economic hardship (Kelsey, 1997). This hardship was experienced throughout the West during this time and compounded in New Zealand by the removal of farming subsidies for inputs (e.g., discounted finance, farm development incentives) and outputs (e.g., supplementary minimum prices). In addition, the effects of globalization during this time resulted in New Zealand's hitherto traditional agricultural trading ties with the United Kingdom being significantly eroded by emergent regional trading blocs such as the European Economic Community. These conditions were further reinforced by waning business confidence in the sector and investment decisions becoming increasingly directed toward the major centres of commerce. With smaller regional centres facing not only a decline in the profitability of primary production, but also a workforce migrating to the main centres, tourism was perceived as a suitable means by which to stem this outbound flow of capital investment and labour (Shone, Horn, Simmons and Moran, 2005).

More recently, an advanced style of neoliberalism has emerged in which governments, arguably in an attempt to reconnect with communities, have refocused the basic unit of economic and social development at the local and regional levels. The overall effect of this restructuring is commonly represented in the academic literature in terms of a shift from local government to local *governance* (Jones, 1998; MacLeod and Goodwin, 1999). This shift to governance is identified as a fundamental feature of the more recent international policy reform discourse, and thus signals a more active role for the state at the local level (Shone and Memon, 2008). In these new circumstances local government now finds itself involved in a range of activities that extend well beyond the traditional provision of roads, collection of rates and rubbish. This expanded range of activities includes social servicing, the protection of community wellbeing, environmental management and economic development (Bush, 1995; Dredge and Jenkins, 2007).

This chapter interrogates the role of the state in regional tourism development, and examines how the role of local government as expanded tourism provider has led to contested understandings about the suitability of the sector to contribute equitably to development objectives at the sub-national level.

Background: Public Policy Transformations in New Zealand

The role and potential of tourism as a contributor to regional growth and development is well established in the academic literature, and is often framed in the context of a politico-economic response to structural changes in national or regional economies. In the New Zealand context, these structural changes speak to a dramatic shift in central–local relations that since the mid-1980s, has seen the formerly prominent role of central government under the hitherto social democratic pattern of Keynesian welfarism supplanted by an expanded role for local government under a transcendental neoliberal public policy framework.

Upon its election in July 1984, the Fourth Labour Government embarked upon a process of reform that fundamentally affected New Zealand's economy and society, replacing the erstwhile social democratic regime with a "textbook case of neoliberalism" (Baragwanath, 2003: 105). In adopting a neoliberal policy framework, New Zealand mirrored the international rejection of Keynesianism occurring in the 1970s and 1980s across the West, exemplified in the rise of 'New Right' conservative governments in the United States, Canada, Britain and West Germany (Baragwanath, 2003; Brohman, 1996; Shone, 2008; 2009; Shone and Memon, 2008; Telfer, 2002). New Zealand, however, went further and faster than any other country in its restructuring programme; both "out-Thatchering Thatcher" in its embrace of market neoliberalism and significantly revamping its governance structures (Haggerty, 2007: 223). Hence, the decision to initiate reforms is not what marked New Zealand's programme as unique, but rather its *extent* (Baragwanath,

2003). The unique nature of New Zealand neo-liberal 'experience' is perhaps best described by Henderson (1996: 13), who notes:

> In no other OECD country has there been so systematic an attempt at the same time (1) to redefine and limit the role of government, and (2) to make public agencies and their operations more effective, more transparent, and more accountable. It is this important extra dimension, as well as the range and scope of reforms that have more obvious counterparts elsewhere that gives the New Zealand programme its special character.

The policy context of the reforms was, in part, a new fabric of relations between the state and civil society. This new fabric consists of neoliberalism in the form of deregulation, fiscal austerity, and the corporatization and privatization of the public sector. While such changes had been justified in terms of the need for fiscal stringency, given the country's high external debt and the failure of the previous policy regime, it is clear, as Boston, Martin, Pallot and Walsh (1996) note, the changes also originate from a marked shift in political philosophy that focuses on the question of the nature and scope of the state. New Zealand thus represents a clear example of the neoliberal shift in political philosophy and policy development. From being the so-called 'social laboratory' of the Western world in the 1930s in terms of social welfare provision, New Zealand became the 'neoliberal experiment' in the 1980s and the 1990s. This historical reversal of social principles and philosophy has singled out New Zealand as a 'successful' experiment pointed to by a number of powerful world policy institutions, such as the World Bank, the International Monetary Fund and the OECD (Fitzsimons, 2000).

This policy shift was accompanied by a significant restructuring of local government in 1989, and further reinforced through a revision of local government roles and responsibilities in 2002. In common with other Western democracies, the principles behind the reforms of local government at this time were heavily influenced by the same imperatives at work elsewhere in the public sector: rational economic actor models of public choice theory (Memon and Thomas, 2006) and New Public Management (Wollmann, 2000; Shone and Memon, 2008). The overall effect of this restructuring has been a shift from a period of relatively centralized regulation and administrative control to a broader governance-oriented role for local government. Perhaps more significantly, this shift has also seen local government assume an increasingly entrepreneurial role in the social and economic development of their constituencies.

In New Zealand, the economies of regional areas were faced with the effects of the reform process with more immediacy and greater acuity than their larger urban counterparts. The declining profitability of the agricultural sector was the principal contributor to this economic hardship (Kelsey, 1997). Such hardship was experienced throughout the West during this time, but was compounded in New Zealand by the removal of farming subsidies for inputs (e.g., discounted finance, farm development incentives) and outputs (e.g., supplementary minimum prices). These conditions were further reinforced by waning business confidence in the sector and investment decisions becoming increasingly directed toward the major centres of commerce. The overall effect of these conditions was that smaller regional centres were facing not only a decline in the profitability of primary production, but also a workforce migrating to the main centres.

However, since the late-1990s there has been a revival of interest in regionalism and regional development strategies in many Western democracies, most notably in the United States and Britain, but also in many internationally peripheral economies such as New Zealand. This interest, while stimulated in no small measure by the election of centre-left 'Third Way' administrations in the West during this time, was influenced more heavily by functional pressures for economic and social regeneration in stimulating demands for an integrative approach to regional governance (Elcock, 2003; Parks and Elcock, 2000). Moreover, it represents an advanced style of neoliberalism in which governments, arguably in an attempt to reconnect with communities, have refocused the basic unit of economic and social development at the local and regional levels (Shone, 2011).

Such an approach allows for a much greater facilitative role for central government in promoting regional development agendas, and provides a suitably permissive policy mandate for local government to engage more readily in 'non-core' activities aligned with stimulating the economic and social wellbeing. Specifically, it allows for "the application of sustainable development at a regional scale, in order to assist individuals, business and communities within regions to identify local opportunities, develop capability to respond to opportunities, and exploit those opportunities" (Schöllmann and Dalziel, 2002: 4). It is in this context of economic and political restructuring that tourism has emerged as a potentially significant contributor to regional development objectives in New Zealand.

This particular discourse has also come to dominate the arena of local economic development. As Benington's and Geddes's (1992: 456) assessment of local economic development strategies throughout the 1980s contends, a feature of market-led neoliberal economic strategy during the 1980s has been a shift in public policy towards explicit or hidden support for growth sectors. The result of such a policy shift for regional locations has been that territorial authorities and their local communities have been compelled to exploit and promote local tourist attractions in an attempt to minimize, halt or reverse economic decline induced by collapse or contraction in more conventional primary or secondary-based sectors (Hopkins, 1998). In the New Zealand context, Kearsley (1998) investigated the changing context for tourism development and highlighted the history of economic challenges facing the country. These challenges, from the beginning of economic restructuring in the late-1970s to the removal of agricultural subsidies in the 1980s, prompted the observation that tourism was seen largely as a suitable means by which to offset the declining profitability of the agricultural sector:

> It seemed, to many small communities, that only tourism was left as a viable course of jobs and community income. Consequently, many farms attempted

to set up tourist ventures, local authorities tried to encourage local festivals and events, and many individuals attempted to set up small enterprises as fishing, guiding or local tours. (Kearsley, 1998: 83)

Significantly, in the case of New Zealand, the neoliberal policy shift during the 1980s and 1990s coincided with a period of significant growth in country's tourism sector. This growth trend has continued to the point where the tourism sector is now a significant and highly visible component of the national economy. The sector accounts for 18.2 per cent of all export earnings and contributes 8.8% of GDP in New Zealand. In addition, it directly supports 4.9 per cent of employment and indirectly supports a further 4.7 per cent of the New Zealand workforce (Tourism Strategy Group, 2011). With the number of international visitors arriving to New Zealand having doubled since 1993, tourism is rightly considered to be a significant growth machine for the national economy. Perhaps unsurprisingly, this growth trajectory has been matched by a growing awareness of the role and potential of the tourism sector to contribute to regional development agendas. The result of this has been significantly increased levels of public sector participation in the tourism sector. This participation, according to Hall (2007), is manifested most notably through the provision and subsidy of destination marketing and promotion by the state for commercial benefit.

Governments thus view the tourism sector favourably as a suitable mechanism by which to stimulate economic activity in regional locations. Indeed, the role and potential of tourism activity to act as a growth pole around which other industry sectors can be developed is well established in the academic scholarship (e.g., Gunn, 1994; Jenkins, Hall and Troughton, 1998). What the literature is less clear about, however, is how the tourism development trajectories of regional locations are impacted when the public sector, in addition to its dual enablement and management roles (Simmons and Fairweather, 2005), also assumes the role of tourism industry entrepreneur. The effect of this pluralism is to create a unique relationship of regulation and ownership of tourism resources, in which the conventional public–private sector differentiation of roles and responsibilities is usurped by a more complex and dynamic manifestation of politics and power at the local level. This in turn has led to the emergence of contested understandings about the appropriate role of the state in the promotion and development of the tourism sector.

Case Study: Regional Tourism Development in the Hurunui District

Research Setting

The Hurunui District is situated in the Canterbury region of New Zealand's South Island. While the social histories of the area reach back over 130 years, the Hurunui District itself is a relatively new creation, having only been gazetted in

1989. This occurred via a process of territorial amalgamation – undertaken as part of a broader process of local government reform – and resulted in the creation of a new territorial local authority: the Hurunui District Council. The district area is largely rural in character, being both sparsely populated (population: 10,476) and occupying a relatively large land area (8,646 km^2). The rural character of the Hurunui is further reflected in the prominent position of the agricultural sector in the district's economic palette. This strong farming presence within the district economy, while now complemented by recent growth in tourism and viticulture, signals the Hurunui's traditional and ongoing links with the agricultural sector. Such is the significance of this relationship with agriculture that local historians claim much of the socio-economic development experienced in the Hurunui is said to have been carried "on the sheep's back" (Gardner, 1983: 433).

The Hurunui's administrative and commercial capital (Amberley, population: 1,305) is located near the south-eastern boundary of the district, approximately 45km to the north of the South Island's largest urban centre and visitor gateway: the city of Christchurch. This geographical proximity not only affords rural producers in the Hurunui ease of access to national and international markets, but it also provides a significant source of visitor flows to, and through, the district. The scale of tourism in the Hurunui is significant when considered against the district's relatively small resident population base, with a total of 928,300 day trips and 617,200 visitor nights made to the district in 2007. Domestic visitors (i.e., New Zealanders) represent a significantly large segment of this visitor market, accounting for 88 percent of day trips and 83 percent of all visitor nights in the Hurunui during this period. The total value of visitor expenditures for this period was estimated to be NZ$93.3 million (Ministry of Tourism, 2008).

Significantly for this case study, the core focus of the Hurunui District's tourism product is centred on the alpine spa village of Hanmer Springs (population: 746). Dominating the village and situated at its centre are the thermal pools for which Hanmer Springs is named and known. This tourism resource – developed and operated as the Hanmer Springs Thermal Pools and Spa (HSTPS) – was vested by the Crown in the Hurunui District Council and gazetted as a recreational reserve in 1990. As such, the Hurunui District Council is the owner and operator of the thermal pool complex. The HSTPS is widely considered to be a highly successful tourism venture, with approximately 550,000 visitors passing through their turnstiles each year. The expenditure from these visitors has generated an operating surplus for the HSTPS of NZ$3.1 million over the period 2005–2008. Moreover, it is anticipated that as the sole shareholder, the financial return to the Hurunui District Council in terms of operating surpluses will total NZ$27 million across a ten-year forecast period 2009–2019 (Hurunui District Council, 2009). The HSTPS thus provides a substantial revenue stream to the district council and financial contribution to be used toward the funding of other reserves in the district area.

While the wider district area is replete with an array of natural attractions and recreational opportunities for the many visitors who traverse the Hurunui, the core focus of the Hurunui tourism 'brand' is firmly centred on Hanmer Springs and its thermal pools. Indeed, its status as visitor destination is the reason that the village has experienced extraordinary levels of growth and urban development at a time when other settlements in the district have been in decline. This discrepant growth trend, coupled with the prominent role of the district council as the apex tourism operator in Hanmer Springs and the Hurunui District, has led to contested understandings about the appropriate level of local government involvement in tourism development. Moreover, the apparent 'asymmetry' of the district's development profile has prompted some stakeholders in the Hurunui to accuse the district council of using the tourism sector to promote development in one part of the district (i.e., Hanmer Springs) at the expense of the wider district area. It is therefore through the unique relationship of ownership and regulation that local government involvement in tourism development in the Hurunui District must be considered.

Research Methodology

This case study utilizes qualitative data drawn from semi-structured interviews with local government, tourism industry and community stakeholder representatives in the Hurunui District during the period August 2008 to June 2009. A total of 34 in-depth interviews were undertaken with key stakeholders during the primary research phase of the case study. These informants were asked to identify the issues and interactions influencing the tourism policy, planning and development process in their experience. Their responses often led to reflections about key people or organizations, the 'place' or role of tourism in the Hurunui District, the political resolve to engage in tourism, the networks and joint arrangements to deliver government and council policies. This has been complemented with the use of secondary sources of information, such as feature articles and letters to the editor in local newspapers, district council planning documents and papers, and ratepayer submissions to council.

Discussion

Tourism as a Public Sector Response to Regional Decline

The Hurunui District, as was the case for many rural areas in New Zealand, experienced a period of significant upheaval in the primary sector during the late 1980s and 1990s. This upheaval was the result of a process of wide-ranging state sector reforms and concomitant government policies directed toward, among other things, the removal of farming subsidies and trade tariffs. Although this more-market approach by central government was typical of a growing trend internationally towards a neoliberal economic perspective, it nonetheless represented a significant threat to the ongoing profitability of the district's economy. The comments of the

CEO of the Hurunui District Council provide a clear picture of the prevailing conditions during this time:

> In 1994, rural New Zealand was facing some difficult issues. The economy was not great, and rural communities were really struggling. We were facing rural decline, and a manifestation of this decline was the closure of post offices, the withdrawal of services and basic lack of interest [from central government]. The rural obituaries were already being written for the smaller townships within the district during this time of change, and the feeling within rural areas was that they had been forgotten, or even worse, abandoned by central government (personal communication).

In addition to the economic instability created through the neoliberalism policies of the 1980s, there was another factor, which served to influence the district council's decision to pursue a tourism 'solution'. A restructuring of the Canterbury region's tourism promotions agency (based in Christchurch) at that time led to uncertainty about the Hurunui's position within the Canterbury tourism 'brand'. This uncertainty and the potential ramifications for the district's fledgling tourism industry proved motivation enough for Hurunui's elected councillors to vote in favour of the establishment of a Hurunui District tourism promotions agency. This confluence of factors is acknowledged by the general manager of this new tourism agency:

> So you've got a number of things happening all at once. And when you put them together you've got a very strong case to go to council and say: "if we don't do this ourselves, and put the money in ourselves, we're going to be left out in the cold. Currently, we've got a local economy that's struggling. We've got obituaries being written about our townships. We need to do something ourselves". (personal communication)

As a consequence of these factors, the district economy was compelled to diversify and broaden its base in order to offset the potential losses from a declining rural sector. For a district that had historically derived its income from primary production, a major shift in thinking was necessary to recognize the potentially valuable role that tourism could play in the Hurunui economy. The Hurunui District Council, realizing that tourism could provide employment and income for local residents while also supporting established local businesses, took the lead in encouraging tourism development. According to the mayor of the Hurunui District, tourism was seen as a way of revitalizing the district in the early 1990s:

> Council members were of the view that tourism might offer a potential for regenerating the Hurunui. The Hurunui was clearly vulnerable to the variations in the farming cycles, and it was important to diversify in order to soften the impacts of those economic cycles. Diversification was seen as an opportunity for looking at a range of interventions, of which tourism was seen at that time as providing the greatest opportunity (personal communication).

Public Sector Funding of Tourism Governance Structures

A significant change in the district council's treatment of tourism occurred in 1995, with the commissioning of a tourism and visitor strategy for the Hurunui District. A major outcome of this strategy was that potential was seen for product triangulation between the wine and food attractions of Waipara, the alpine spa attractions of Hanmer Springs (both positioned within the Hurunui) and the marine-based attractions of the neighbouring Kaikoura District. After a period of discussions with the Kaikoura District Council, the tourism promotions alliance was formalized and touring route between the above-noted attractions was created. This coincided with the establishment of a Hurunui District tourism promotions agency known as Alpine Pacific Tourism. The primary role of this agency is to promote the Hurunui District as a visitor destination to both the domestic and international visitor markets. Subsidiary to this role is the provision of marketing assistance to individual member subscribers of Alpine Pacific Tourism through a variety of mechanisms and forums at their disposal.

The challenge for the Hurunui District Council in creating this tourism structure and brand was centred principally on issues of funding. The initial establishment and subsequent operating budgets of the district's tourism promotions agency were funded for some time via local government taxes (known as *rates*) collected unilaterally from all district ratepayers. While this funding mechanism was deemed suitable by the district council, which argued that the benefits of tourism activity would eventually 'trickled down' to all in the community, there was growing disquiet about the equity of the district's tourism funding model. As recounted by several research informants, it was the case that many rural landowners felt that they – through their 'general' rate levy – were subsidizing those in the tourism industry. The district mayor, who notes that this situation did not sit comfortably with ratepayers in an economic environment where the 'spirit' of user-pays was still prevalent, acknowledges this sentiment:

> Well, in the early days of the tourism board and tourism structure of this council, it originally set that model up based on funding from the general rate, which meant that every ratepayer was paying into this, and that was being paid on capital value. So, if you like, large landowners and farmers were paying more in outright dollar terms than urban people. There was at the time other issues going on between the council and its rural landowners, but this flowed over into their animosity towards paying a general rate to tourism. So the early days of this tourism funding model did anything but galvanize the district. It actually drove it further apart and absolutely drove a wedge into this district (personal communication).

Arguably, the main catalyst for the proposed changes to the tourism-funding model was precipitated by an increasingly fractious relationship between the district council and the rural sector. The origins of this disquiet, while centred principally on the increasing ability of the council to impose various caveats on farming land-use practices, were nonetheless amplified by a desire for a fairer system of tourism funding. As noted by farming representatives in the district:

> The backlash from the Hurunui District Council "throwing money and attention at tourism" was based on the conviction that local council rates and levies should be targeted at specific users and activities. Rather than have a unilateral approach to council funding, those industries, which benefit from council spending in a particular area should have an accordingly proportionate amount of their local council rates directed towards that area of council activity. (personal communication)

In the eyes of rural landowners, many of whom regarded the flow-on benefits of tourism to the wider district area as being tenuous at best, this targeted approach to funding the district council's tourism-related activities represents a more equitable basis by which to bear the financial burden of the council's tourism 'folly'. In 2002, as a response to a growing concern among local ratepayers regarding the sourcing of funding for district tourism promotions activities from the general rate, the district council announced its intention to revise the tourism-funding model. To this end, a new equity-based funding system that specifically targeted tourism operators and associated service industries was implemented in 2003 and continues on to the present day.

Contested Tourism Development Objectives

The centrality of Hanmer Springs' thermal pools to the wider district and regional area is well recognized by a number of research informants, who note that without the dynamism of the thermal pools, Hanmer Springs as an area, Hurunui as a district, and Canterbury as a region, would lose a substantial point of difference. However, while the ongoing promotion of Hanmer Springs and the HSTPS are critical to the successful development of the Hurunui tourism product, it need not be the case that little attention should be given by the district's promotions agency to other aspects of the local tourism industry. The words of an industry representative succinctly capture the crux of this sentiment:

> Currently, in terms of promoting tourism in the Hurunui it seems that all roads inevitably lead to Hanmer Springs. But it doesn't have to always be the case. The Hurunui has a wide range of tourism attractions to offer potential visitors, yet the focus of the council's tourism promotions seems to be firmly fixed on Hanmer Springs. The council should also be encouraging visitors to spend more time in other parts of the district. But it just doesn't seem to happen, because ultimately the power to make it happen rests at the council chambers in Amberley. But the power has always been in Amberley. (personal communication)

While the potential of secondary or lower-order destinations within the district to contribute to the growth trajectory of tourism development is not in dispute, the position of Hanmer Springs as centre of tourist activity and location of council-owned tourism business interests has resulted in contested understandings about the township's role in 'Brand Hurunui'. The following comment by a research informant helps illustrate this point:

> When people think of tourism in the Hurunui, more often than not they think of Hanmer Springs and the thermal pools. Well, the Hanmer Springs Thermal Reserve belongs to the council; in other words, to all the ratepayers. There is a little bit of money that comes out of that and goes into recreational reserves [throughout the district], but the great part of it is sunk back into the pools and more money is borrowed to develop Hanmer Springs. Every three years it seems that it has to be refurbished and reignited again to attract more people and to keep them coming back. So a great majority of the income, of the earnings, never sees the light of day to benefit the district. And people say: "where is the benefit to us? Everything is going to Hanmer Springs". (personal communication)

This perception of district council bias towards development in Hanmer Springs at the expense of the wider district area has been characterized by a number of informants as a 'West-East' divide. As explained by several research informants, this divide represents, in its most basic form, the remnants of historical territorial divisions, which existed prior to the creation in 1989 of the Hurunui District. The 'West' is typically more pro-tourism because they gain the most benefit from tourism activity in the district. The 'East' is typically more resistant to tourism development, particularly that which is undertaken or funded by the district council. This is due largely to the comparatively low levels of tourism activity and economic benefit from tourism experienced in the eastern reaches of the district area. The following comment provided by a district councillor from the eastern part of the district area captures the depth of this divide:

> The politics of North Canterbury are still at work in the Hurunui. It's not as pronounced as it used to be, but it's still there. There is a divide. And mainly the divide is created by Hanmer Springs getting too much. And in the past they had good reason. Even in town planning now, Hanmer Springs usually gets everything they want, no problems. And we're having a hell of a job getting the Amberley town concept plan passed. Development in Hanmer Springs just doesn't seem to be held up by the usual council checks and balances like other townships in the district. It just doesn't seem at that fair to me. (personal communication)

It must be noted that stakeholders within the Hanmer Springs community also acknowledge the contrary views contained within this West-East binary. Not surprisingly, however, the views expressed by Hanmer stakeholders differ significantly to those of their 'eastern' counterparts. The following excerpt provides an apt example:

> Places throughout the district are terribly jealous of Hanmer Springs. But does Hanmer have everything its own way? No, it doesn't. In fact, the reality is that getting support for Hanmer from around the council table is tremendously difficult. But the rest of the district has to face up to the reality of the situation. In Hanmer's small corner of the district there are millions of dollars being generated by over 500,000 visitors to the thermal pools every year. And that's the true value of Hanmer Springs to the Hurunui District, whether the rest of the district likes it or not. (personal communication)

The above-noted quotes indicate the existence of two separate issues with respect to the manifestation of tourism and local government policy in the Hurunui District; the apparent focus of district promotions on Hanmer Springs; and the perceived inequitable manifestation of power relations between tourism stakeholder groups in the district. Moreover, the position of the district council as both owner and operator of the HSTPS and its ongoing support of development in Hanmer Springs has served to further entrench its role in tourism promotion and development. This stance has proven to be highly inflammatory for local ratepayers, many of whom view local government involvement in tourism as tangible evidence of council resources being used to favour one part of the district over another.

Conclusion

This chapter has argued that the tourism sector presently occupies a prominent position within New Zealand's economic landscape. The antecedents of this prominence can be traced back to the nation's earliest colonial history, but is more recently linked to a period of neoliberal-inspired public policy shift during the 1980s and 1990s. This policy shift coincided with a period of sustained growth in tourist arrivals to New Zealand at a time when the nation's hitherto dominant agricultural sector was experiencing a period of economic hardship as a direct consequence of neoliberal public policy. This prominence of the tourism sector is also experienced at the sub-national level, as illustrated in the case study of the Hurunui District. Specifically, the tourism sector is recognized as being contributor to district and regional economies, as well as being a source of employment at the community level.

This chapter has also argued that the tourism experiences of regional locations such as the Hurunui District are inextricably linked to the broader forces of change at the international and national levels. Put simply, local government involvement in the Hurunui District's tourism sector represents a locally derived response to global forces of change. Indeed, the interconnectedness that so marked New Zealand's early development as a polity continues to impart its influence on the livelihoods and futures of regional communities throughout the country. An appreciation of the broader context under which tourism development occurs is therefore central to better understanding the role and potential for tourism to contribute to the development objectives of regional locations. As noted earlier in this chapter, the growing prominence given to tourism development by local government can be traced to a period of profound transformation in public policy ideology in the 1980s. Arguably, the most significant impact of this transformation has been manifested as the new role for local authorities to provide for the economic and social well-being of their constituent communities. Prominent in this shifting focus for local government has been the active support for a range of sunrise industries, including tourism.

More broadly, this chapter has shown that governments are increasingly using the tourism sector as a tool by which to offset declines in other sectors of regional economies. The use of tourism for this purpose in the Hurunui District reflects, in turn, wider national and international trends that identify the tourism sector as a key lever by which to address issues of regional decline within the discourse of sustainable communities. However, the experience of the Hurunui District suggests that far from being a panacea for regional development, the promotion of tourism development by local government can result in a 'new' range of challenges for stakeholders in destination areas. In the Hurunui District, these challenges include conflict surrounding the funding mechanisms of the district's tourism governance structure; contested understandings about the appropriate role of local government in tourism development; and, the ability of the tourism development to contribute equitably to broader regional development objectives. This last issue is of particular salience in the Hurunui case study, where destination development in Hanmer Springs appears to be promoted at the expense of regional development across the district area. The presence of these challenges manifestly illustrate that as well as being utilized as a response to a changing politico-economic conditions, the tourism sector itself can also be regarded as an agent of change in its own right within destination regions.

On this point, the academic literature appears unanimous in its characterization of tourism as an agent of change; be it economic, social, cultural or environmental. Importantly, however, that same body of scholarly literature cautions against premature judgements against the tourism sector as the primary instigator of change within host communities. Typically, tourism development is one of many factors, which combine to create the conditions of change within destination areas. Other factors may include political ideologies and public policy responses, economic cycles of growth and decline, socio-cultural dynamism, and macro-regional influences such as 'globalization'. Therefore, rather than being a linear or causal relationship, the literature describes the need to contextualize the conditions within which tourism development occurs. According to Hess (2004), one of the central notions in this contextualization of change is the concept of the 'embeddedness' of economic action into wider institutional and social frameworks. This concept of embeddedness, when viewed from a societal perspective, argues that economies are not 'stand-alone' entities. Rather, they exist within a network of social and cultural institutions, which dictate their existence, and shape of development. This is the case for the development trajectory of the tourism sector in the Hurunui District.

References

Baragwanath, B.L. (2003). *Fortress-Dwellers to Global Players? Globalisation and New Zealand: Description, Discourse and Action*. Unpublished Doctoral Thesis. Lincoln University, New Zealand.

Benington, J. and Geddes, M. (1992). Local economic development in the 1980s and 1990s: Retrospect and prospects. *Economic Development Quarterly*, 6(4), 454–63.

Boston, J., Martin, J., Pallot, J. and Walsh, P. (1996). *Public Management: The New Zealand Model*. Auckland: Auckland University Press.

Brohman, J. (1996). *Popular Development: Rethinking the Theory and Practice of Development*. Oxford: Blackwell.

Bush, G. (1995). *Local Government and Politics in New Zealand* (2nd ed.). Auckland: Oxford University Press.

Dredge, D. and Jenkins, J. (2007). *Tourism Planning and Policy*. Milton, Qld: John Wiley.

Elcock, H. (2003). Regionalism and Regionalisation in Britain and North America. *British Journal of Politics and International Relations*, 5(1), 74–101.

Fitzsimons, P. (2000). Neoliberalism and 'Social Capital': Reinventing Community. *Area Symposium. Neoliberalism, Welfare and Education: "The New Zealand Experiment": Critique and Critical Transformations*. New Zealand Association for Research in Education. AREA Conference, New Orleans.

Gardner, W.J. (1983). *The Amuri: A County History* (2nd ed.). Culverden, NZ: Amuri County Council.

Gunn, C. (1994). *Tourism Planning: Basics, Concepts, Cases* (3rd ed.). Washington DC: Taylor & Francis.

Haggerty, J.H. (2007). "I'm not a greenie, but … ": Environmentality, eco-populism and governance in New Zealand. Experiences from the Southland whitebait fishery. *Journal of Rural Studies*, 23(2), 222–37.

Hall, C.M. (2007). *Tourism Planning: Policies, Processes and Relationships* (2nd. Ed.). Harlow: Pearson Prentice Hall.

Henderson, D. (1996). *Economic Reforms: New Zealand in an International Perspective*. Wellington: New Zealand Business Roundtable.

Hess, M. (2004). 'Spatial' relationships? Towards a reconceptualization of embeddedness. *Progress in Human Geography*, 28(2), 165–86.

Hopkins, J. (1998). Signs of the post-rural: Marketing myths of a symbolic countryside. *Geografiska Annaler: Series B, Human Geography*, 80(2), 65–81.

Hurunui District Council (2009). *Draft Hurunui Long Term Community Plan 2009–2019*. Accessed 20 April 2009 from: http://www.hurunui.govt.nz/ Documents/Publications/Draft%20Hurunui%20Community%20Plan%20 (LTCCP)%202009%20-%202019/18%20-%20Council%20Activities%20 -%20Hanmer%20Springs%20Thermal%20Pools%20and%20Spa.pdf.
Jenkins, J., Hall, C.M. and Troughton, M. (1998). The restructuring of rural economies: Rural tourism and recreation as a government response. In R. Butler, C.M. Hall and J. Jenkins (eds) *Tourism and Recreation in Rural Areas*. Chichester: John Wiley, 43–68.
Jones, M. (1998). Restructuring the local state: Economic governance or social regulation? *Political Geography*, 17(8), 959–988.
Kearsley, G. (1998). Rural tourism in Otago and Southland, New Zealand. In R. Butler, C.M. Hall and J. Jenkins (eds) *Tourism and Recreation in Rural Areas*. New York: John Wiley, 81–95.
Kelsey, J. (1997). *The New Zealand Experiment: A World Model for Structural Adjustment?* Auckland, NZ: Auckland University Press.
MacLeod, G. and Goodwin, M. (1999). Reconstructing an urban and regional political economy: On the state, politics, scale and explanation. *Political Geography*, 18(6), 697–730.
Memon, P.A. and Thomas, G. (2006). New Zealand's new Local Government Act: A paradigm for participatory planning or business as usual. *Urban Policy and Research*, 24(1), 135–44.
Ministry of Tourism (2008). *Regional Data: Hurunui RTO 2008–2014*. Wellington, NZ: Ministry of Tourism. Accessed 21 April 2009 from: http://www.tourismresearch.govt.nz/By-Region/South-Island/Hurunui-RTO-2008---2014/.
Parks, J. and Elcock, H. (2000). Why do regions demand autonomy? *Regional and Federal Studies*, 10(3), 87–106.
Schöllmann, A. and Dalziel, A. (2002). *Rediscovering Regions: Regional Development from a Central Government Policy Perspective*. Paper presented to the New Zealand Association of Economists Conference.
Shone, M.C. (2008). *Tourism, Regional Development and the 'New Regionalism': The Case of the Hurunui District, New Zealand*. Proceedings of the New Zealand Tourism and Hospitality Research Conference (NZTHRC). Lincoln University, 2–5 December. Hanmer Springs, Canterbury, New Zealand.
Shone, M.C. (2011). Local government entrepreneurship in tourism development: The case of the Hurunui District, New Zealand. In D. Dredge and J. Jenkins (eds) *Stories of Practice: Tourism Policy and Planning*. Aldershot: Ashgate, 153–72.
Shone, M.C. and Memon, P.A. (2008). Tourism development and public policy paradigms: From neo-liberalism to the new regionalism. *Local Economy*, 24(4), 291–305.
Shone, M.C., Horn, C.M., Simmons, D.G., and Moran, D. (2005). Adapting to tourism: Community responses to tourism in five New Zealand tourism destinations. In D.G. Simmons and J.R. Fairweather (eds) *Understanding the*

Tourism Host-Guest Encounter in New Zealand: Foundations for Adaptive Planning and Management. Christchurch: EOS Ecology, 83–106.

Simmons, D.G. and Fairweather, J.R. (2005). Conclusions: Planning and managing for sustainable tourism. In D.G. Simmons and J.R. Fairweather (eds) *Understanding the Tourism Host-Guest Encounter in New Zealand: Foundations for Adaptive Planning and Management*. Christchurch: EOS Ecology, 257–66.

Telfer, D.J. (2002). The evolution of tourism and development theory. In R. Sharpley and D.J. Telfer (eds) *Tourism and Development: Concepts and Issues*. Clevedon: Channel View Publications, 35–78.

Tourism Strategy Group (2011). *New Zealand Tourism Strategy 2015*. Wellington: Ministry of Economic Development.

Wollmann, H. (2000). Local government systems: From historic divergence towards convergence? Great Britain, France and Germany as comparative cases in point. *Environment and Planning C: Government and Policy*, 18(1), 33–55.

Chapter 5

Developing Markets – the Neoliberalization of Tourism Structures in Jordan: The Example of Aqaba Special Economic Zone

Nicolai Scherle and Markus Pillmayer

Tourism, that is our bread and butter. We cannot live without it.

A Jordanian interview partner

"No other country has been declared dispensable as often as the Kingdom of Jordan", wrote the German Middle East expert Perthes (2002: 241) from the renowned German Institute for International and Security Affairs. A typical product of colonialism, whose national boundaries were drawn according to colonial era considerations, Jordan has often been labelled as an artificial entity without much of a future that threatens to implode because of both endogenous and exogenous limits to its stability. Even though Jordan belongs to the middle income economies according to the categories of the World Bank (2012), its economic power is considered at least as unfavourable as its political and geographical location as a buffer state squeezed in between a large number of trouble spots (Bouziane and Lenner, 2011; El Ouazghari, 2011). A large proportion of the generated income does not result from the country's own production factors or ones based in the country; rather, the state and its citizens are highly dependent on foreign financial inputs. Measured in terms of its population, Jordan is one of the largest beneficiaries of international development and/or financial aid; a fact that is reflected paradigmatically in the concentration of foreign NGOs in the country (Harmsen, 2008; Talal, 2004). Moreover, traditionally a large proportion of private income and wealth derives from remittances from migrant workers, who often have returned after years or decades from the economically powerful Gulf States (Perthes, 2002; Schlumberger, 2002; El Namaki, 2008; Istaiteyeh, 2011).

In view of its exceptionally challenging political and economic structures, Jordan has increasingly attempted in the last two decades to improve economic conditions for both local businesspeople and foreign investors. Moreover, the Jordanian royal family recognized earlier than many other governments in the Arab world that economic discontent can rapidly turn into a general crisis of legitimacy of the state and its institutions (Perthes, 2002; Zorob, 2011). In these circumstances, it is hardly surprising that, at least at the time of this chapter's writing, the political implications of the Arab Spring have had comparatively little effect on the Hashemite Kingdom. It is in this context that former Prime Minister Rawabdeh's plea to the House of

Representatives in 1999 must be seen: "The Jordanian economy has moved from the phase of slow growth to that of regression. The recession is felt by every citizen. It is useless to deny or justify it by any theory ... our circumstances, living conditions, and limited sources of income make the negative effects of the recession more than the citizen can bear. Therefore, there must be urgent steps to stop the regression and return to quick growth" (cited in Nsour, 2002: 25).

One of the main reform steps that the Jordanian government initiated at the beginning of the 21st century was the establishment of the so-called Aqaba Special Economic Zone (ASEZ). The hope being that this would result in a sustained economic upswing whose effects would spread far beyond this southern Jordanian city on the Red Sea. King Abdullah II is cited as saying in a speech to the ASEZ Board of Commissioners: "We hope the ASEZ will bolster the national economy, cut unemployment rates and attract foreign investment" (cited in Kardoosh, 2005: 18). Following the example of China, the establishment of the Special Economic Zone in Aqaba was geared to a regional and regulatory development concept that was to go far beyond classic industrial development. As the Chinese example makes impressively clear, special economic zones are not only free-market experiments in planned economies. In many cases, their markedly pro-business conditions adhere to neoliberal policies that, have lost much of their attractiveness since the last economic and financial crisis.

In this chapter, we would like to trace the current transformation of tourism structures in Jordan from a problem-centred perspective. The Hashemite Kingdom is a textbook example of a welfare state based on rent capitalism that in the last two decades has committed itself to neoliberal ideals, embracing primarily market forces. The Aqaba Special Economic Zone (ASEZ), declared on the Red Sea around the turn of the millennium, will serve as our example. Its highly pro-business conditions are intended to intensify the development of tourism, which in view of the shortage of natural resources and manufacturing is the most important economic sector in the county. We will present the assessments of experts interviewed in the framework of a research project supported by the German Research Foundation (DFG) dealing with the internationalization of the tourism industry in Jordan.

Economic Change under the Conditions of Welfare State Rent Capitalism?

Like so many other Arab states, Jordan's economic and social system is still characterized by rent capitalism to an extent that should not be underestimated. The developmental paradigm of rent capitalism implies not only a deformation of economic structures, including the entire societal orientation, but also a rent-seeking mentality among the elite and hence also among local entrepreneurs (Krueger, 1974; Barham and Kopp, 2001; Scherle, 2011). This system is pointedly feudalistic, at least from a Western perspective. It is associated with a very influential state whose self-conception is that of a welfare state with highly paternalistic business structures in which profits are not reinvested as much as they are siphoned off (Schmid, 1991; Kuran, 2004; Ahmed et al., 2006). Investments to maintain or even increase productivity of an operation are largely alien to rent capitalism, meaning that this economic and social system is in many regards parasitic in character (Bhagwati, 1982; Chatelus, 1987; Mensching and Wirth, 1989). Barham (2002: 283), a geographer teaching at the University of Jordan, gets to the heart of the matter when he states in connection with Jordan:

> The state itself, as was the case with many rent-seeking states in the region, provided welfare services and employment to the population at large, irrespective of qualification or need. Furthermore, such benefits were differentially accessible through patronage and influence, as a result of persistent social and political traits – the well-known wasta system. The system, which dominated whole sectors of the Kingdom's political and economic life, severely restricted the opportunities open to qualified and creative people. The system certainly provides the state with an effective means of control and influence but it undermines all economic or even managerial efficiency.

In 1999, King Hussein designated his son Abdullah, who was only 37 at the time, as his successor, contrary to the expectations of political observers, who were betting on his brother Hassan. At the time, this was in many regards a political sensation – particularly because many experts saw in the young successor a pro-western reformer whom they thought capable of reforming the Hashemite Kingdom both politically and economically. In fact, especially at the beginning of his reign, Abdullah II focussed on intensified technological and economic modernization of the country. A reflection of this was the establishment of an Economic Consultative Council (ECC) that was to advise the king personally and simultaneously to initiate and carry out the most important economic reforms (Harrigan and El-Said, 2000; Barham, 2002; Schlumberger, 2002). This met with opposition, most notably from the traditional elite with their highly nepotistic relationships, who benefitted most from the traditional system. The more so as only a comparatively small proportion of the members of the council came from the leading family clans, or rather the bloated government bureaucracy, and the choice of members was based less on whether they belonged to specific social groups than on their personal qualifications.

Among the ambitious powers represented in the new economic council was a quite remarkable initiative, the Young Entrepreneurs Association, which was launched by the liberal German Friedrich Naumann Foundation (*Friedrich-Naumann-Stiftung für die Freiheit*) and in many regards embodied a generational change (Amalu, 2010; Istaiteyeh, 2011). Its members differed positively from the often rather fusty bureaucrats of Jordan's traditional economic associations and their rent capitalistic mindset. Most of them not only belonged to a young generation often socialized abroad, they also represented comparatively new and innovative businesses ranging from graphic design to software production to procuring venture capital. Much more important, however, was the fact that these actors did not merely focus on their own business interests, but were equally motivated by a desire to elicit change in Jordan (Perthes, 2002).

This aspiration ultimately resulted in the proclamation in 2000 of the so-called Vision 2020, a policy paper that envisioned a doubling of the per capita income within the next 20 years. The focus was to be on modern technologies. The sights were consistently set on export-oriented growth, increasing competitiveness, consistent development of infrastructure, optimization of human resources and, not least, a reform of public administration structures, which – quite in accordance with neoliberal ideas – were perceived as a main obstacle to the development of entrepreneurial activities in a globalized world (Knowles, 2005; Istaiteyeh, 2011). "In fact," Perthes (2002: 260) writes in the context of the reform efforts under Abdullah II "for a while after the new king assumed office, especially after he appointed a new pro-business government one year later, it appeared as if Jordan had fallen into a kind of globalisation frenzy."

As desirable and necessary as many of the envisioned reforms were, one should not overlook the fact that in the zeal for reform, many goals were only partially achieved or fell by the wayside. Moreover, the pro-business course of the Jordanian government repeatedly obscured, particularly from the perspective of the West, the lack of a political desire to reform, as the following quotation from Mednicoff (2002: 104) illustrates:

> The fact that Jordan faces a strong challenge to create and anchor its niche in the global economy is not in itself an argument about political liberalization. Indeed, economic growth is used by governments to justify limited political openness at least as much as it encourages democratization. However, in a small economy such as Jordan's with limited financial clout to defy international expectations, there is more reason to believe in a link between the country's dependence on the world economy and steps towards liberalization. This is because, however selectively or even hypocritically, wealthy advanced economies and multilateral economic actors frequently link business or aid to privatization, human rights or political accountability.

To the present day, little has changed about this ten-year-old assessment; consequently, the Jordanian royal family's desire to reform still appears highly ambivalent.

Between the National Tourism Strategy and the Special Economic Zone: The Development of Tourism in Aqaba

Aqaba lies on the Red Sea in the extreme south-west part of the Hashemite Kingdom. The port traditionally serves as the most important place of entry or exit for goods to and from Jordan. In this context, it should be noted that Aqaba is Jordan's only access to the sea. With its mere 27 kilometres of coastline, the country is otherwise in many regards a classic landlocked country. From a geostrategic perspective, this gives the city an importance that should not be underrated (Barham, 1999; Hejazeen, 2007; Hopfinger and Pillmayer, 2013). The enormous importance of the city as a seaport and trading post reaches back to ancient Biblical, Roman and Byzantine times. Moreover, after Muhammad conquered it in 630–31, the city developed into an important way station for Egyptian Muslims making the pilgrimage to Mecca. After World War I and the defeat of the Ottoman Empire, Great Britain annexed the port city and placed it under the administration of the Transjordanian Authority (Gradus, 2001). During the era of the British protectorate, Aqaba served as an important operation base for the flamboyant political activities of Lawrence of Arabia (Murphy, 2011).

With Jordan's independence in 1946, Aqaba finally became an integral part of the Hashemite Kingdom, though for a long time neighbouring Saudi Arabia also laid claim to the city. Not until 1965 – in conjunction with an exchange of territory – did Saudi Arabia recognize Jordan's authority over Aqaba (Gradus, 2001). The most important milestone in Aqaba's recent history was the proclamation of the city as a so-called Special Economic Zone. The Jordanian government pins its hopes on a significant economic upswing for the city and the surrounding areas that will affect not only the traditional economic sectors of trade and logistics, but above all tourism, which in consideration of the country's lack of natural and industrial resources is currently seen as a key economic driver (Hejazeen, 2007; Hopfinger and Pillmayer, 2013).

This raises the question to what extent a city that previously made its name primarily as a port city – not least as an important transhipment point for oil – qualifies as a tourism destination. The dual profile, as a port on the one hand and a tourist destination on the other, is one of the crucial challenges in the future economic development of Aqaba. With a coastline of only 27 kilometres, permanent conflicts of interest between the two roles are to be expected. Nevertheless, in the past years, Aqaba has increasingly succeeded in making a name for itself as a tourism destination, in spite of the competing destinations of Eilat in Israel and Taba in Egypt only a few kilometres away.

This positive development can be attributed primarily to two factors. One is the excellent conditions for snorkelling and diving on Jordan's Red Sea coast, and the other is its position as the main urban destination in the so-called Golden Triangle. In addition to Aqaba, the Golden Triangle comprises Petra, the world famous UNESCO cultural heritage site, and Wadi Rum, which was immortalized by Lawrence of Arabia in his autobiography *Seven Pillars of Wisdom* and is deemed one of the most awe-inspiring desert landscapes in the world. The three destinations are so close to each other that both the members of the Jordan Tourism Board and the local actors have gradually recognized the enormous potential as a bundled "product", not least with regard to the development of tourism, marketing and the exploitation of synergies (Pillmayer and Scherle, 2012). This circumstance is reflected in the National Tourism Strategy adopted by the Ministry of Tourism and Antiquities (2011: 55), which for the first time follows a regional cluster approach that has also proved effective in other destinations:

> By applying a strategic, nationally-linked and well-planned and promoted cluster approach to regional tourism destinations within Jordan, a wide range of new, cluster-specific experiences will be added, which attract prioritized tourism segments and niche markets. This will increase visitor length of stay, boost expenditure, expand economic opportunities and generate more income for local communities.

In 2001, the Jordanian government created a Special Economic Zone. In the words of Farole (2008: 27), Special Economic Zones are "demarcated geographic areas contained within a country's national boundaries where the rules of business are different from those that prevail in the national territory. These differential rules principally deal with investment conditions, international trade and customs, and taxation; whereby the zone is given a business environment more liberal and effective than that of the national territory." The intention was to clearly signal, especially to foreign investors, the desire for economic reforms. As Imad Fakhoury, the ASEZ commissioner for investment, stated during the foundation phase of the Special Economic Zone:

> We expect the ASEZ to make Aqaba a key engine for Jordan's economic growth ... we want to see Aqaba deliver the full potential of its existing infrastructure and serve as a gateway to the global economy for investors. The combination of the ASEZ's location, its incentives, its one-stop-shop approach for investors and the opportunities opened up by Jordan's easy access to the world's major markets, including both the US and the EU, should make it a great business, logistics and leisure destination. (cited in Kardoosh, 2005: 17)

From both a theoretical and a practical perspective the establishment of Special Economic Zones has developed into a widespread concept, or instrument, of regional development and system transformation in an increasingly interconnected world (Orrego Vicuña, 1989; Busch, 1992; Litwack and Qian, 1998; Aggarwal, 2006; Nallathiga, 2008). Along with the Special Economic Zones created in developing and newly industrialized countries, the concept experienced an enormous boom in central and eastern Europe after the fall of the Iron Curtain (in this regional context cf. especially Dörrenbächer, 1991; Palit and Bhattacharjee, 2008; Carter and Harding, 2011; Farole, 2011). The theoretical basis was the insight that economic growth is not a process that is distributed equally over all regions of a country (Röhl, 2004). This insight prompted the

Swedish economist Myrdal (1957) already in the 1950s to develop a theory of unbalanced or cumulative growth. The neoclassical growth theory prevailing until then was always oriented towards equilibrium because of the diminishing returns of the production factors labour and capital. This meant that a higher growth rate was expected for regions with a low level of prosperity because of a shortage of capital than for highly developed economies if proportionately the same amount was invested. Even if diverse limiting assumptions such as differences in the savings and investment rate were taken into account, in the opinion of its critics, the neoclassical theory was not supported by the observed development processes, especially in developing and newly industrialized countries. Against this backdrop, Myrdal developed the hypothesis of a "circular causation" of regional growth that can accelerate cumulatively.

Mainly in adherence to Perroux' (1955) concept of development poles, it is assumed that in Special Economic Zones specific incentives will promote the economic activities in a territorially and legally delimited region. There are two main ways in which this occurs, but they do so in combination rather than separately (Busch, 1992). On the one hand, financial incentives, for instance tax concessions, exemption from customs duties, or the granting of loans on preferential terms, can be used to encourage businesses to invest in the Special Economic Zone. On the other hand, the regulation of Special Economic Zones can be changed (deregulation), for instance to implement pro-business laws on competition, planning, contract and labour (Wong and Chu, 1984; Ge, 1999; Groß, 2006; Muchlinski, 2011). Whereas proponents of Special Economic Zones praise the preferential treatment of a particular region within a sovereign state as an innovative tool of regional economic policy, critics primarily see the negative implications of the progressive neoliberalization of the economic and social structures. Ong (2006: 19), for instance, points out:

> While the state retains formal sovereignty, corporations and multilateral agencies frequently exert de facto control over the conditions of living, laboring, and migration of populations in special zones. As the administrative controls, citizenship, and territoriality once fused in a sovereign state are teased apart, we see what are in fact overlapping sovereignties. The neoliberal exception thus pries open the seam between sovereignty and citizenship, generating successive degrees of insecurity for low-skilled citizens and migrants who will have to look beyond the state for the safeguarding of their rights.

As Table 5.1 illustrates, in the Aqaba Special Economic Zone the focus is predominantly on financial incentives, although pro-business deregulation is being promoted with an unbureaucratic one-stop-shop policy.

Table 5.1   Key incentives for businesses to relocate to the Aqaba Special Economic Zone (ASEZ)

- exemption from custom duties on imports
- absence of a social services tax, annual land and building taxes on value-added property
- 5 per cent tax rate on net business income (compared to 35 per cent for the rest of Jordan), except income generated from banking, insurance and land transport activities
- 7 per cent sales tax only levied on the consumption of personal goods and hotel/restaurant services (as opposed to a 13 per cent levy for other parts of the country).

Source: Adapted from Kardoosh (2005).

The goals pursued by the Aqaba Special Economic Zone Authority (ASEZA) with the establishment of the Special Economic Zone – for instance that of creating a globally competitive investor-friendly environment or the efficient utilization of entrusted resources in harmony with a master plan to internationally recognized best practices – were rather broad. Nevertheless, very soon after the project was announced it became obvious that it would meet with opposition in Jordan. For example, a study published by the Center for Development Research of the University of Bonn (Kardoosh, 2005: 17) dealing with the economic legislation in the Aqaba Special Economic Zone states:

> Opponents were concerned about a range of issues, including the possibility of heavy Israeli investment, moral issues (the possibility of the establishment of casinos, for example) and fears that Aqaba's special status will undermine Jordanian sovereignty over a large area of the country. ... Nevertheless, alarm bells continued ringing in Jordan over the ambitious government plan for Aqaba into a duty-free special economic zone. Aqaba's proximity to Israel was fanning passions. Aqaba was seen as 'very sensitive' as it shares borders with Israel and Saudi Arabia and is the country's only port. Several MPs expressed concern that custom-made legislation for the ASEZ will undermine sovereignty, consecrating 'Aqaba's separation from the rest of Jordan.' Deputy Salameh Al Hiyari was blunter. 'It is as if we will set up a state in a state'.

Neoliberalism Rules? Experts' Perspectives on the Development of Tourism in the Aqaba Special Economic Zone

In the course of this interdisciplinary project supported by the German Research Foundation (DFG), which deals with the internationalization of tourism structures in Jordan from an incremental perspective, particular attention was paid to the development of tourism in the Aqaba Special Economic Zone. The rationale consisted of the following considerations: first, in the context of the Jordanian tourism strategy outlined in the previous section, Aqaba plays a key role in the future development of tourism, both as an urban destination in the Golden Triangle and as the country's only seaside destination. Second, the establishment of the Special Economic Zone is a truly paradigmatic illustration of the increasing neoliberalization of the Jordanian economic structures. The latter aspect appears especially interesting, because Jordan's economic and social structures are still considered those of a classic rent-seeking state. Selected experts from the fields of politics, economy and tourism were asked in semi-structured interviews to explain their assessments of the current transformation processes in the Special Economic Zone. The following quotations from the interviews carried out with 17 experts in the period between March and October 2011 are a distillation of their assessments of the Jordanian economic policies in the Special Economic Zone and the current development of tourism in Aqaba.

First we will quote an official representative of the Aqaba Special Economic Zone Authority (ASEZA), which functions as the key strategic and operative authority of the Special Economic Zone and whose six member commission is named by the government and reports directly to the Prime Minister:

> Aqaba and especially Jordan are following a very neoliberal policy, to open markets and to attract international investors. We have 6000 years of economic zone in Aqaba due to the fact that people for thousands of years have conducted commerce within this area. So I believe in liberalizing, opening up markets to get investors and providing at least job opportunities for the local people. That is the way to go. Is this a good way? I am not quite sure but it is a matter of fact that we have learned a lot of this from the US, which always used Jordan as some kind of base for their operations in this region.

What appears remarkable in this comment is not only the fact that our interview partner points out the increasing neoliberalization of Jordanian economic policies in the past years, but that he also raises the question whether such an economic concept is the correct path for the Hashemite Kingdom to follow. Because of the traditionally close economic connections between the US and Jordan, due to the important geostrategic position of Jordan in this politically unstable region, neoliberal concepts were accepted relatively rapidly compared to the neighbouring states (in particular Syria and Iraq) (El Ouazghari, 2011; Fathi, 1994; Knowles, 2005). Additionally, the deceased King Hussein had an American wife and the Jordanian royal family continues to have private contacts to the US, a fact that most likely encouraged the diffusion of neoliberal ideas. The following statement by a prominent tourism expert, who teaches at one of the country's most prestigious tourism academies, should be interpreted against this background:

> As long as King Abdullah rules with his government, which is very conservative, not much will change. The king can dismiss the cabinet at any moment. He did it three, four times in recent times – and he usually does it so that he can bring in more people with neoliberal ideas. Obviously, this doesn't please everybody. Moreover, such ideas are always associated with Western business practices, which either appear suspicious to most people or are simply rejected. Following the motto: Everything that comes from the West is bad! Sometimes that is unfortunately true!

This citation not only illustrates the extraordinary power traditionally issuing from the Jordanian royal family, which continues to be far from the ideals of a Western-style constitutional monarchy; it also reveals the proactive manner in which the king and his highly dependent government are attempting to break up the old economic structures based on rent capitalism (Beblawi, 1990; Parker, 2009; Berger, 2011). Here we should again mention the Young Entrepreneurs Association, which was frequently perceived as a neoliberal entrepreneurial spearhead for liberalized market conditions adhering chiefly to the laws of globalization and competition. At this point, we would also like to note that in recent years the opposition to the intensified neoliberalization of Jordan's economic structures has been concentrated primarily in two groups. One is the traditional elite, who naturally benefitted most from the economic structures of rent capitalism. The other is Islamistic groups, who are also finding an increasingly receptive audience in Jordan – particularly among the losers of the ongoing globalization processes (Pillmayer, 2014). Particularly the latter fear an increasing "sell-out" of Jordanian interests for the benefit of foreign – in particular Western – investors. Any observer, however, who expects to meet such criticism exclusively from persons who do not profit from the transformation processes, stands to be corrected. For instance, the director of one of the leading architecture and city planning offices in Jordan stated:

> There is too much foreign money, too much investment in the market. For me, personally, the market is overheated. Imagine the huge construction sites we have here in Jordan. Abdali in Amman, the Lagoon at the Dead Sea, Ayla, Saraya and Marza Zayed down in Aqaba. All projects are on hold or even had to be abandoned. Partners changed, disappeared from one day to another, there are bills still to pay and we still are in an economic and financial crisis. This more and more without any kind of judgment must come to an end. Otherwise, everything will blow up. And then?

Precisely such statements, moreover from a comparatively business-friendly representative, are grist to the mill of the critics of unbridled neoliberalism, which from their – occasionally too generalized – perspective serves solely the entrepreneurial interests of globalized capital. Many investors actually thought, similarly to some politicians at both local and national level, that Aqaba, with its intensified promotion of transport, logistics and tourism once initiated a very successful differentiation of its economic structures persisting for a number of years, could develop into a second Dubai (Elsheshtawy, 2010; Schmid, 2009; Schmid et al., 2011).

Similarly critical of the recent economic policy developments in Jordan is the assessment by the following expert from an international development aid organization, who is responsible for Aqaba Community and Economic Development:

> I do not think it is a good idea to open Jordan to every kind of market, to create these kind of special economic zones we have in Jordan now. We need investments and exchange because we have no real goods to trade. But not every kind of concessions! Sometimes I have the feeling that too many people only want to make fast money and have dollar signs in their eyes. But what is the price we have to pay? I fear that one day we will wake up and recognize that it was a bad idea to turn everything loose, without any kind of control. We need control about what is going on in our market because we have an increase in prices, in taxes etc. Life is becoming so expensive, who can still afford it? We are not in Europe; we are in the Middle East!

Although during the interview this expert welcomed many of the economic policy reforms initiated under King Abdullah II, especially in view of the increasing internationalization of the Jordanian tourism structures, on the whole it was clear that she desired stronger regulation on the part of the Jordanian government, which she felt should lead to the taming of uncontrolled market mechanisms. Such demands are also not uncommon in Western states, for example in the context of greater regulation of the banking sector during economic crises. Nevertheless, this expert particularly appreciated the strong promotion of tourism in the Aqaba Special Economic Zone, which she expected would lead to a differentiation of the economic structures of the country given its lack of natural resources. She anticipated that combining the destinations of Petra, Wadi Rum and Aqaba with their quite varied tourist profiles within the umbrella brand "Golden Triangle" and raising its profile would lead to increasing synergy. In view of the implications of the Arab Spring and the civil unrest in Syria, which – at least in the perception of the media (Sönmez, 1998; Cousins and Brunt, 2002; Al-Hamarneh and Steiner, 2004) – could well spread to the neighbouring states of Lebanon, Turkey and Jordan, the decreasing demand is increasingly leading to a rethinking of potential target groups (Center for Middle Eastern & North African Politics, 2011; Pillmayer, 2014). For instance, the Head of Investor Relations and Marketing Department, who represents the Aqaba Development Cooperation (ADC) remarked:

> We are also working on introducing new types of tourism. For example, we have noticed that we cannot completely rely on Europeans and Americans. They are very sensitive in terms of the Middle East; too much, from my point of view.

So now, there is an idea of going towards or establishing a couple of resorts that cater especially for the Islamic type of tourism. You have separated pools for men and women where each family can have their own private pool, for example. So we are thinking about Sharia compliance because we have to fill this gap we always have during crises. We have some potential and reliable investors from Qatar and Saudi Arabia who are deeply interested. Aqaba is very close to Saudi Arabia and they would be happy if they could invest here. And they want to.

Even if it cannot be predicted whether this statement will only be a short-term trend in response to the most recent political developments in the region or whether it is an increasingly promising strategy, it should be obvious that, currently, business is far from usual in the Aqaba Special Economic Zone. For the time being at least, the vision of a Jordanian Dubai on the Red Sea that was floating around in the minds of many political actors and strategic investors has receded into the distance. As a quote by a medium-scale entrepreneur highlights, local small and medium-sized enterprises do not regret this: "Jordanian tourism lives on its small-scale structures, which are characterized almost exclusively by family businesses. Anonymous investors aiming at short-term returns do not fit in with our culture. Seriously, don't the failed construction projects in Aqaba speak for themselves?"

Conclusions

Since the outbreak of the Arab Spring, the Arab world is in a phase of fundamental historical change. Nevertheless, this change is not as fast, as profound and as comprehensive as large parts of the population would like it to be, as foreign politicians and managers consider necessary and as many of the traditional elite fear. Even though the effect of the Arab Spring so far on Jordan is relatively minimal, the Hashemite Kingdom represents anything but political and economic standstill. Comparatively prudent foreign domestic policies under Abdullah II have bestowed upon the country a moderate transformation process that clearly differs from the explosive developments in most of the neighbouring states. In addition, the reform-minded economic policies in many regards contrast with Jordan's persisting economic and social structures based on rent capitalism. These economic policies include an undeniable affinity to neoliberal economic concepts that advocate stronger deregulation, the dismantling of welfare state structures and largely pro-business tax policies (Peck and Tickell, 2002; Peck, 2004; Altvater and Mahnkopf, 2007; Carroll, 2010). This affinity is reflected in the constitution of the Young Entrepreneurs Association and in the establishment of the Aqaba Special Economic Zone (ASEZ).

As many of the expert opinions regarding the establishment of the Special Economic Zone in Aqaba showed, the recent economic developments in this southern Jordanian city are seen exceedingly critically. People not only fear a gradual loss of sovereignty to foreign investors, they also criticize the lack of sustainability of investments adhering to capital market criteria. The ongoing economic and financial crisis serves as a warning. In fact, a large number of major tourist projects are currently on hold or have been entirely stopped. In this situation, it is hardly surprising that critical observers increasingly question the system and ponder fundamentally to what extent the capital market controlled interests of transnational global players are compatible with the needs of small and medium-sized enterprises – many of which, moreover, are still in the thrall of the paradigm of rent capitalism. Aggravating this situation is the fact that tourist demand from the important European and North American source markets is declining as a result of the recent political developments in the region, leading many to reconsider potential target groups. As a local hotelkeeper remarked, "perhaps we will have to get used to having the chador increasingly compete with the bikini at the swimming pool." That this kind of perspective definitely has advantages for the Jordanian tourism industry is obvious. There are two key advantages: first, an intensified inner-Arabian tourist demand has been observable for a number of years, not least because of the increasing social and economic importance of the middle class in many Arab states. Second, it would make the Jordanian tourism industry less dependent on the strong fluctuations in demand in the European and North American source markets in response to crises. At any rate, it will continue to be fascinating to observe the developments in tourism in Jordan, especially in the Aqaba Special Economic Zone. One insight of the neoliberalization of Jordan by means of the special economic zone of Aqaba has been gained: a Dubai on the Gulf of Aqaba is still very remote and whether it is even worth pursuing remains more than questionable.

References

Aggarwal, A. (2006). Special economic zones: Revisiting the policy debate: A discussion of the pros and cons of the controversial. *Economic and Political Weekly*, 41(43/44), 4533–6.

Ahmed, Z.U., Julian, C.C., Baalbaki, I., and Hadidian, T.V. (2006). Firm internationalisation and export incentives from a Middle Eastern perspective, *Scandinavian Journal of Hospitality and Tourism*, 13(4), 660–69.

Al-Hamarneh, A. and Steiner, C. (2004). Islamic Tourism: Re-thinking the strategies of tourism development in the Arab World after September 11th. *Comparative Studies of South Asia, Africa and the Middle East*, 24(1), 18–27.

Altvater, E. and Mahnkopf, B. (2007). *Grenzen der Globalisierung: Ökonomie, Ökologie und Politik in der Weltgesellschaft*, Münster: Westfälisches Dampfboot.

Amalu, N (2010). A Voice for Young Entrepreneurs. In Center for International Private Enterprise (ed.) *Strategies for Policy Reform, Volume 2 – Engaging Entrepreneurs in Democratic Governance*. Washington DC: CIPE, 40–44.

Barham, N.F. (1999). Jordanien. Eine geographische Einführung. In G. Shanneik (ed.) *Die Beziehungen zwischen der Bundesrepublik Deutschland und dem Haschemitischen Königreich Jordanien*. Bonn: Shanneik, 13–28.

Barham, N. (2002). Sectoral actors in the Jordanian economy. In G. Joffé (ed.) *Jordan in Transition*. London: Hurst and Company, 278–97.

Barham, N. and Kopp, H. (2001). Tourismusentwicklung im Rentenstaat am Beispiel von Petra, dem Brennpunkt des jordanischen Tourismus. *Erdkunde*, 55(3), 228–43.

Beblawi, H. (1990). The Rentier state in the Arab world. In G. Luciani (ed.) *The Arab State*. London: Routledge, 85–98.

Berger, L. (2011). The Missing Link? US policy and the international dimensions of failed democratic transitions in the Arab world. *Political Studies*, 59(1), 38–55.

Bhagwati, J.N. (1982). Directly unproductive, profit-seeking (DUP) activities. *Journal of Political Economy*, 90(5), 988–1002.

Bouziane, M. and Lenner, K. (2011). Protests in Jordan: Rumblings in the Kingdom of Dialogue. In Center for Middle Eastern & North African Politics (ed.) *Protests, Revolutions and Transformations – the Arab World in a Period of Upheaval*, Berlin: Freie Universität Berlin, 148–65.

Busch, B. (1992). *Sonderwirtschaftszonen als Instrument der Systemtransformation*. Cologne: Deutscher Instituts-Verlag.

Carroll, W.K. (2010). *The Making of a Transnational Capitalist Class: Corporate Power in the Twenty-first Century*. London: Zed Books.

Carter, C. and Harding, A. (eds) (2011). *Special Economic Zones in Asian Market Economies*. London: Routledge.

Center for Middle Eastern & North African Politics (ed.) (2011). *Protests, Revolutions and Transformations – the Arab World in a Period of Upheaval*. Berlin: Freie Universität Berlin.

Chatelus, M. (1987). Rentier or producer economy in the Middle East? The Jordanian response. In B. Khader and A. Badran (eds) *The Economic Development of Jordan*. London: Croom Helm, 2004–220.

Cousins, K. and Brunt, P. (2002). Terrorism, tourism and the media. *Security Journal*, 15(1), 19–32.

Dörrenbächer, H. (1991). Sonderwirtschaftszonen: Ein Beitrag zur wirtschaftlichen Entwicklung der UdSSR? *Osteuropa-Wirtschaft*, 36(2), 81–105.

El Namaki, M.S.S. (2008). *Strategy and Entrepreneurship in Arab Countries*. New York: Palgrave Macmillan.

El Ouazghari, K. (2011). Jordanien: Reform statt Revolution. *Aus Politik und Zeitgeschichte*, 61(39), 24–6.

Elsheshtawy, Y (2010). Redrawing Boundaries: Dubai, an Emerging Global City. In Y. Elsheshtawy (ed.) *Planning Middle Eastern Cities: An Urban Kaleidoscope in a Globalizing World*. London: Routledge, 169–99.

Farole, T. (2011). *Special Economic Zones in Africa: Comparing Performance and Learning from Global Experience*. Washington, DC: The World Bank.

Fathi, S.H. (1994. *Jordan – an Invented Nation?* Hamburg: Deutsches Orient-Institut.

Ge, W. (1999). Special economic zones and the opening of the Chinese economy: Some lessons for economic liberalization. *World Development*, 27(7), 1267–85.

Gradus, Y. (2001). Is Eilat-Aqaba a bi-national city? Can economic opportunities overcome the barriers of politics and psychology? *GeoJournal*, 54(1), 85–99.

Groß, S.R. (2006). *Freizonen als Instrument evolutorischer Strukturpolitik.* Bayreuth: P.C.O.

Harmsen, E. (2008). *Islam, Civil Society and Social Work: Muslim Voluntary Welfare Associations in Jordan between Patronage and Empowerment.* Leiden: ISIM.

Harrigan, J. and El-Said, H. (2000). Stabilisation and structural adjustment in developing countries: The case of Jordan and Malawi. *Journal of African Business*, 1(3), 63–110.

Hejazeen, E. (2007). *Tourism and Local Communities in Jordan: Perception, Attitudes and Perspectives.* Munich: Profil.

Hopfinger, H. and Pillmayer, M. (2013). Tourismus in Jordanien – aktuelle Tendenzen und zukünftige Herausforderungen. In H. Kopp (ed.) *Jordanien und Deutschland: Über die Vielfalt kultureller Brücken.* Wiesbaden: Reichert, 169–76.

Istaiteyeh, R. (2011). *Economic Development and Highly Skilled Returnees: The Impact of Human Capital Circular Migration on the Economy of Origin Countries: The Case of Jordan.* Kassel: University Press.

Kardoosh, M.A. (2005). The Aqaba Special Economic Zone, Jordan: A Case Study of Governance. Center for Development Research, Bonn University. http://www.zef.de/fileadmin/webfiles/downloads/projects/politicalreform/The_Aqaba_Special_Economic_Zone_.pdf. Accessed 7 November 2012.

Knowles, W. (2005). *Jordan Since 1989: A Study in Political Economy (Library of Modern Middle East Studies).* London: Tauris.

Krueger, A. (1974). The political economy of the rent-seeking society. *American Economic Review*, 64(3), 291–303.

Kuran, T. (2004). *Islam and Mammon: The Economic Predicaments of Islamism.* Princeton, NJ: Princeton University Press.

Lawrence, T.E. (1997). *Seven Pillars of Wisdom.* Hertfordshire: Wordworth.

Litwack, J.M. and Qian, Y. (1998). Balanced or unbalanced development: Special economic zones as catalysts for transition. *Journal of Comparative Economics*, 26(1), 117–41.

Mednicoff, D. (2002). Monarchical stability and political liberalization: Connections between Jordan and Morocco. In G. Joffé (ed.) *Jordan in Transition.* London: Hurst and Company, 91–110.

Mensching, H. and Wirth, E. (1989). *Nordafrika und Vorderasien.* Frankfurt: Fischer.

Ministry of Tourism and Antiquities (2011). *Jordan National Tourism Strategy,* http://www.mota.gov.jo/en/portals/0/NTS_2011–2015_English.pdf. Accessed 7 November 2012.

Muchlinski, P. (2011). SEZs: A policy tool in search of a new agenda? In C. Carter and A. Harding (eds) *Special Economic Zones in Asian Market Economies.* London: Routledge, 15–37.

Murphy, D. (2011). *Lawrence of Arabia.* Colchester: Osprey Publishing.

Myrdal, G. (1957). *Economic Theory and Under-Developed Regions.* London: Duckworth.

Nsour, M. (2002). Governance, economic transition and Jordan's national security. In G. Joffé (ed.) *Jordan in Transition.* London: Hurst and Company, 23–44.

Ong, A. (2006). *Neoliberalism and Exception: Mutations in Citizenship and Sovereignty.* Durham: Duke University Press.

Orrego Vicuña, F. (1989). *The Exclusive Economic Zone: Regime and Legal Nature under International Law.* Cambridge: Cambridge University Press.

Palit, A. and Bhattacharjee, S. (2008). *Special Economic Zones in India: Myths and Realities.* London: Anthem Press.

Parker, C. (2009). Tunnel-bypasses and minarets of capitalism: Amman as neoliberal assemblage. *Political Geography,* 28(2), 110–20.

Peck, J. (2004). Geography and public policy: Constructions of neoliberalism. *Progress in Human Geography,* 28(3), 392–405.

Peck, J. and Tickell, A. (2002). Neoliberalizing space. *Antipode,* 34(3), 380–404.

Perroux, F. (1955). Note sur la Notion de 'Pôle de croissance'. *Economie Appliquée,* 7, 307–20.

Perthes, V. (1982). *Geheime Gärten: Die neue arabische Welt.* Berlin: Siedler.

Pillmayer, M. and Scherle, N. (2012). Jordan's Golden Triangle: New diversification strategies in response to current transformation processes. In A. Kagermeier and J. Saarinen (eds) *Transforming and Managing Destinations: Tourism and Leisure in a Time of Global Change and Risks.* Mannheim: MetaGIS-Systems, 49–61.

Pillmayer, M. (2014). *Internationalisierung in der Tourismuswirtschaft: Das Beispiel Jordanien.* Wiesbaden: Springer Gabler.

Saraya Aqaba (2010). *Press CD.* Aqaba.

Scherle, N. (2011). Tourism, neoliberal policy and competitiveness in the developing world: The case of the Masterplan of Marrakech, in J. Mosedale (ed.) *Political Economy of Tourism.* London: Routledge, 207–24.

Schlumberger, O. (2002). Transition to Development. In G. Joffé (ed.) *Jordan in Transition.* London: Hurst and Company, 225–53.

Schmid, C. (1991). *Das Konzept des Rentier-Staates. Ein sozialwissenschaftliches Paradigma zur Analyse von Entwicklungsgesellschaften und seine Bedeutung für den Vorderen Orient.* Münster: Lit.

Schmid, H. (2009). *Economy of Fascination: Dubai and Las Vegas as Themed Urban Landscapes.* Berlin: Borntraeger.

Schmid, H., Sahr, W-D. and Urry, J. (eds) (2011). *Cities and Fascination: Beyond the Surplus of Meaning.* Farnham: Ashgate.

Sönmez, S.F. (1998). Tourism, terrorism, and political instability. *Annals of Tourism Research*, 25(2), 416–56.

Talal, Basma bint (2004). *Rethinking an NGO: Development, Donors and Civil Society in Jordan.* London: Tauris.

Wong, K.Y. and Chu, D.K. (1984). Export processing zones and special economic zones as generators of economic development: The Asian experience. *Geografiska Annaler, Series B. Human Geography*, 66(1), 1–16.

World Bank (2012). *World Development Report 2013: Jobs.* Washington, DC: World Bank Publications.

Zorob, A. (2011). Aufstand in der arabischen Welt: Wirtschaftliche Hintergründe und Perspektiven. In Center for Middle Eastern & North African Politics (ed.) *Protests, Revolutions and Transformations – the Arab World in a Period of Upheaval.* Berlin: Freie Universität Berlin, 62–81.

Chapter 6

Ecotourism as the Focus of the Neoliberal Tourism Project in India

Kevin Hannam and Maharaj Vijay Reddy

The political and economic theory of neoliberalism has become associated with the proposition that entrepreneurship should be maximized within an institutional framework that allows the greatest degree of freedom for entrepreneurs whilst limiting the role of the state in intervening in market forces. Following this ideology, since the early 1990s the liberalization of the Indian economy has led to significant changes in its urban and rural landscapes and livelihoods as well as notable resistance to these changes, which have been well documented. However, little attention has been paid explicitly to the role neoliberalist ideologies have played in terms of tourism. This chapter seeks to examine this through an analysis of the role of the state in developing ecotourism in India. In particular, the chapter critically examines the development of the Ecotourism Guidelines by the Ministry of Environment and Forests of the Government of India. Firstly, the chapter examines how the relationships between nature and neoliberalism have been theorized.

Theorising Neoliberalism and Nature

The neoliberalization of nature can be defined as a process whereby non-human phenomena are increasingly subject to market-based systems of management and development (Castree, 2003, 2007; Duffy, 2008). Early critiques of the effects of neoliberalism on nature came from a political ecology perspective that examined the politics of environmental change in the Third World in terms of certain problems, concepts, socio-economic characteristics and regions, or used a combination of these (Bryant, 1992; Peet and Watts, 1996; Bryant and Bailey, 1997; Peluso and Watts, 2001). As Bryant and Bailey (1997: 3) pointed out:

> Political ecologists appear to agree on two basic points … Firstly, they agree that the environmental problems facing the Third World are not simply a reflection of policy or market failures … but rather are a manifestation of broader political and economic forces. … [A] second area of agreement among political ecologists is the need for far-reaching changes to local, regional and global political-economic processes …

Political ecologists are thus highly sceptical of the merits of concepts such as sustainable development, partly because of the way that such ideas have become swiftly incorporated into the dominant discourses of global organizations, nation-states and multi-national corporations without much change at grassroots level. This is largely because of the foregrounding of the political in political ecology research. Moreover, this is all the more apparent in Third World contexts where the colonial legacy of commodification and land degradation has led to the continuation of social and environmental conflicts in the post-colonial era. Ultimately, a political ecology approach is grounded in a historical and material analysis of the often complex and unequal relations of power within any environmental context.

More recent theorists of neoliberalism have continued to study the impact of neoliberalism on nature and the environment, as Heynen and Robbins (2005: 6) have critically noted: "[r]evolutions in law, policy, and markets are accelerating the ongoing commodification of natural things, laying bare the structurally driven and environmentally destructive tendencies of capitalism." They go on to discuss how the encounter between neoliberalism and nature also draws attention to sometimes overlooked scalar dialectics of political economic change. The inherent connections between city and country, local and extra-local, and regional and national, intensify as spatially complex environmental processes (e.g., animal migration, carbon diffusion, and water flows) encounter various scales of human-imposed economic structures, such as property rights, markets, and regulation. Resistance against the environmentally destructive forces of neoliberalization also operates at and produces a range of geographic scales – feedbacks and responses that emerge from both human and non-human communities" (Heynen and Robbins, 2005: 7).

Hence, they argue that it is only by critically examining these diverse connections, processes and resistances to neoliberalism that the relations between economy and nature can be fully understood. From a tourism perspective, meanwhile, Rosaleen Duffy (2008: 327) has analysed the effects of neoliberalism and argues that ecotourism in particular, "relies on the neoliberalisation of nature through the transformation of natural resources into privately owned and globally 'marketable goods'." This is a point, which we shall return to in our analysis of ecotourism in India.

The Neoliberalism Project in India

Historically, India has been a country that has had a large state apparatus in direct contrast to contemporary ideologies of liberalism. The extension of State activity from the late nineteenth century onwards disrupted local patterns of power and protest, and made the State more obtrusive and disliked by local communities. It provided new issues and arenas for the ambitious to fight over, and started to link up provincial centres and peripheries as never before. The relationships between the State and society in India can be seen as the product of a series of practices based upon the accumulation of knowledge about India and the creation of disciplinary forms of power. Whilst it is broadly true to say that the British

Indian State was ultimately based upon a monopoly over the means of force and violence, after 1857 only a calculated display of such despotic and coercive power was considered necessary to create an awareness of its authoritarian power (Bhattacharya, 1986). In the formulation and implementation of policies and laws, the element of coercion was moderated by the desire to secure consent and conciliate oppositional forces. As a result, the legitimating of British rule became the abiding concern of the State, operationalized primarily through various discursive means such as the codification of laws (Washbrook, 1981).

The emergence of a true bureaucratic State – high in disciplinary power and relatively low in despotic power – rests with the re-configuration of the Indian State after independence and federalization (Hannam, 1998). The Congress State formation that emerged after independence retained many of the features of the British Indian State but was somewhat different in a number of respects. In particular, Nehru and others argued that the practice of central or national planning was crucial to their vision of economic development. As Ron Inden (1995: 268) has noted: "[p]lanning was the utopian principle through which Nehru and his government hoped to embody the foundational Reason of democratic socialism and hence bring about economic development. ... The utopian practices they proceeded to use, however, were based on the illusion that scientific and technical knowledge were certain and complete and that existing knowledges of the people were of no use."

However, the role of the independent Indian State, whilst increasingly bureaucratic in form, has not remained stable. Indeed, after 25 years of national planning, the Indian bureaucratic State formation turned towards ever more subtle, diffused methods of governance involving increased popular participation in the State's activities. In response to changes in the world economy, the Indian State has launched its new economic policy since 1991and thus restructured or liberalized the Indian economy by allowing greater administrative autonomy and a wider role for private finance and entrepreneurship (Pedersen, 2000; Ahmed et al., 2011). Nevertheless, the Indian State still retains many of the features from the colonial period in terms of its apparatus, supplemented by national five year plans. Thus, the meshing of a neoliberal ideology with a strong state apparatus has led to India's unique development path with particular implications for tourism (Hannam and Diekmann, 2011).

India's new economic policy framework mirrored the standard structural adjustment measures as advocated by the International Monetary Fund and the World Bank and was widely perceived as resulting in faster rates of economic growth in India. However, such headline growth rates mask ever-widening economic disparities and increasing poverty levels (Patnaik, 2007). As Ahmed et al. (2011: 1–2) note: "neoliberal growth has come at the expense of high levels of smallholder indebtedness, mounting unemployment, and a declining natural resource base." Neoliberalism, in the Indian context, can look very different to those people who have been displaced by the so-called economic miracle. Global institutions have arguably worked in conjunction with local state elites to reinforce dominant class and caste positions (Ahmed, 2011). In particular, "the liberalization of imports of capital goods and components required for a number of commodities catering to luxury consumption, especially of electronics and automobiles" reinforced class and caste disparities (Chandresekhar, 2010).

Neoliberalism and Tourism in India

As a direct result of the economic liberalization reforms of the 1990s, tourism was singled out as a priority sector for economic investment and a new tourism policy was developed. In 2002, the Ministry of Tourism formulated the 'National Tourism Policy' providing a strategy for tourism development that considered tourism as one of the major elements for national economic growth. Key aspects of this policy were:

> To:
> Position tourism as a major engine of economic growth;
> Harness the direct and multiplier effects of tourism for employment generation, economic development and providing impetus to rural tourism;
> Focus on domestic tourism as a major driver of tourism growth.
> Position India as a global brand to take advantage of the burgeoning global travel trade and the vast untapped potential of India as a destination;
> Acknowledges the critical role of private sector with government working as a pro-active facilitator and catalyst;
> Create and develop integrated tourism circuits based on India's unique civilization, heritage, and culture in partnership with States, private sector and other agencies and
> Ensure that the tourist to India gets physically invigorated, mentally rejuvenated, culturally enriched, spiritually elevated and "feel India from within. (MoT, 2002)

More recently, (1997–2002) this plan has been interpreted as involving primarily the development of large-scale tourism resorts at selected destinations in line with neoliberal ideologies of mega-developments. However, half of all expenditure is earmarked for overseas marketing and publicity. This has led to the (re)development and (re)branding of many of its destinations as the Indian government has begun to recognize the potential importance of tourism to the Indian economy and has begun to invest in tourism infrastructure (Raguraman, 1998; Bandyopadhyay and Morais, 2005). Developing foreign tourism arrivals is seen as the main focus, partly because of the need for foreign currency. The State is beginning to recognize that domestic tourism has grown rapidly in recent years, both in size and sophistication, due to the emergence of a dynamic urban middle class with disposable income.

The Ministry of Tourism has viewed cultural and heritage tourism as its central focus and aims to provide visitor facilities particularly for foreign tourists around specific monuments and heritage sites. It has identified a growing market in pilgrimage tourism for both the domestic and diaspora markets. However, more recently it has also given some limited attention to diversification and the development of nature-based tourism.

A key aspect of India's contemporary tourism governance since 2002 has thus been a change from a primary function of regulating tourism and the supply of facilities for domestic tourists towards a global destination branding strategy. As Kant (2009: 4) notes: "[u]ntil 2002, India had eighteen tourism offices abroad. There was no positioning, common branding or a clear precise message. One foreign office called it 'Spiritual India' another termed it 'Cultural India' and the third 'Unbelievable India'." The development of a single 'mother' brand for India's tourism was seen as important in the face of Asian competition following the events of 9/11 (Kant, 2009). Kant (2009: 16) further notes that the campaign involved "more than just advertising", which, in fact, played only a marginal role. The brand-building process comprised personal relationships with international tour operators and journalists, partnerships, promotions, contests, use of interactive media and an aggressive communication strategy. ... In reality, the 'Incredible India' campaign encompassed a new corporate culture ... "

Indeed, one of the key so called 'successes' of the Incredible India campaign has been that it has helped to change the perception in the West of India as a developing country with 'poverty problems' towards a perception of India as an emerging destination with contemporary values (Bandyopadhyay and Morais, 2005; Kant, 2009). Moreover, Sunil (2009, cited in Kant, 2009: 20) argued that the campaign headlines "such as 'not all Indians are polite, hospitable and vegetarian' are more than just witty advertising copy. They are symptomatic of a much bigger social phenomenon – an optimistic and extroverted new India, eager to make its presence felt in the global community." However, this arguably masks the reality of the neoliberal project. Indeed, Bandyopadhyay and Morais (2005) have highlighted the dissonance between the nationally given image of India and the image India portrays to Western countries, in particular the United States.

In early 2009, the tourism ministry launched a new tourism policy emphasizing the importance of domestic tourism and allocating new funding for this initiative, as they wish to continue to "encourage domestic tourists to visit unexploited tourist destinations in various states and thereby, project India as an attractive multi dimensional tourist destination" (MoT, 2009). Alongside this, however, they also wish to attempt to open up new markets in neighbouring countries, such as Singapore, Korea and China. Thus, tourism to, out and within India has undergone some important changes in recent years. The Indian tourism industry has had to adapt on the one hand to a rising numbers of international visitors and on the other hand to an increase of domestic tourism due to the growth of its middle class within the country. It is also recognized that as its economy continues to grow at a rapid rate, India will also become one of the most important countries in terms of future outbound tourism, as its middle classes look to visit destinations abroad.

In its most recent Annual Report, meanwhile, India's Ministry of Tourism (2010) has further articulated its plans for the development and branding of tourism in India. It notes that: "[t]he Ministry, in its efforts to deliver responsive governance has initiated some measures. It is the first Ministry to have a Performance Agreement signed between the Secretary (Tourism) and the senior officers of the Ministry of the rank of Joint Secretary and above. This agreement lays down timelines for implementation of specific tasks by the officers. This has culminated in the Results Framework Document for the Ministry being hosted in the official" (MoT, 2010: 8).

This statement is important as it signifies a shift in terms of tourism governance in India, as well as the Indian State's thinking more generally, towards a Western system of using performance indicators as a method of public governmentality.

In terms of furthering brand development, meanwhile, the current Annual Report of the Ministry of Tourism in India notes the importance of online marketing activities as part of its integrated marketing strategy. Moreover, it "undertook a series of promotional initiatives to minimize the negative impact of the global economic meltdown and the terrorist attack in Mumbai and to promote tourism to India" (MoT, 2010: 64). These have included various 'road shows' in developing markets such as Russia, Scandinavia, Australia and the Middle East focusing, in particular, on showcasing adventure tourism, nature-based tourism, health tourism, sports tourism (emphasising New Delhi hosting the Commonwealth Games) as well as India's cuisine as niche tourism sectors (MoT, 2010).

Neoliberalism and Ecotourism in India

Rosaleen Duffy (2008: 329) has argued that the "neoliberalisation of nature is nowhere more apparent than in the faith in ecotourism as a means of 'delivering' sustainable development" in the developing world. Furthermore, she notes that: "[e]cotourism especially suffers from being promoted as a kind of magic bullet which can simultaneously hit multiple targets" (Duffy, 2008: 330). Indeed, we can see this in various 'critiques' of the relations of tourism and nature in India. For example, both Maikhuri et al. (2000) and Singh and Singh (2004) note how in the Nanda Devi biosphere in the Indian Himalayas human-nature conflicts can be resolved by ecotourism which "will not only help to resolve the local people-policy conflicts and improve the local economy but will also help to achieve the biodiversity conservation goal" (Maikhuri et al., 2000: 333) and that the "development of sound ecotourism can resolve this conflict and bring park and people together" (Singh and Singh, 2004: 43). Whilst these critiques are laudable and do raise issues of resistance to state policies which control and discipline minority populations in India's national parks (Hannam, 2004), they fail to address the wider issue of the neoliberal project of ecotourism, which masks more global market inequalities. Indeed, as we shall see below, India's government has recently published a draft national policy for the development of ecotourism, which at face value would address some of the criticisms that these authors put forward.

In June 2011, the Ministry of Environment and Forests of the Government of India published the draft 'Ecotourism Guidelines' following a period of consultation with 'wildlife experts' and 'tourism practitioners' – mostly from the private sector. Like the 'magic bullet' alluded to above, the Minister of Environment and Forests,

Mr Ramesh, in his foreword to the Guidelines states that: "These guidelines fulfil multiple objectives. They are important because as we know, most wilderness areas in India are fragile ecosystems that provide important ecosystem services, and at the same time remain important tourism attractions. Ecotourism is tourism that is compatible with these fragile landscapes, while providing enhanced livelihoods to local communities." The Guidelines go on to state that:

Healthy natural ecosystems are critical to the ecological well-being of all living entities, and especially for the economic security of people. Ecotourism has the potential to enhance wilderness protection and wildlife conservation, while providing nature-compatible livelihoods and greater incomes for a large number of people living around natural ecosystems. This can help to contribute directly to the protection of wildlife or forest areas, while making the local community stakeholders and owners in the process (MoEF, 2011: 3).

The Guidelines, in the main, rely on the definitions of ecotourism set out by the International Ecotourism Society, which have been extensively critiqued (see Butcher, 2006). Each regional State in India is instructed in the Guidelines that it must develop an ecotourism strategy in relation to its protected areas. Furthermore, each state government should "develop a system by which gate receipts from Protected Areas should be collected by the Protected Area management, and not go as revenue to the State Exchequer." But that "the welfare of wildlife and Protected Areas/ biodiversity takes precedence over tourism" (MoEF, 2011: 4–5). In terms of implementation and management a 'Local Advisory Committee (LAC)'

must be constituted for each Protected Area by the State government. The LAC will have the following mandate:

• To review the State Ecotourism Strategy with respect to the Protected Area and make recommendations to the State government

• To ensure site specific restrictions on buildings and infrastructures in private areas in close proximity to core/critical tiger habitat/National Park/Sanctuary or buffer zone, keeping in mind the corridor value.

• To advise local and state government on issues relating to development of ecological-tourism in non-forest areas of ecological tourism zones etc.

• Regularly monitor all tourist facilities falling within 5 km of a Protected Area vis-à-vis environmental clearance, area of coverage, ownership, type of construction, number of employees etc, for suggesting mitigation/retrofitting measures if needed.

• Regularly monitor activities of tour operators to ensure that they do not cause disturbance to animals while taking visitors into the Protected Area. (MoEF, 2011: 6)

This represents a further shift in terms of the neoliberal governmentality of India's national parks as the rise in monitoring of activity further extends the state's surveillance of human activities in these areas.

The Guidelines also provide specific instructions for the restriction of tourism activity in India's Tiger Reserves. This has led to criticism from tour operators who have seen this as a particular threat arguing that:

> First, wildlife tourism offers an informal monitoring and anti-poaching programme through passive viewing by visitors. Second, it has a significant impact on the perceived status of a park and its ability to attract local, governmental or international funding. Third, it enhances the motivation and quality of a park's rangers and management. And finally, wildlife tourism creates perceived 'economic zones', where forests and their wildlife are valued as living ecosystems rather than as firewood, bushmeat or agricultural land. (Matthews, 2009: 50)

Nevertheless, such critiques that promote tourism fail also to see the wider neoliberal marketization of the national parks as part of the problem. The international funding that has often supported the economic liberalization of India's national parks. As Duffy (2008: 333) argues: "ecotourism is being developed in a manner which conforms to externally produced and driven models to suit the global marketplace; this in turn means that it may be difficult for local communities to negotiate effectively for forms of ecotourism that meet their specific needs."

Conclusions

Since the early 1990s, the liberalization of the Indian economy has led to significant changes in its urban and rural landscapes and livelihoods as well as notable resistance to these changes not least due to tourism development strategies. This chapter has analysed the role of the state in the terms of the recent development of ecotourism policy in India. While specific cases of human-environment conflicts in India can be charted, the wider issue of neoliberalism and its effects need to be further analysed in relation to tourism policies and processes in India. Moreover, the connections between neoliberalism and governmentality need to be further discussed.

References

Ahmed, W., Kundu, A. and Peet, R. (eds) (2011). *India's New Economic Policy: A Critical Analysis*. London: Routledge.
Bandyopadhyay, R. and Morais, D. (2005). Representative dissonance: India's self and western image. *Annals of Tourism Research*, 32(4), 1006–21.

Bhattacharya, N. (1986). Colonial state and agrarian society. In S. Bhattacharya and R. Thapar (eds) *Situating Indian History*. New Delhi: Oxford University Press.

Bryant R. (1992). Political ecology: An emerging research agenda in third-world studies. *Political Geography*, 11(1), 12–36.

Bryant, R. and Bailey, S. (1997). *Third World Political Ecology*. London: Routledge.

Butcher, J. (2006). Natural capital and the advocacy of ecotourism as sustainable development. *Journal of Sustainable Tourism*, 14(6), 629–44.

Castree, N. (2003). Commodifying what nature? *Progress in Human Geography*, 27(2), 273–92.

Castree, N. (2007). Neo-liberalising nature 1: The logics of de- and re-regulation. *Environment and Planning A*, 40(1), 131–52.

Chandrasekhar, C. (2010). From dirgisme to neoliberalism: Aspects of the political economy of the transition in India. *Development and Society*, 39(1), 29–59.

Duffy, R. (2008). Neoliberalising nature: Global networks and ecotourism development in Madagascar, *Journal of Sustainable Tourism*, 16(3), 327–44.

Hannam, K. (1998). *The Indian Forest Service: A Cultural Geography*. PhD Thesis. University of Portsmouth.

Hannam, K. (2004). Tourism and forest management in India: The role of the state in limiting tourism development. *Tourism Geographies*, 6(3): 331–51.

Hannam, K. and Diekmann, A. (2011). *Tourism and India*. London: Routledge.

Heynen, N. and Robbins, P. (2005). The neoliberalization of nature: Governance, privatization, enclosure and valuation. *Capitalism, Nature, Socialism*, 16(1), 5–8.

Inden, R. (1995). Embodying God: From imperial progresses to national progress in India. *Economy and Society*, 24(2), 245–78.

Kant, A. (2009). *Branding India: An Incredible Story*. New Delhi: HarperCollins.

Maikhuri, R., Rana, U., Rao K., Nautiyal, S. and Saxena, K. (2000). Promoting ecotourism in the buffer zone areas of Nanda Devi Biosphere Reserve: An option to resolve people—policy conflict. *International Journal of Sustainable Development & World Ecology*, 7(4), 333–42.

Matthews, J. (2009). Can tourism save India's tigers. *The Geographical Magazine*, January, 49–50.

MoEF (2011). *Draft Guidelines for Ecotourism in and around Protected Areas*. New Delhi: Government of India.

MoT (2002). *National Tourism Policy*. New Delhi: Government of India.

MoT (2009). *Guidelines for the Scheme of Market Development Assistance for Promotion of Domestic Tourism*. New Delhi: Government of India.

MoT (2010). Annual Report. New Delhi: Government of India.

Patnaik, U. (2007). Neoliberalism and rural poverty in India. *Economic and Political Weekly* 42(30), 3132–50.

Pedersen, J. (2000). Explaining economic liberalization in India: State and society perspectives. *World Development*, 28(2), 265–82.

Peet, R. and Watts, M. (eds) (2004). *Liberation Ecologies*. London: Routledge.

Peluso, N. and Watts, M. (eds) (2001). *Violent Environments*. Cornell: Cornell University Press.

Raguraman, K. (1998). Troubled passage to India. *Tourism Management*, 19(6), 533–4.

Singh, T.V. and Singh, S. (2004). On bringing people and park together through ecotourism: The Nanda Devi National Park, India. *Asia Pacific Journal of Tourism Research*, 9(1), 43–55.

Washbrook, D. (1981). Law, state and agrarian society in colonial India. *Modern Asian Studies*, 15(3), 649–721.

Chapter 7
The Changing Nature of National Parks under Neoliberalization

Dzingai K. Nyahunzvi

It is well-documented that protected areas worldwide face a litany of problems that include underfunding, pressures from tourism developments, population growth, overgrazing, farming, mining and urbanization (McNeeley, 1994; IUCN, 2000; Balmford and Whitten, 2003; Font et al., 2004). A protected area is defined in this chapter as "an area of land and/or sea dedicated to the preservation and maintenance of biological diversity and of natural and associated cultural resources and managed through legal or other effective means" (IUCN, 1994: 7). Beginning with some Western countries from the 1970s, neoliberal governance approaches have been adopted on a large-scale in response, in part, to the chronic underfunding that protected areas worldwide face (Leal and Fretwell, 1997; Font et al., 2004).

It is worth noting that neoliberalism is an ambiguous and heavily contested term that has defied a universal definition. In this chapter, neoliberalism refers to a philosophy that celebrates the primacy of market forces and private property rights as an efficient allocation mechanism of resources (Harvey, 2005). This economic philosophy was adopted in some Western countries such as the USA and Britain in different forms, starting from the 1970s as a result of disenchantment with Keynesian economics (Telfer, 2002; Shultis, 2005). The latter emphasized an interventionist role by the state in the post-World War II era economies. With regard to developing countries, the adoption of neoliberalism was mainly a post-1980s phenomenon usually at the instigation of International Financial Institutions (IFIs) such as the World Bank (Haque, 1999; Bond and Dor, 2003). At this juncture, it seems appropriate to facilitate the reader's interpretation of this chapter by declaring my political allegiances early. On a personal level, I have reservations with neoliberalism, particularly the increased poverty and inequities that it has come to be associated with (Harvey, 2005). Rather, I find neo-structuralism with its strong emphasis on the regulatory powers of the state as a more appropriate development paradigm.

For the purposes of this chapter, the term neoliberalization will be used in place of neoliberalism to signify that it is a context-specific process rather than a universal phenomenon, in line with current academic thinking (e.g. Igoe and Croucher, 2007; Castree, 2008a, b). The application of neoliberal development orthodoxy in biodiversity conservation will be referred to as neoliberal conservation after

Igoe and Brockington (2007). Thus, the term neoliberal conservation collectively refers to the various modes of protected area governance that include conservation easements, public-private partnerships (PPPs), outsourcing, marketization, commercialization and privatization.

It is necessary to note that there are varied meanings and interpretations ascribed to the various governance modes of neoliberal conservation mentioned above. Two modes of neoliberal conservation are particularly relevant in this study and need to be operationally defined, namely commercialization and privatization. Commercialization is known by various other terms in the literature including outsourcing, contracting-out, competitive sourcing and commercial tourism-protected area partnership. In this chapter, the term commercialization will be used in place of the above-cited terms and will be taken to mean the adoption of business principles and practices in the management of a protected area including outsourcing part or all of the functions performed by the protected area agency to the private sector (de la Harpe et al., 2004). Privatization is another term that has loose definitions and interpretations but for the purposes of this study, it will be taken to mean a change of ownership of a protected area from the public to the private sector together with the subsequent management of the protected area on a commercial basis (Crompton, 1998).

It has been argued that the critical shortage of state funding for conservation has led to *inter alia*, the existence of "paper parks and animal slums," poor service provision and environmental degradation in several countries (Child et al., 2004: 163). With specific reference to Africa, it is argued that " ... the underfunding of national park agencies is now probably the single most important threat to the conservation of the areas under their control" (de la Harpe et al., 2004: 190). It is further claimed that protected area agencies even in affluent countries such as the USA's National Park Service (NPS) face chronic underfunding (de la Harpe et al., 2004).

The foregoing discussion captures some of the core arguments advanced in favour of neoliberal conservation in general and the commercialization of national park agencies in particular. Admittedly, it appears that state funding for conservation is inadequate and has progressively decreased in several countries (Font et al., 2004). However, decreased and inadequate state funding is generally closely associated with the adoption of neoliberal policies by several countries, worldwide (King, 2009). In light of this, I contend that there is a strong relationship between the commercialization of park agencies and neoliberalization.

Following the 'dominant conservation narrative' described above, there has been increased adoption of neoliberal conservation worldwide (Igoe and Brockington, 2007). Indeed, it has been argued that the commercialization of national parks is the only "viable, practical and sustainable" option for Africa (de la Harpe et al., 2004: 189). At the same time, the neoliberalization of nature in general is seen as a 'common sense approach' (Heynen et al., 2007). Furthermore, neoliberal conservation is touted as a 'win-win' strategy that satisfies a range of protected areas' stakeholders including but not limited to the taxpayer, local communities, tourists, local and non-local private sector companies and investors, the physical environment, IFIs and international development and environmental organizations (Grandia, 2007; Igoe and Brockington, 2007).

Within this context, it is only in the past decade that there has emerged a "new but fast-growing geographical research literature about neoliberalising nature" (Castree, 2008b: 153). This literature is predominantly case study-based and involves diverse resources and contexts (Heynen et al., 2007; Castree, 2008a, b). The dominant theme emerging from this literature is that there still exists limited "evidence-based critiques" (Castree, 2008b: 154) of the neoliberalization of nature in specific contexts (Duffy, 2008). This limited research is incongruous with the tremendous pressure that exists for protected area agencies to adopt neoliberal conservation (Buckley, 2004; Darcy and Wearing, 2009; Wilson et al., 2009). Furthermore, very few studies have assessed the implications of conservation policies within the context of neoliberalization (Igoe and Brockington, 2007). Based on the foregoing research gaps and omissions, this chapter critically examines the development and conservation implications of South African National Parks' (SANParks) 'Commercialization as a conservation strategy' at Kruger National Park (KNP). In doing so, it responds to appeals for research that exposes the nature and character of "actually existing neoliberalism" (Brenner and Theodore, 2002: 351).

Unpacking Representations of KNP's Commercialization Process

The 'Commercialization as a conservation strategy' (hereafter, KNP's commercialization process) was implemented in 2000. It involved seven concession sites meant for the construction and operation of five star lodges in KNP, two sites in Addo Elephant National Park, two in Table Mountain National Park and a hotel management contract in Golden Gate Highlands National Park (Fearnhead, 2003). The commercialization process also led to the outsourcing of SANParks' entire stock of shops and restaurants to the private sector. In KNP banking and car hire services, the management of the entire fleet of the park's vehicles, internet cafes, security services and two picnic sites were also outsourced. These services were considered peripheral to the primary conservation mandate of the organization. The park retained the following functions that were deemed as core functions, research, human resources, marketing, finance, information communication technology, people and conservation, conservation, the wilderness trail (a 21-day walking safari package) and the rest of the accommodation units that mainly cater for domestic tourists (Fearnhead, 2003; Mabunda, 2004).

SANParks is a protected area agency with the mandate to run South Africa's 21 national parks. The objectives of KNP's commercialization process were to *inter alia*, generate additional funding for conservation, economically empower Historically Disadvantaged Individuals (HDIs) through investment and employment opportunities in concessions, reduce the cost of service delivery and improve service provision through outsourcing part of the tourism services to the private sector (Fearnhead, 2003, 2007; Spenceley, 2004; van Jaarsveld, 2004; Varghese, 2008). The term HDIs refers to South African citizens who according to racial classification in the apartheid era, did not have the right to vote or had restricted voting rights immediately prior to the 1994 elections (SANParks, 2000).

The rationale for the adoption of the commercialization process was that the democratic government faced a wide array of pressing social needs, hence it was argued that it could not afford the 'luxury' of supporting nature conservation (Fearnhead, 2003; Mabunda, 2004). In the case of SANParks, the government supported it with an R59m subsidy per annum (Cock and Fig, 2000). A related issue raised was that the government had progressively reduced its funding over the years leading to a backlog in the maintenance of park infrastructure and reduced budgets for capital projects (Mabunda, 2004).

It is further documented that the floods that affected KNP in 2000 leading to its closure for ten months, precipitated a serious financial crisis as the park generated about 80 per cent of SANParks' revenue (Mabunda, 2011). As result of this financial crisis, the government from March 24–26, 2000 convened a stakeholder meeting to discuss a new vision for SANParks. It is advanced that at this meeting the government "articulated the need for SANParks to prepare for the eventual weaning from state funding and urged the entity to re-think new models of leveraging its resources and establish new sustainable revenue generation options to achieve future financial self-reliance" (Mabunda, 2011: np). Prior to these discussions, it is worth noting that a team of consultants had produced the 'McKinsey Business Consultants Report for SANParks' in 1999, which recommended that SANParks should embark on commercialization as a result of reduced government appropriations (Mabunda, 2004, 2011).

There are further arguments that service delivery prior to commercialization was costly, inefficient and not tailored to meeting the increased foreign visitors and the emerging black middle class (Fearnhead, 2003; Mabunda, 2004, 2011). Commercialization was also articulated as a means to allow HDIs, "in particular those from local communities living adjacent to national parks" (Fearnhead, 2003: 2) to derive benefits from SANParks' estates on the recognition that, traditionally, only white-owned businesses were allowed to do business with SANParks (Cock and Fig, 2000). It was also envisaged that the provision of goods and services by the private sector, would allow SANParks to concentrate on its core mandate of conservation (Fearnhead, 2003; Mabunda, 2004). It was further reasoned that the state did not "have the skills, attitudes and incentives that drive successful businesses" (Fearnhead, 2003: 2). Besides, a lack of a shareholder base and enabling legislation meant that SANParks was not able to raise additional capital, as would a private company (Fearnhead, 2003).

However, there are some dissenting views to these documented 'official narratives.' The use of the latter phrase captures the important point that these views are expressed by government representatives i.e. mostly SANParks' managerial employees. It is also in line with the contention that in dealing with representations of environmental discourses, there is a need to pay attention to "the power of language, social interests and networks in defining 'truth' and how regimes of truth become institutionalised through practices" (Jeanrenaud, 2002: 114). Ferreira and Harmse (1999) contend that SANParks' business performance was positive prior to commercialization, with KNP registering some one million visitors per year and a net income of R155m (US$25m) annually that enabled it to self-fund its tourism operations. However, Fearnhead (2003) challenges this positive assessment by pointing out that contrary, all departments except conservation performed poorly whilst productivity and service levels were low and costly in relation to industry norms. Mabunda (2004) concurs and further contends that the annual subsidy to SANParks for the period 1993/1994–2002/2003 did not increase in line with inflation.

In contrast, King (2009) links the mid-1990s commercialization of the Mpumalanga Parks Board (MPB) (another South African protected area agency) to the neoliberal macroeconomic policy adopted by the democratic government in 1996 in place of a social democratic programme. In stating this, King (2009: 408) laments the limited use of institutional ethnographies in contemporary literature to either "understand how [conservation policies] are created and rationalised by powerful organisations and networks [e.g. SANParks]" or to "understand how organisations construct and institute particular [conservation] discourses and policies." King (2009: 409) further asserts, "the commercialisation push within the MPB mirrored a general trend towards neoliberal decentralisation in the Global South." This assertion suggests that KNP's commercialization process is not informed by internal factors alone. Another view is provided by Mohany and van Zyl (2002) who point to the stiff competition KNP faced from private lodges that border it as compelling SANParks to embark on commercialization as a 'business survival strategy'.

The above analysis demonstrates that there are contrasting documented views regarding the rationale behind the adoption of the commercialization process. The same contested views are found both within and outside SANParks in terms of whether the commercialization process was necessary or justified at all, including the direction it took (Mabunda, 2004; Varghese, 2008). Here, I concur with King's (2009) perspective and further argue that we should go beyond the 'official narratives' to the source i.e. neoliberalization, in order to understand the shift to the private sector in the provision of goods and services by several protected area agencies worldwide. If we do this, we will see the pervasive influence of such organizations as the World Bank and the IMF in the 'neoliberal turn' in several developing countries since the 1980s. The shift to the private sector by protected area agencies can then be meaningfully interpreted as part of the wider process to establish 'open' economies in developing countries as advocated by the World Bank and IMF. Taking this approach, may enable us to make sense out of the 'official narrative' that suggests that the democratic government wanted to save money and channel it to pressing social needs yet, ironically, the source of all life on earth is biodiversity. Thus, it seems that it is not by coincidence that almost all of southern Africa's protected area agencies embarked on commercialization almost at the same time i.e. from the 1980s after the adoption of SAPs (see de la Harpe et al., 2004). Elsewhere, it is instructive that Büscher and Dressler (2012: 367) note that a " ... even more important driver of the congruency between the design and implementation of [conservation] approaches has been the simultaneous global rise and influence of neoliberalism." In similar vein, it can be argued that 'official narratives' do not acknowledge that the reduced levels of state funding for conservation in South Africa were part of a deliberate policy that started in the 1980s when the apartheid government adopted neoliberal policies. Put differently, I argue here that a changing political ideology is at the heart of KNP's commercialization process.

Since the launch of KNP's commercialization process in 2000, a small but growing literature (e.g. Fearnhead, 2003, 2007; Spenceley, 2004; van Jaarsveld, 2004; Saporiti, 2008; Varghese, 2008), largely authored by SANParks managers has emerged. This prior research articulates the principal features of the process and evaluates the development and conservation outcomes and implications of the commercialization process concluding that it is largely a win-win process. The characterization of KNP's commercialization process as largely a win-win process meant that it was seen as benefiting everyone. To illustrate, tourists would benefit from superior service delivery and cheaper tourist experiences, the state would make cost-savings with conservation paying for itself, concession fees would be a risk-free source of funding as opposed to state-funding and local communities would benefit from the investment and employment opportunities opened up by the commercialization process. It is within this context that the term win-win is used throughout the chapter.

It is important to note that some of the prior research dwells on preliminary outcomes as the studies were undertaken at a time when the commercialization process had just been implemented (e.g. Child et al., 2004; Mabunda, 2004; Spenceley, 2004; van Jaarsveld, 2004). On the same note, both this and recent research (e.g. Fearnhead, 2007; Varghese, 2008) were not based on direct engagement with stakeholders at the 'coal-face' of neoliberal practice at KNP. Although this pioneering literature provides some important insights into the commercialization process, there is a definite need for studies that incorporate 'coal-face' perspectives. Such studies address the observed absence of extensive research that provides multi-voiced, embodied and reflexive accounts of neoliberal conservation (Castree, 2008a, b; Himley, 2008). Most importantly, prior research has not located KNP's commercialization process within a neoliberal lens thereby potentially limiting our understanding of its wider ramifications. Rather, prior research has followed the trend observed in the wider literature of evaluating PPPs or commercialization "through conceptual lenses that emphasize either the administrative, managerial, financial or technical dimensions of this reform strategy" thereby overlooking "a host of political issues and tensions" it raises (Flinders, 2005: 215).

The findings presented in this chapter are based on qualitative materials drawn from semi-structured interviews held with tourists, concession and SANParks' employees as well as residents of Belfast village. Interviews were restricted to those who were willing to participate in the research or those who gave their informed consent. The interviews were stopped as soon as theoretical saturation was reached as recommended for qualitative research by Jennings (2005). It is necessary to note that hereafter, the term SANParks employees is used to refer to both head office and KNP employees whilst the term concession managerial employee refers to concessions' owners and managers who were interviewed. The rest of the concession employees interviewed are referred to as concession non-managerial employees. The above terms have been used to protect the identity of the research participants; this was guaranteed as a pre-condition for participating in the study. Personal observations and experiences were another source of the qualitative materials used in this study together with document analysis. Document analysis started before the interviews and continued alongside the interviews as more secondary data was availed to the researcher by SANParks and concession employees.

Description of the Study Sites

The fieldwork involved interviewing SANParks employees based at the Pretoria head office and at KNP as well as concession managers and employees and tourists. KNP is a world-renowned park, located in the north-eastern part of South Africa in Mpumalanga Province. The park is one of 21 national parks under the ambit of SANParks, generating almost 80 per cent of the organization's revenue (Mabunda, 2004). This shows the financial importance of KNP to SANParks; part of its revenue is used to subsidise the costs of running the other 16 loss-making national parks (Mabunda, 2004). KNP is able to generate a lot of revenue because it attracts over one million visitors per year due to its wealth of tourist assets that include important cultural heritage sites and a range of flora and fauna.

There are four considerations that make neoliberal theory an appropriate lens to use for such study sites as KNP. First, it must be recognized that the KNP 'space' is conceptualized in this study as an 'embattled zone' dominated by a network of competing state and non-state actors, who reside in and beyond the borders of South Africa. Second, KNP is among the 'pioneering parks' in Africa in terms of embracing the provision of tourism goods and services by the private sector at a period that generally coincides with the adoption of neoliberal policies in several developing countries. Third, South Africa is a case of "neoliberalisation from above" (Büscher and Dressler, 2012: 368) i.e. the democratic government established a deliberate policy to adopt neoliberal reforms. Finally, it has been observed that South Africa:

... retains landscapes of significant biological diversity and unique physical features that have become part of the global conservation consciousness. [The country is at the] forefront of combining community development with biodiversity conservation whilst experiencing the thrust of global neoliberalisation. ... in this setting, the rural poor have faced massive disenfranchisement as a result of major structural adjustments, not least by state, NGO, and private sector driven conservation efforts. (Büscher and Dressler, 2012: 369)

Interviews were also conducted in Belfast village; one of the three rural settlements (including Justicia and Huntingdon) that are located on the 'doorstep' of KNP, just less than ten kilometres from the Paul Kruger Gate on the main highway to the urban settlement of Hazyview.

Findings and Discussion

Field evidence suggested that SANParks' employees saw a range of benefits from the commercialization process from income generation to improved efficiencies. Document analysis confirmed these observations including the fact that the commercialization process was incomparable to even some Western nations' in terms of its positive financial and environmental outcomes. However, other testimonies revealed that although some concessions were thriving, others suffered from low occupancies and lack of awareness and knowledge of possible sources of technical and financial assistance. In addition, some tourists and SANParks employees confirmed reservations evident in prior research (e.g. Mabunda, 2004) surrounding the quality of service and pricing of goods by some of the concessionaires.

This study found evidence of the complexities associated with the day-to-day management of the concessions; a range of problems including lodge concession managers' high labour turnover and the failure by some SANParks employees to treat concessionaires as business partners were noted. The latter shows the absence of the necessary 'buy-in' among some SANParks employees with regards to the commercialization process.

Most of the concession managers were satisfied with the performance of their businesses although there were concerns raised regarding the adverse effects of unanticipated factors such as the 2009 global recession. Concession managers also emphasized the need on the part of SANParks to ensure an enabling business environment and to treat concessionaires as 'business partners.' The study further found some evidence of limited attention that had been paid to concessionaires' empowerment obligations, with some concession managers even indicating that there should be a renegotiation of the obligations. Factors that were cited for the limited progress in terms of empowerment obligations included the perceived lack of black employees with managerial potential and the lack of capacity and reliability among local suppliers. Some testimonies of the concession non-managerial employees indicated that the jobs they gained could only help them to cope with rather than to eliminate poverty and that job security was a cause of concern due to the global recession. In contrast, concession managerial employees gave testimonies that indicated their commitment to abide and even exceed the stipulated environmental obligations.

There were some highly pertinent findings from my interactions with Belfast village residents. Most of the Belfast participants perceived KNP as not benefiting them at either a personal or communal level. Indeed, KNP was seen as promoting enclave tourism and imposing far greater costs than benefits as it was pointed out that only a few people from the village had gained park employment. Moreover, some of the participants did not see park employment as radically transforming the lives of those who had gained employment at KNP.

Belfast participants further indicated that there were poor levels of interaction with the park and expressed their desire for the park to play a greater developmental role than it had. The study also found evidence of political disempowerment as the research participants pointed out that neighbouring communities did not have any direct influence on the management of KNP. In addition, most research participants perceived the existing Park Forum (a representative organization of KNP's publics that was formed by SANParks) as lacking legitimacy whilst others expressed ignorance of its existence. There were other testimonies to the effect that KNP management had not availed the necessary information regarding entrepreneurial opportunities that had been opened up by the commercialization process.

Six key implications of KNP's commercialization process were identified that are restated and further clarified below. First, one of the key implications emerging from the field evidence is that contrary to previous conceptualizations of KNP's commercialization as largely a win-win solution (e.g. Fearnhead, 2003, 2007; Spenceley, 2004, 2005, 2006; van Jaarsveld, 2004; Saporiti, 2008; Varghese, 2008), it should be regarded as a political process that determines stakeholders' access to ecological resources and subsequently socio-economic opportunities. Thus, KNP's commercialization process did not only raise additional funding for conservation, empower neighbouring communities and lower the cost of service provision as the prior research suggests (e.g. Fearnhead, 2003; 2007; Spenceley, 2004; Varghese, 2008) but it also created "winners and losers" among its stakeholders in terms of capturing the resultant socio-economic opportunities (Nyahunzvi, 2010a: 66). By applying a neoliberal lens to national park management, we also see that the commercialization process became the means through which some KNP's stakeholders became further integrated into the global neoliberal system.

Judging by the limited amount of employment created in relation to the total population in neighbouring communities (there are some five million black people living in villages adjacent to the park), it is evident that the majority from neighbouring communities found no role to play at all. Whilst it appeared that local and non-local elites possibly benefited most from the commercial opportunities offered by the commercialization process. This, in turn has negative implications for KNP's conservation mandate as dependence on natural resources among the majority in the neighbouring communities persists, as do the unmet expectations of deriving benefits from protected areas in the post-apartheid era.

Second, KNP's commercialization process empirically demonstrates how the state actively ensures that the capitalization of nature proceeds unhindered through *inter alia* the creation and enforcement of private property rights thereby changing human-nature relations. As Duffy and Moore (2010: 746) observe, " ... wildlife and landscapes are produced, reproduced and redesigned as tourist attractions. In the process they are commodified and drawn in to the global tourism marketplace as products to be consumed." In this way, SANParks and private capital were able to generate considerable income through the commercialization process that repackaged KNP as a tourist destination whose tourism services were in part now under the 'competent' management of the private sector. Judging from the outstanding revenues generated at KNP alone through the commercialization process, it is understandable why many protected area agencies are making or being pressured to make the 'neoliberal turn' (Buckley, 2004; Darcy and Wearing, 2009; Wilson et al., 2009).

However, risks emanating from the less controllable macro-meso environmental factors such as the 2009 global recession threatened to derail the outstanding financial gains that had been made at KNP. The implication drawn from the above is that contrary to claims by some prior researchers (e.g. de la Harpe et al., 2004; Varghese, 2008), the commercialization of national parks is not a win-win solution but at best a mixture of risks and benefits. To further support the above conclusion, field evidence also showed that commercialization at KNP was not a risk-free process that always delivered superior and affordable recreational experiences; a common claim made in favour of private sector provision of goods and services in protected areas (More, 2005). In line with this, some tourists complained of poor service delivery and higher prices.

Third, this study found evidence of the influence of contextual factors on neoliberalization in line with assertions by several researchers (e.g. Brenner and Theodore, 2002; Mansfield, 2004; Castree 2008a, b; Himley, 2008; Duffy and Moore, 2010). As an example of the path-dependent nature of neoliberalization, empowerment obligations were incorporated into concession contracts thereby making KNP's commercialization process politically acceptable to the black constituency. The empowerment obligations required concessionaires to *inter alia*, effect changes in the ownership and management patterns of their businesses through preferential employee recruitment policies, the training and upgrading the skills of black employees and establishing backward economic linkages with local communities (Fearnhead, 2003, 2007; van Jaarsveld, 2004; Varghese, 2008). In line with this thinking, it can equally be concluded that the appeal of KNP's commercialization process was that it was framed like the Broad Based Black Economic Empowerment (BBBEE) Act of 2003, in that it had a "latent 'stakeholder' character ... [that] allows it to be accepted as an instrument of (relative) change even within the broad dictates of neoliberal economic policy" (Ponte et al., 2007: 950). The foregoing adaptation of the commercialization discourse at KNP supports the contention that "neoliberalisation adapts to context-specific processes, values, ideas and institutions" (Duffy and Moore, 2010: 762).

More importantly, I argue that the presentation of the commercialization process as largely a win-win solution benefiting a range of stakeholders as projected by prior research (e.g. Fearnhead, 2003; 2007; Spenceley, 2004; Varghese, 2008) can be considered as part of the discursive practices that have been used to legitimize it (Nyahunzvi, 2010b). That is, commercialization was packaged in such a way that not only appealed to diverse interests but was morally difficult to challenge. The presentation of commercialization as a process that addressed development needs in local communities meant that it became a powerful discourse. The framing of the commercialization process mirrors the packaging of ecotourism; "a narrative of salvation; nature and local people are saved through the actions of ecotourists, and parks are the temples to which morally aware consumers flock to do good" (Campbell et al., 2008: 213). It is important to note that discourses can be used to facilitate the acceptability of specific human-nature relations (Escobar, 1996) and "are reflections of power relations; those with power [e.g. KNP management] assert their discourses, thereby determining what will count as truth and knowledge for all society" (Campbell et al., 2008: 202). I further argue that through this dominant discourse, other ways besides viewing KNP as a source of jobs and investment opportunities are silenced or marginalized thereby maintaining powerful actors' vantage position and access to natural resources (Nyahunzvi, 2010b).

Field evidence suggests that the development outcomes of the commercialization process were not different from other strategies that are similarly framed on South Africa's neoliberal development orthodoxy. That is, it appeared that elites benefited most whilst only a few people from neighbouring communities could secure employment or investment opportunities. Seen in this light, KNP's commercialization process did not offer a livelihood option to the majority of people living in neighbouring communities (Nyahunzvi, 2010a). This was partly due to the sheer numbers of people who lived in adjacent communities coupled with the lack of resources required to capture the investment and employment opportunities opened up by the commercialization process among the locals. Moreover, it appeared that there were inadequate support mechanisms for local entrepreneurs and concessionaires seemed not to have fully complied with the stipulated empowerment obligations. In comparative terms, apart from the Spatial Development Initiatives (SDIs), the commercialization process appears to draw strong parallels with South Africa's Working for Water (WfW) programme which " ... offers a limited and transitory route out of poverty" (Hope, 2006: 152) and to only a few households in rural communities. The WfW similarly attempts to fuse conservation and development by employing the poor from local communities to remove high water consuming alien plants (DWARF, 1997).

Fourth, the implication of the above analysis is that this study lends qualified support to Castree's (2008b: 163) assertion " ... that nature's neoliberalisation is a project driven by political economic elites that marginalises the poor and calls forth resistance. Such resistance, in turn, can reconfigure the project in its specific geographical manifestation." The support is qualified because the poor in South Africa appear to offer ineffective resistance to neoliberal development orthodoxy. The ineffective resistance is often expressed in sporadic street demonstrations instead of other means such as through the electoral system as happened in some Latin American countries where several political parties that espoused neoliberal policies were voted out of power in the past decade.

Fifth, the study found evidence of Schilcher's (2007: 94) notion of "false empowerment" i.e. " ... empowerment at a lower structural level which does not touch upon higher levels, or more perversely reinforces structural constraints at higher levels." That is, the commercialization process does not address structural constraints that produce and reinforce poverty and inequities as well as biodiversity loss in rural South Africa. The failure to address these structural constraints means that any gains made by locals in the commercialization process may be eroded. Overall, it can also be argued that KNP's commercialization process strengthens and perpetuates a system (i.e. the global capitalist system) that several researchers (e.g. Magubane, 2004; Harvey, 2005) argue creates poverty and inequities as a condition for its continued existence. This assertion is in line with Duffy and Moore's (2010: 743) observation that the "tourism industry is one means by which nature is neoliberalized, since it allows neoliberalism to target and open up new [capitalist] frontiers in nature ... "

Finally, in terms of the broader neoliberalization of nature literature, this study's findings suggest that KNP's commercialization process had mixed socio-economic and environmental outcomes. The mixed consequences recorded at KNP are consistent with some prior studies (e.g. Loftus and McDonald's (2001) study of water privatization in Argentina, Bakker's (2003) study of water privatization in England, and Bury's (2004) study of gold mining in Peru). The implication of the foregoing is that this study lends weight to Castree's (2008b) contention that the neoliberalization of nature does not result in negative outcomes only.

However, to judge whether the positive outcomes outweigh the negative at KNP or *vice versa* is difficult and contentious. To illustrate, how do we relate the gain by SANParks in terms of additional funding for conservation to the limited economic empowerment of Belfast village residents to give an overall assessment of the commercialization process? The same question was posed by Castree in relation to Bakker's (2003) study of the privatization of water:

> How are we to weigh the fact of more English and Welsh customers enjoying higher water quality against the increase in water cut-offs among a group of poorer households? Do we tabulate these effects in aggregate (at the national or regional levels)? Or do we focus on the *experienced* effects of water privatisation among a range of water consumers? (2003: 166)

Whilst, any decision reached concerning the above is subject to debate, one of the dominant themes emerging from this study of KNP's commercialization is that contrary to assertions by its proponents, the neoliberalization of nature is rarely a win-win solution.

Conclusion

One of the key themes emerging from this study is that neoliberalization transforms protected areas such as national parks into further frontiers of capitalist expansion. This in turn means that such spaces might see increased multi-actor struggles over ecological resources. Judging from this case study, it would appear that poverty-stricken villages living adjacent to national parks seem to be the least able to compete for a share of these resources compared to other stakeholders. Furthermore, this case study suggests that the hegemonic claims made by proponents of neoliberal conservation do not always coincide with 'coal-face' perspectives of neoliberal practice. The above analysis suggests the need for the critical adoption of neoliberal conservation by protected area agencies.

In terms of further studies, this study needs to be complemented by future comparative studies that recognize the contested and politicised nature of neoliberal governance approaches. This would also establish the extent to which this case study can be generalized to other geographic regions and socio-economic and political systems. Further research opportunities lie in studies that involve other stakeholders that were not included in this study. The latter, include distant stakeholders such as the ruling elite, environmental organizations, local and non-local concession shareholders and international financial institutions (IFIs). Brown (2002: 10) points out the importance of engaging these 'remote' stakeholders when he states; " ... in many circumstances very powerful actors are not in the immediate vicinity [of a protected area] ... [yet] they may significantly influence the way in which the resources are used." This field of study would profit from longitudinal perception studies; in this study, this approach was prevented by time and financial constraints. A related issue is the need to address the existing dearth of studies surrounding stakeholder relationships in commercial tourism-protected area partnerships in general (Wilson et al., 2009) and 'coal-face' perspectives of neoliberalization in particular.

References

Bakker, K. (2003). *An Uncooperative Commodity: Privatising Water in England and Wales.* Oxford: Oxford University Press.

Bakker, K. (2005). Neoliberalising nature? Market environmentalism in water supply in England and Wales. *Annals of the Association of American Geographers*, 95(3), 542–65.

Balmford, A. and Whitten, T. (2003). Who should pay for tropical conservation and how should the costs be met? *Oryx*, 37(2), 238–50.

BBBEE (Broad-Based Black Economic Empowerment) Act 53 of 2003. Pretoria: Government Printer.

Bek, D., Binns, T. and Nel, E. (2004). 'Catching the development train': Perspectives on 'top-down' and 'bottom-up' development in post-apartheid South Africa. *Progress in Development Studies*, 4(1), 22–46.

Bond, P. and Dor, G. (2003). Neoliberalism and poverty reduction strategies in Africa. Discussion Paper for the Regional Network for Equity in Health in southern Africa (EQUINET). Accessed 27 February 2015, http://www.equinetafrica.org/bibl/docs/DIS4trade.pdf.

Brenner, N. and Theodore, N. (2002). Cities and the geographies of "actually existing neoliberalism." *Antipode*, 34(3), 356–86.

Brown, K. (2002). Innovations for conservation and development. *The Geographical Journal*, 168(1), 6–17.

Buckley, R. (2004). *Innovative Funding Mechanisms for Visitor Infrastructure in Australian National Parks. In A natural partnership: Making National Parks a Tourism Priority.* Sydney: TTF Australia and CRC for Sustainable Tourism.

Bury, J. (2004). Livelihoods in transition: Transnational gold mining operations and local change in Cajamarca, Peru. *The Geographical Journal*, 170(1), 78–91.

Büscher, B. and Dressler, W. (2012). Commodity conservation: The restructuring of community conservation in South Africa and the Philippines. *Geoforum*, 43(3), 367–76.

Büscher, B. and Dressler, W. (2007). Linking neo-protectionism and environmental governance: On the rapidly increasing tensions between actors in the environment-development nexus. *Conservation and Society*, 5(4), 586–611.

Campbell, L.M., Gray, N.J. and Meletis, Z.A. (2008). Political ecology perspectives on ecotourism to parks and protected areas. In K.S. Hanna, D.A. Clark and D.S. Slocombe (eds) *Transforming Parks and Protected Areas: Protected Area Policy and Management in a Changing World.* New York and London: Routledge, 200–21.

Castree, N. (2008a). Neoliberalising nature: The logics of deregulation and reregulation. *Environment and Planning A*, 40(1), 131–52.

Castree, N. (2008b). Neoliberalising nature: Processes, effects and evaluations. *Environment and Planning A*, 40(1), 153–73.

Child, B., McKean, S., Kiss, A., Munthali, S., Jones, B., Mutsambiwa, M., Castley, G., Patton, C., Magome, H., Pangeti, G., Fearnhead, P., Johnson, S. and Chilikusha, G. (2004). Park agencies, performance and society in southern Africa. In B. Child (ed.), *Parks in Transition: Biodiversity, Rural Development and the Bottom Line.* London: Earthscan, 125–63.

Cock, J. and Fig, D. (2000). From colonial to community-based conservation: Environmental justice and national parks of South Africa. *Society in Transition*, 31(1), 22–35.

Crompton, J. (1998). Forces underlying the emergence of privatisation in parks and recreation. *Journal of Parks and Recreation Administration*, 16(2), 88–101.

Darcy, S. and Wearing, S. (2009). Public-private partnerships and contested cultural heritage tourism in national parks: A case study of the stakeholder views of the North Head Quarantine Station (Sydney, Australia). *Journal of Heritage Tourism*, 4(3), 181–99.

de la Harpe, D., Fearnhead, P., Hughes, G., Davies, R., Spenceley, A., Barnes, J., Cooper, J. and Child, B. (2004). Does commercialisation of protected areas threaten their conservation goals? In B. Child (ed.), *Parks in Transition: Biodiversity, Rural Development and the Bottom Line*. Gland: IUCN, 186–216.

Duffy, R. and Moore, L. (2010). Neoliberalising nature? Elephant-back tourism in Thailand and Botswana. *Antipode*, 42(3), 742–60.

Duffy, R. (2008). Neoliberalising nature: Global networks and ecotourism development in Madagascar. *Journal of Sustainable Tourism*, 16(3), 327–44.

DWARF (Department of Water Affairs and Forestry) (1997). *The Working for Water Programme, Annual Report 1996/97*. Pretoria: Department of Water Affairs and Forestry.

Eagles, P.F.J. (2008). Governance models for parks, recreation and tourism. In K.S. Hanna, D.A. Clark and D.S. Slocombe (eds) *Transforming Parks and Protected Areas: Protected Area Policy and Management in a Changing World*. London: Routledge, 39–61.

Escobar, A. (1996). Constructing nature: Elements for a poststructural ecology. In R. Peet and M. Watts (eds) *Liberation Ecologies*. London: Routledge, pp. 46–8.

Fearnhead, P. (2003 September). Commercial tourism concessions: A means of generating income for South African National Parks. Paper presented at the Vth World Parks Congress: Sustainable Tourism Stream, Durban, South Africa.

Fearnhead, P. (2007). Concessions and commercial development: Experience in South African National Parks. In R. Bushell and P.F.J. Eagles (eds) *Tourism and Protected Areas: Benefits beyond Boundaries*. Wallingford, UK and Cambridge, USA: CABI, 301–14.

Ferreira, S.L.A. and Harmse, A.C. (1999). The social carrying capacity of Kruger National Park, South Africa: Policy and practice, *Tourism Geographies*, 1(3), 325–42.

Flinders, M. (2005). The politics of public–private partnerships. *The British Journal of Politics & International Relations*, 7(2), 215–39.

Font, X., Conchrane, J. and Tapper, R. (2004). *Pay per Nature View: Understanding Tourism Revenues for Effective Management Plans*. Leeds: Leeds Metropolitan University.

Grandia, L. (2007). Between Bolivar and bureaucracy: The Mesoamerican biological corridor. *Conservation and Society*, 5(4), 478–503.

Haque, M.S. (1999). The fate of sustainable development under neoliberal regimes in developing countries. *Political Science Review*, 20(2), 197–218.

Harvey, D. (2005). *A Brief History of Neoliberalism*. Oxford: Oxford University Press.

Heynen, N., McCarthy, J., Prudham, S. and Robbins, P. (2007). Introduction: False promises. In N. Heynen, J. McCarthy, S. Prudham and P. Robbins (eds)

Neoliberal Environments: False Promises and Unnatural Consequences. New York: Routledge, 1–22.

Himley, M. (2008). Geographies of environmental governance: The nexus of nature and neoliberalism. *Geography Compass*, 2(2), 433–51.

Hodge, G.A. and Greve, C. (2007). Public–private-partnerships: An international review. *Public Administration Review*, 67(3), 545–58.

Hope, R.A. (2006). Water, workfare and poverty: The impact of the Working for Water Programme on rural poverty reduction. *Environment Development and Sustainability*, 8(1), 139–56.

Igoe, G. and Brockington, B. (2007). Neoliberal conservation: A brief introduction. *Conservation and Society*, 5(4), 432–49.

Igoe, G. and Croucher, B. (2007). Conservation, commerce, and communities: The story of Community-based Conservation Management Areas in Tanzania's northern tourist circuits. *Conservation and Society*, 5(4), 534–61.

Igoe, J., Neves, K. and Brockington, D. (2010). A spectacular eco-tour around the historic bloc: Theorising the convergence of biodiversity conservation and capitalist expansion. *Antipode*, 42(3), 486–512.

IUCN, (1994). *Guidelines for Protected Area Management Categories*. Gland: IUCN.

IUCN, (2000). *Financing Protected Areas: Guidelines for Protected Area Managers*. Gland: IUCN.

Jeanrenaud, S. (2002). Changing people/nature representations in international conservation discourses. *IDS Bulletin*, 33(1), 111–22.

Jennings, G.R. (2005). Interviewing; a focus on qualitative techniques. In B.W. Ritchie, P. Burns and C. Palmer (eds) *Tourism Research Methods*. Wallingford: CABI, 99–118.

King, B.H. (2009). Commercialising conservation in South Africa. *Environment and Planning A*, 41(2), 407–24.

Leal, D. and Fretwell, H.L. (1997). Back to the future to save our parks. *PERC Policy Series no. PS-10 (June)*. Montreal: Property and Environment Research Centre.

Loftus, A.J. and McDonald, D.A. (2001). Of liquid dreams: A political ecology of water privatisation in Buenos Aieres. *Environment and Urbanisation*, 13(2), 179–99.

Mabunda, D.M. (2004). *An Integrated Tourism Management Framework for the Kruger National Park, South Africa*. Unpublished PhD Thesis, University of Pretoria, Pretoria.

Mabunda, D.M. (2011). *Commercialisation Strategy: Safari Hotels*. Accessed 11 April 2011, http//www.sanparks.org/forums/viewtopic.

Magubane, Z. (2004). A revolution betrayed? Globalisation, neoliberalisation and the post-apartheid state. *The South Atlantic Quarterly*, 103(4), 658–71.

Mahony, K. and van Zyl, J. (2002). The impacts of tourism investment on rural communities: Three case studies in South Africa. *Development Southern Africa*, 19(1), 83–103.

Mansfield, B. (2007). Privatisation: Property and the remaking of nature-society relations. *Antipode*, 39(3), 393–405.

McNeely, J.A. (1994). Protected areas for the 21st century: Working to provide benefits to society. *Biodiversity and Conservation*, 3(5), 390–405.

Mohamed, G. and Roberts, S. (2008).Weak links in the BEE chain? Procurement, skills and employment equity in the metals and engineering industries. *Journal of Contemporary African Studies*, 26(1), 27–50.

Moore, S.A. and Weiler, B. (2009). Tourism-protected area partnerships: Stoking the fires of innovation. *Journal of Sustainable Tourism*, 17(2), 129–32.

More, T. (2005). From public to private: Five concepts of park management and their consequences. *The George Wright Forum*, 22(2), 12–20.

Nyahunzvi, D.K. (2010a). Winners and losers: Local perceptions of Kruger National Park's commercialisation. In A. Reis, C. Jellum, B. Lovelock, and A. Thompson (eds) *Proceedings of the 2010 Centre for Recreation Research Symposium – Recreation Values and Natural Areas*. Dunedin: Centre for Recreation Research, 64–8.

Nyahunzvi, D.K. (2010b). *A Review of my PhD Steps*. Paper presented at the PhD Departmental seminar series, University of Otago, Dunedin, New Zealand.

Ponte, S., Roberts, S. and van Sittert, L. (2007). Black Economic Empowerment: Business and the state in South Africa. *Development and Change*, 38(5), 933–55.

SANP, (2000). *Visions of Change: Social Ecology and South African National Parks*. Johannesburg: Development Communications Company in association with South African National Parks.

Saporiti, N. (2008). Managing national parks: How public–private partnerships can aid conservation. Viewpoint: Public policy for the private sector. Accessed 4 April 2010, http://rru.worldbank.org/ Public Policy Journal.

Scheyvens, R. (1999). Ecotourism and the empowerment of local communities. *Tourism Management*, 20(2), 245–9.

Schilcher, R. (2007). *Supranational Governance of Tourism: Aid, Trade and Power Relations between the European Union and the South Pacific Island States*. Unpublished PhD Thesis, University of Otago, Dunedin, New Zealand.

Shultis, J. (2005). The effects of neo-conservatism on park science, management and administration: Examples and a discussion. *The George Wright Forum*, 22(2), 51–8.

Spenceley, A. (2004). Responsible nature-based tourism in South Africa and the commercialisation of Kruger National Park. In D. Diamantis (ed.), *Ecotourism: Management and Assessment*. London: Thomson Learning, 267–80.

Spenceley, A. (2005 March). *Tourism Investment in the Great Limpopo Conservation Area: Scoping Report*. Report to the Transboundary Research Initiative. Accessed May 12, 2008, http://anna.spenceley.co.uk/files/Tourism%20InvestmentGLTFCAMar05.pdf.

Spenceley, A. (2006). Tourism in the Great Limpopo Transfrontier Park. *Development Southern Africa*, 23(5), 649–67.

Telfer, D.J. (2002). The evolution of tourism and development theory. In R. Sharpley and D.J. Telfer (eds) *Tourism and Development: Concepts and Issues*. Clevedon: Channel View Publications, 35–78.

van Jaarsveld, A. (2004). *Application in terms of regulation 16.8 of the Public Finance Management Act (PFMA), 1999, dealing with Public-private partnerships for approval of amendment and variation of agreements for the concession contracts*. Pretoria: SANParks.

Varghese, G. (2008). Public-private partnerships in South African national parks: The rationale, benefits and lessons learned. In A. Spenceley (ed.), *Responsible Tourism: Critical Issues for Conservation and Development*. London: Earthscan, 69–83.

Wilson, E., Nielsen, N. and Buultjens, J. (2009). From lessees to partners: Exploring tourism public-private partnerships within the New South Wales National Parks and Wildlife Service. *Journal of Sustainable Tourism*, 17(2), 269–85.

Chapter 8

Social Tourism: From Redistribution to Neoliberal Aspiration Development

Lynn Minnaert

In 2011, *The Express*, a British tabloid newspaper, reported that social tourism is 'a scheme that, on the face of it is caring and kind but which rewards those who don't necessarily deserve help, and only serve to perpetuate the dependency culture that is the root of many of our social problems' (*The Express*, 1st November 2011). The article rages against 'scroungers' and 'layabouts', and presents social tourism as 'holidays on the social' for those 'with a plasma screen television of less than 42 inch'. This article is an appropriate illustration for this chapter, as it exemplifies the neoliberal turn in views on welfare policy that dominates many sections of the press and public opinion today. The chapter will start by introducing the concept of social tourism, and will discuss how social tourism provision has changed from its original nature as a redistributive measure, to its current interpretation as a developer of neoliberal aspirations.

Social Tourism: Definitions and Implementations

Minnaert et al. (2007, 2009, 2011) define social tourism as tourism with an added moral value, of which the primary objective is to benefit the host or the visitor in the tourism exchange. In practice, social tourism for disadvantaged families usually refers to budget-friendly holidays in the own country, or in some cases day trips to theme parks, museums and attractions, that are funded or made available at highly reduced rates, by charities or agencies in the public sector, often in cooperation with partners in the tourism sector. The field of social tourism is blighted by fuzzy definitions, despite the fact that it has existed as a concept for at least 60 years (Diekmann and McCabe, 2011). Due to the diverse processes and organizational structures in which social tourism has developed and been implemented in the different countries of the European Union (including voucher systems, holiday grants and public–private partnership structures), the concept has been interpreted very differently in different countries. In several countries and regions of mainland Europe (France, Belgium, Spain, Portugal) for example, social tourism initiatives are often (co-)funded by the public sector – either via direct grants or public–private partnerships (European Economic and Social Committee

(EESC), 2006). In the UK and the USA, social tourism is not usually part of public policy and is mostly provided via charitable bodies.

A justification for the provision of social holidays via the public sector is the notion, supported by a number of European institutions, that everyone has the right to basic tourism provision (EESC, 2006: 69), and the assumption that "social tourism clearly promotes integration, greater knowledge and personal development" (EESC, 2006:76). Haulot (1982: 208), includes this aspect in his definition of social tourism: 'Social tourism ... finds justification in that its individual and collective objectives are consistent with the view that all measures taken by modern society should ensure more justice, more dignity and improved enjoyment of life for all citizens' (Haulot, 1982: 208). The view that social tourism is something modern societies 'should ensure' is a principle that is advocated in a number of countries in Europe. This view however is by no means universal: in many countries, tourism is seen as a luxury, a discretionary activity to which no right exists (Minnaert et al., 2011).

The Neoliberal Turn in Welfare Policies: From Expectation to Aspiration

Neoliberalism 'refers to the policies and processes whereby a relative handful of private interests are permitted to control as much as possible of social life in order to maximise their personal profit' (Chesney in Chomsky, 1999: 7). Chesney (*ibidem*) argues that the term itself is relatively unknown with the general public, and that neoliberal initiatives, for example in the press, are often discussed in much more positive terms, 'as free market policies that encourage private enterprise an consumer choice, reward personal responsibility and entrepreneurial initiative, and undermine the dead hand of the incompetent, bureaucratic and parasitic government, that can never do good even if well intended, which it rarely is'.

The quote above highlights key neoliberal values such as submission to the 'free market' and the celebration of 'personal responsibility' in all realms. Neoliberals make a clean and definitive distinction between 'sociological excuses' and 'individual responsibility' (Wacquant, 2009): although persons may be born in unequal circumstances, this does not diminish the responsibility of each person to become an 'aspirational citizen' (Raco, 2009). Welfare beneficiaries 'are considered morally deficient unless they periodically provide visible proof to the contrary' (Wacquant, 2009: 15) – this attitude is often accompanied by a trend towards elimination of public aid programmes, 'on grounds that their recipients must be snatched from their culpable torpor by the sting of necessity' (Wacquant, 2009: 51).

These views have clear implications on the perceived roles and responsibilities of the welfare state. The U.S. is often seen as a prototypical neoliberal regime, and here it seems that rather than of a welfare state, 'one should speak of a *charitable state*, inasmuch as the programmes aimed at vulnerable populations have at all times been limited, fragmentary and isolated from other state activities, informed as they are by a moralistic and moralizing conception of poverty as a product of the individual failings of the poor. The guiding principle of public action in this domain is not solidarity but *compassion*; its goal is not to reinforce social bonds, and still less to reduce inequalities, but at best to relieve the most glaring destitution and to demonstrate society's moral sympathy for its deprived yet deserving members' (Wacquant, 2009: 42). 'The American state is the prototype of the 'residual welfare state' to the extent that it offers support only in response to the cumulative failures of the labour market and the family, by intervening on a case-by-case basis through programmes strictly reserved for vulnerable categories that are deemed 'worthy': ex-workers temporarily pushed out of the wage-labour market, the handicapped and severely disabled, and, subject to varying restrictive conditions, destitute mothers of young children' (Wacquant, 2009: 46).

Although there are significant differences between the American and European implementations of the welfare state (and indeed, even within Europe considerable differences exist), a trend towards the increased adoption of Neoliberal policy views in Europe is noticeable. In the UK for example, Raco (2009) argues that policy makers have moved from an 'expectational' to an 'aspirational' view of citizenship. In the 'expectational' view, the relationship of the state with the individual takes the shape of a social contract, and the state shows a commitment to ensure the well-being of its citizens. 'In short, boundaries of citizenship [are] drawn to reflect a politics of expectation that defined what the state could and should do for its citizens (Raco, 2009: 438). In the 'aspirational' view of citizenship however, state intervention is rolled back and the objective of social policy should be, as far as possible 'to clear away the barriers that prevent those at the bottom from being able to achieve their aspirations' (Giddens in Raco, 2009: 439). 'These ideas presume a new citizenship contract, based upon responsibilities as well as rights. The state helps provide citizens with the resources to make their own lives, but in return they have to recognize their obligations towards the community' (Giddens, 2003: 3–4).

Levitas' Three Discourses in Social Policy

The Neoliberal views on society as described above have far-reaching implications for the formulation of policies dealing with social exclusion. Levitas (1998) analysed different accents of social exclusion under New Labour in the UK and organized them in a system of three discourses. A first discourse she describes is the *redistributionist* discourse (RED), which intertwines social exclusion with poverty. It emphasizes poverty as a prime cause of exclusion and implies a reduction of poverty through increases in benefit levels. It contrasts exclusion with citizenship, and addresses the social, political, cultural and economic aspects of citizenship, so that it can also be described as a general critique of inequality. It aims to remove the factors that produce inequality and to redistribute resources and power (Levitas, 1998: 14).

A second discourse of social exclusion is the *moral underclass discourse* (MUD), which concentrates on the cultural explanations of poverty. It presents the underclass or socially excluded as culturally distinct from the mainstream, and focuses on the behaviour of the poor rather than on the structure of the whole society. It implies that benefits arc bad, rather than good, for their recipients, and encourage "dependency". Levitas (1998: 210) describes this discourse as "gendered", stating that it is about idle criminal young men and single mothers. Basically, this is the discourse that focuses on the effects of social exclusion (e.g. teenage pregnancy, benefit dependency, substance abuse etc.), and transforms these in a sort of "culture" of the underclass, representing it as a cause rather than a result of their exclusion.

The third discourse mentioned by Levitas is the *social integrationist discourse* (SID), linking inclusion to labour and market attachment. It narrows the definition of social inclusion or exclusion to participation in paid work. It does not imply a reduction of poverty by an increase in benefit levels, and obscures the inequalities between paid workers (Levitas, 1998: 26).

The remainder of this chapter will argue that social tourism provision has moved, since its first expressions to its current conceptualization and interpretation in Europe, from a Redistributionist to a Moral Underclass discourse of social exclusion. Over time, it will be shown that the rationale for provision and the projected outcomes of the social tourism intervention have significantly changed.

Social Tourism: From a Redistribution to a Moral Underclass Discourse[1]

Early Beginnings

The origins of social tourism can be dated back to the emergent industrialized societies at the end of the 19th century. It is difficult to identify a single factor, or set of factors, or one or more specific interests, which lead to the uneven development of social tourism, and the roles of different institutions in Europe. However, the rapid process of industrialization leading to overcrowded and unhealthy conditions in cities undoubtedly prompted a significant increase in interest for the health and social conditions of workers and their families at this time. Also, tourism was beginning to develop as a commercial sector in response to increased mobility due to the introduction of the rail networks. Even though most workers had to work six days each week and leisure time was often organized by the dominant class, holidays now became accessible for the highest earners in the working class. "Although poverty was widespread in the rapidly expanding industrial cities,

---

1   This overview of the history of social tourism is based on L. Minnaert, A. Diekmann and S. McCabe (2011), Defining Social Tourism and its historical context, in S. McCabe, L. Minnaert and A. Diekmann (eds) *Social Tourism in Europe: Theory and Practice*, Bristol: Channel View Publications.

some working people were able for the first time to accumulate savings to pay for holidays" (Sharpley, 1999: 47).

The first isolated initiatives began to appear that allowed disadvantaged workers or their children to go on a holiday. The pioneers of social tourism in Europe were often socio-educational and religious organizations. In the UK, "following the impoverishment of the British aristocracy, a series of well-kept properties surrounded by big parks was put on the market at very low prices, representing only a small percentage of their former value. In this way several organizations, especially the 'Co-operative Holiday Association' and the trade unions have acquired properties that were later turned into family holiday homes" (Lanquar and Raynouard, 1986: 14). Other initiatives concentrated on inner-city children who were taken to the countryside or the seaside by charities, which were seen as beneficial to their health (CESR, 1999).

Social tourism thus emerged alongside 'traditional' or mainstream, commercial tourism. Not being a commercial product per se however, social tourism expanded strongly in countries with a well-developed social system, in particular in France, Belgium, Germany and Eastern European countries. Organized by unions and other social welfare and health structures these initiatives aimed to provide access to holidays for all based on a clear ideological understanding of the place of holidays in the wellbeing of individuals in society (such as children) and people's rights to free time as a reward for providing their labour.

In the second half of the 19th century the middle class promoted holiday tourism as a beneficial activity in relation to sport and health tourism (e.g. British Alpine Club, 1857). These were followed by the creation of youth movements and the development of specific accommodations, such as youth hostels (e.g. '*Deutsches Jugendherbergwerk*' in, 1900). At the same time, in France and Switzerland, Christian movements ran the first holiday camps for disadvantaged children.

Social tourism was not yet a concern for the public authorities. A pivotal point in the development of popular tourism was the 1936 Holiday with Pay Convention, put forward by the International Labour Office in Geneva. Article 2.1 of this convention states that "every person to whom this convention applies shall be entitled after one year of continuous service to an annual holiday with pay of at least six working days". The Holiday with Pay Convention is generally considered as the starting point for social tourism in Europe (Lanquar and Rayouard, 1986, Chauvin, 2002), even though it took many countries a number of years to actually implement the terms of the convention into national legislation. The UK is an example: "Private holidays-with-pay agreements between employers and workers proliferated throughout the 1920s and 1930s, and despite the slump, holidays-with-pay became a major industrial negotiating point. It was appreciated however that for millions of working people this could only be attained through legislation. The resulting campaign did not succeed in pushing legislation through Parliament until 1938, and only after a Royal Commission" (Walvin, 1978: 143). Tourism now became desirable for a large number of people, and the holiday was on its way to becoming part of the national "lifestyle". During the Second World War, this process slowed down, but the holiday with pay legislation was implemented for most workers across Europe after the war ended. This is also when public authorities started subsidizing social tourism, which was, and still is, in many countries controlled by associations, workers councils, popular educational movements and collectives (Chauvin, 2002).

The earliest forms of social tourism were thus inspired by a Redistributionist view on social exclusion. Holidays were increasingly democratized and social tourism provision stemmed from a desire to make travel opportunities available to all layers of society. Although public policy (via the implementation of the Holiday with Pay Convention) was a central driver for the development of social tourism on a larger scale, it transpires that the implementation was largely in the hands on non-governmental and semi-governmental organizations.

Social Tourism Matures

The years following the Second World War were the heyday for social tourism in Europe. The period between 1950 and 1980 is described in French as the "*trente glorieuzes*", the glorious 30. Traditional social tourism was based around the holiday centre in mainland Europe, and around the holiday camp in Britain. The holiday centres on the mainland (e.g. in France, Belgium and Italy) created a product that was new, desirable and affordable and helped towards a democratization of holidaymaking. Traditionally they offered a stay in full board with all entertainment and activities included. In many cases, the sector had a socio-educational or even socio-political aspect. The organized activities on holiday were often inspired by the ideals of the popular educational movements, and sometimes had a strong militant character (Jolin, 2003). The holidaymakers stayed in rather basic accommodation at low rates, which were often tiered dependent on the income level of the holidaymaker, and usually helped with the daily chores. Most holiday centres were run by charities or unions, maybe resulting in very bureaucratic management. Still they developed according to the changing needs of their public, many switched from full board to half board, the visitors had more freedom when choosing their activities, and help with the chores was no longer required (Chauvin, 2002: 67). It is certainly no coincidence that these changes occurred when commercial tourism became more accessible to people from weaker economic backgrounds.

During the same period, social tourism in the UK was also on the rise. The holiday camps in Britain show certain similarities with the holiday centres on the mainland (they offered basic accommodation, full board, with all entertainment included), but there are also great differences. First, they were mostly run on a commercial basis. Camps built by education authorities, trade unions or charities existed but were far less common. Second, although the first large camps were introduced in the 1930s, the heyday of holiday camps came later, in the 1950s and the 1960s. Third, whereas in Europe the camps had adaptable rates, depending on family size and income, the British camps had one fixed rate. "During the 1930s, when the average weekly wage was about £3, some of the simpler camps were charging 50 shillings (£2.50) per head, a competitive rate though still beyond the means of the lowest paid and unemployed" (Hardy, 1990: 550).

During these *"trente glorieuzes"*, a number of international organizations were launched (e.g. Federation of Popular Travel Organisations -IFPTO-, 1950; Federation of International Youth Travel Organisations-FIYTO-, 1956). The creation of these international bodies was accompanied by the launch of different declarations and the organization of conferences on social tourism. In 1963, a number of organizations that aimed to provide a permanent platform where social tourism issues could be discussed at an international level established BITS, the *Bureau International du Tourisme Social* (International Bureau of Social Tourism). Its goal was to "further the development of social tourism within an international framework, by coordinating the tourist activities of its members, and informing them on all matters relating to the evolution of social tourism around the world" (www.bits-int.org). (The organization changed its name to ISTO (International Social Tourism Organisation) in 2010).

The period of 1950–1980 shows clear differences in the approaches of many mainland European countries compared to the provision of social tourism in the UK. Whereas in mainland Europe the Redistributionist discourse persists, the UK develops a much stronger private sector involvement in social tourism whereby participation is based on ability to pay and free market principles. The absence of tiered, means-dependent pricing structures in the UK highlights this most clearly. Although, as stated before, the social tourism sector developed in both areas simultaneously to the commercial tourism sector, it becomes clear that there are starker distinctions between the two sectors on the European continent, whereas the two sectors share more similarities in the UK.

Signs of Decline

After the '*trente glorieuzes*', social tourism went through a period of transformation and reorientation. This was mainly due to changes affecting the traditional target group for social tourism, manual workers: they were increasingly able to take holidays in the commercial circuit, because of the low prices mass tourism could offer. In many cases, it transpired that traditional social tourism establishments found it hard to match the low price offered abroad. Manual workers were now no longer by definition excluded from the commercial tourism industry, and other groups took their place: the unemployed, one-parent families, young families on low incomes etc. Since the 1980s, tourism for persons with disabilities or restricted mobility has also received more attention.

The above shows that as the commercial tourism sector became able to offer holidays at competitive prices for the majority in society, social tourism began to focus more and more on marginalized groups who were unable to be served by this private sector provision. A tension in the Redistributionist view on social tourism becomes apparent at this stage as social tourism schemes are aimed at smaller and more marginalized groups – the focus gradually shifts to the view of tourism as a type of 'intervention' to support their inclusion into mainstream society. The value of the holiday now no longer lies in the tourism experience itself, but in the impacts it can have on beneficiaries after their return. Holidays are increasingly seen as motivational and transformative – this view supports the Moral Underclass Discourse of social exclusion, rather than the Redistributionist Discourse.

As mass tourism grew in importance, the negative effects of mass tourism on local ecosystems and cultures received increasing attention, and a desire for more sustainable forms of tourism became apparent. Social tourism organizations such as ISTO acknowledged the benefits the tourism industry can bring, and expressed it as their aim to transfer these benefits to communities who can either gain economically from tourism, or who are at risk to be negatively affected by the commercial tourism circuit. ISTO for example has introduced the concept of 'solidarity tourism' as a part of social tourism, 'introducing a sense of solidarity between the tourist and the host population, confirming that social tourism is opposite to invasive mass tourism that overburdens local resources' (Bélanger and Jolin, 2011).

By incorporating new aspects into the concept of social tourism, ISTO aimed to stay current and relevant in a changing society. This highlights that over time, social tourism is not a static, but a dynamic concept. To avoid becoming obsolete, social tourism organizations had to face the challenges new socio-economic factors posed, and adapt to address them successfully. In recent years, interest in social tourism has steadily increased. As Mignon (2002) points out: "We have gradually evolved, in just a few years, from a period in which social tourism was perceived as, let's be frank, obsolete, negative or reductive, to a situation in which the notions of social policy, solidarity and durable development are, in contrast, viewed very positively – an evolution which, at the same time, puts the concept of social tourism back at the heart of the most up-to-date initiatives".

Current Interpretations

Two recent interpretations of social tourism can be found in the European Commission's 'Calypso' programme and the work of the All Party Parliamentary Group on Social Tourism in the UK. Both examples illustrate that when the public sector shows a renewed interest in social tourism, achieving economic aims and supporting tourism as a business sector are key motivations.

The clearest expression of the current interest in social tourism is the 'Calypso' project of the Directorate General of Enterprise and Industry in the European Commission. Social tourism has been of interest to the EU since the 1990s, but since 2009 has the focus been on social tourism as a means of lowering seasonality within the accommodation sector. The Calypso programme aims to put into action some of the outcomes of the Lisbon Treaty and the objectives of the Tourism

Sustainability Group of the EU. Calypso is presented as having both social and economic goals. The social goals of Calypso are focused on European citizenship, cultural exchange, improving the quality of life of 'less privileged citizens', offering a break from routine, and broadening mental horizons. Calypso has four distinct target groups: senior citizens, families facing financial or other pressures, youth and persons with disabilities (Calypso, 2011).

The Calypso programme is an initiative of the DG Enterprise and Industry – as such, it is unsurprising that economic goals play a major role in the conceptualization of this project. The project's aim is described as:

> By facilitating tourism access in European Destinations for society groups for which going on holiday represents a difficult or even impossible undertaking, social tourism strengthens the tourism industry's revenue generation potential. It enables off-season tourism to be developed, particularly in regions where tourism is well developed but highly seasonal, whilst giving the opportunity to relatively unknown, small or emerging destinations to promote their offer amongst a wider spectrum of the European population. (http://ec.europa.eu/enterprise/sectors/tourism/calypso/index_en.htm)

The economic goal of Calypso is the implementation of a social tourism scheme lowering seasonality in the accommodation sector by fostering at the same time intra-European mobility for specific target groups (Diekmann et al., 2011). The economic rationale for the Calypso programme is 'To create more and better jobs in the tourism sector (respect for tourism sustainability challenges; strengthening full-time employment prospects as opposed to seasonal part-time work; improving employment conditions by stressing the importance of a qualitative work environment throughout the entire tourism supply chain)'. (http://ec.europa.eu/ enterprise/sectors/tourism/calypso/general/index_en.htm)

The Calypso programme thus firmly reconceptualizes social tourism as an intervention with social as well as economic benefits in established economies. Social tourism is now presented as an economic regeneration measure, with relatively widely defined target groups: apart from the category of 'families facing financial or other pressures', income is not proposed as a central factor for social tourism participation. The focus has moved from marginalized, disadvantaged groups – this can be seen as a neoliberal turn, presumably to avoid that the 'least powerful are perceived to be benefitting 'unfairly' from an overly generous welfare system' (Raco, 2009: 439). Target groups have been identified who are perceived to be 'deserving' – not coincidentally these are target groups where the ability to pay may be higher and there may be more suppressed demand than within more marginalized sections of society (for example the long-term unemployed).

A similar trend can be discerned in the UK, where an All Party Parliamentary Group (APPG) on Social Tourism was formed in 2010 to review the potential of social tourism. The APPG, headed by Paul Maynard MP, published its findings in 2011 in a report entitled 'Giving Britain a Break: Inquiry into the social and economic benefits of social tourism'. From the title, it becomes clear that economic benefits are also here seen as key justifications for the eventual facilitation of social tourism.

In keeping with the 'aspirational' view on citizenship, state involvement in social tourism is proposed to be rolled back to minimal intervention: 'Several contributors in the enquiry stressed the need for some form of central Government action on social tourism in the UK, but would prefer it to act as a facilitator rather than taking a coordinating role' (APPG Social Tourism, 2011: 3).

This view is supported in the following comment from John Penrose MP, Minister for tourism and Heritage. He firmly dismissed a Redistributionist view of social tourism on the basis that this would prove unpopular with the general public. He also highlights the difficulty in discerning who would be 'deserving' groups in society who would be allowed to benefit from social tourism:

> The Government is not in apposition to fund or subsidise holidays and, equally, previous Governments of all parties have not found any money to do so either. ... Outright subsidies would prove unpopular with taxpayers who have to tighten their purse-strings, and there would also be the practical issue of determining eligibility and thresholds. (APPG Social Tourism, 22)

The previous Government adopted a similar approach, as exemplified by the quote below from Lord Davies of Oldham, the Parliamentary Under-Secretary of DEFRA in 2010. He refers explicitly to the need for families to be able to make their own choices:

> France, Spain and Italy have integrated social tourism into their social welfare policy, providing holidays for those on low income. We have taken a rather different view on the question of improving life for the less well-off in our society ... We prefer to ensure that increased resources are available for families to make their choices. (APPG Social Tourism, 22)

Consumer choice and choice-based welfare are again key characteristics of a neoliberal and aspirational approach to citizenship and welfare. Rather than proposing redistribution as a way to reduce inequalities in society, the state acts as an 'enabler', allowing citizens to aspire to be non-dependent, middle-class members of society.

Conclusion

This chapter has highlighted how the concept of social tourism has changed considerably from its redistributionist beginnings to its current, more neoliberal interpretations. Although there are still many organizations across Europe (and beyond) which offer opportunities to marginalized groups to participate in travel, the political discourse around the concept has clearly shifted towards social tourism as a measure of economic regeneration, that aims to unlock supressed demand and attract tourists to destinations in decline.

Social outcomes are still presented as justifications for provision: both the Calypso project and the report of the APPG mention potential social outcomes that can result from social tourism participation. How these social objectives will be achieved however, particularly for groups in society who arguably need them the most, is not explored in either case – both presume that social benefits will accrue naturally from tourism participation. Minnaert et al. (2009) however highlighted that for these social benefits to develop, support structures need to be in place before, during and after the holiday for the most vulnerable groups. Neither these support measures nor these vulnerable groups receive much attention in the most recent interpretations of social tourism, whereas the development of economic benefits is explored in much more detail.

Although the European Economic and Social Research Council proposed a right to basic tourism provision for all, it is clear from the above that this is not the line taken by the DG Enterprise and Industry, nor by the APPG on social tourism. This more redistributionist stance is replaced by a focus on personal responsibility – only those who are considered to fulfil their responsibilities in society as aspirational consumers are considered deserving. The focus on personal responsibility is a characteristic of neoliberal views on exclusion and welfare, which tends to emphasize that in Redistributionist welfare approaches 'the balance between rights and responsibilities moves too far towards rights and away from responsibilities. At that point the incentive to work hard and play by the rules is undermined' (Millburn in Raco, 2009: 439). From the above, it has become clear that the rules referred to are those of Neoliberalism – and social tourism is increasingly subject to these rules too.

References

All Party Parliamentary Group on Social Tourism (2011). *Giving Britain a Break. Inquiry into the Social and Economic Benefits of Social Tourism.* London: APPG Social Tourism.

Bélanger, C. and Jolin, L. (2011). The International Social Tourism Organisation: Working towards a right to tourism and holidays for all. *Current Issues in Tourism*, 14(5), 475–82.

CESR (1999). *Le tourisme social et associatif dans la région de Nord-Pas-de-Calais.* Nord-Pas-de-Calais: CESR.

Calypso (2011). *Calypso Widens Europe's Travel Horizons.* Brussels: European Commission, DG Enterprise and Industry.

Chauvin, J. (2002). *Le tourisme social et associatif en France.* Paris: l'Harmattan.

Chomsky, N. (1999). *Profit over People: Neoliberalism and Global Order.* New York: Seven Stories Press.

Diekmann, A. and McCabe, S. (2011). Systems of social tourism in the European Union, a comparative study. *Current Issues in Tourism*, 14(5), 417–30.

Diekmann, A., McCabe, S. and Minnaert, L. (2011). Social Tourism Today: Stakeholders, and Supply and Demand Factors. In S. McCabe, L. Minnaert and A. Diekmann (eds) *Social Tourism in Europe: Theory and Practice*. Bristol: Channel View, 35–52.

European Economic and Social Committee. (2006). *Opinion of the Economic and Social Committee on Social Tourism in Europe*. Brussels: EESC.

Giddens, A. (ed.) (2003). *The Progressive Manifesto*. Cambridge: Polity Press.

Hardy, D. (1990). Sociocultural dimensions of tourism history. *Annals of Tourism Research*, 17(4), 541–55.

Jolin, L. (2003). Le tourisme social, un concept riche de ses evolutions. *Le tourisme social dans le monde*, Édition spéciale 40ème anniversaire: 141.

Lanquar, R. and Raynouard, Y. (1986). *Le Tourisme Social*. Paris: Presses Universitaires de France: Paris.

Levitas, R. (1998). *The Inclusive Society? Social Exclusion and New Labour*. Palgrave: Basingstoke.

Mignon J. (2002). *Introductory Conference to the Mexico BITS*, 13 May. Tourism for All World Congress, Mexico.

Minnaert, L., Maitland, R. and Miller, G. (2011). What is social tourism? *Current Issues in Tourism*, 14(5), 403–15.

Minnaert, L., Maitland, R. and Miller, G. (2009). Tourism and social policy – The value of social tourism. *Annals of Tourism Research*, 36(2), 316–34.

Minnaert, L., Maitland, R. and Miller, G. (2007). Social tourism and its ethical foundations. *Tourism Culture and Communication*, 7(1), 7–17.

Raco, M. (2009). From expectations to aspirations: State modernization, urban policy, and the existential politics of welfare in the UK. *Political Geography*, 28(7), 436–44.

Sharpley, R. (1999). *Tourism, Tourists and Society*. Huntingdon: Elm Publications.

The Express (2011). *Now it's Holidays for the Poor Funded by the Taxpayer.* 1st November 2011.

Wacquant, L. (2009), *Punishing the Poor: The Neoliberal Government of Social Insecurity.* Durham, NC: Duke University Press.

http://www.bits-int.org.

http://ec.europa.eu/ enterprise/sectors/tourism/calypso/general/index_en.htm

Chapter 9

Enacting Neoliberal Discourses through Heritage Tourism in Ghana

Francis Offeh and Kevin Hannam

Ghana has been recognized as one of the most popular destinations in Africa for western tourists and especially for African-Americans due to the significance of heritage tourism based upon the historical connections due to the slave trade (Teye and Timothy, 2004). Indeed, despite a relative lack of adequate infrastructure and access, Ghana's 15-Year National Tourism Development Plan (1996–2010) recognized the potential of the Slave Route Project for the promotion of ethnic/heritage tourism (MoT/DR, 2006). Moreover, particular attention has been focused on tourism development in Ghana as part of the strategies by the Ghanaian government to diversify the economy away from mining and agriculture. Currently tourism is the fourth foreign exchange earner for Ghana contributing about $1.4 billion in 2008 and this constituted 6.2 per cent of Gross Domestic Product (Offeh, 2010).

Some tourism researchers have investigated tourism development in Ghana but the focus of this research has been primarily on the heritage experience of the slave castles on the Ghanaian coast (Bruner, 1996; Teye and Timothy, 2004). While Bruner's study (1996) investigated tourists to the Elmina Castle in terms of the contested representations and meanings that tourism has brought to the Ghanaian coast, Teye and Timothy (2004) develop this further in terms of the links back to the African-American Diaspora in their methodologically innovative analysis of tourist guidebooks at Elmina Castle. Victor Teye et al., (2002) have also conducted a study in the central region of Ghana on residents' perception towards tourism development and found that both the local residents and workers in the tourism industry had a negative perception of tourism. More recently, Amuquandoh (2010) has focused on residents understandings of tourism in the Bosomtwe Basin of Ghana. Nevertheless, all of this work has primarily focused on either the experiences of tourists, or the perceptions of residents.

Instead, this chapter focuses on the role of neoliberalism as a discourse and how it has been enacted in terms of the promotion of heritage tourism development and particularly the impact that this has had in terms of what has been termed 'institutional commodification'. We begin by discussing the ways in which neoliberal discourses and practices have been theorized. We then note the context of neoliberalism in Ghana and go on to critically examine the discourses of neoliberal tourism from the Ministry of Tourism and Diasporan Relations. Finally, we examine how these discourses are enacted through the support of USAID in terms of the institutional commodification of the informal economy through heritage tourism projects in the Ashanti Kingdom of Ghana.

Theorizing Neoliberal Discourses and Practices

As Bob Jessop (2002) has noted, discourses of neoliberalism have involved calls for: "the liberalization and deregulation of economic transactions; the privatization of state-owned enterprises and state-provided services; the use of market proxies in the residual public sector; and the treatment of public welfare spending as a cost of international production, rather than as a source of domestic demand. As a political project, it seeks to roll back forms of state intervention associated with the mixed economy and the welfare state" (Jessop, 2002: 452). Nevertheless, "it also involves enhanced state intervention to roll forward new forms of governance ... that are purportedly more suited to a market-driven ... globalizing economy. This typically involves the selective transfer of state capacities upwards, downwards, and sideways, as intervention is rescaled in the hope of securing conditions for a smoothly operating world market and to promote supply-side competitiveness on various scales above and below the national level" (Jessop, 2002: 452).

In practice, this has led to "a range of policies intended to extend market discipline, competition and commodification throughout all sectors of society" (Brenner and Theodore, 2002: 350). The irony is though, that while neoliberalism as an ideological project puts forward a utopian vision of the market free from government interference, in reality neoliberalism as it actually exists in practice involves "a dramatic intensification of coercive, disciplinary forms of state intervention in order to impose market rule" (Brenner and Theodore, 2002: 352). Moreover, frequently under these circumstances, "a period of institutional searching and regulatory experimentation ensues in which diverse actors, organizations, and alliances promote competing hegemonic visions, restructuring strategies, and development models" (Brenner and Theodore, 2002: 356). As we shall see, this involves the reworking of traditional institutional arrangements in order to make space for new institutional strategies as neoliberalism is 'rolled out' (Raco, 2005; Lockie and Higgins, 2007).

Neoliberalism and Tourism in Ghana

Neoliberalism in Ghana was initially implemented through structural adjustment policies of the Rawling's government from the mid-1980s onwards (Chalfin, 2008), with tourism development being seen as central to 'resuscitating' the Ghanaian economy (MoT/DR, 2006:11). Decentralization was seen as crucial to the development planning of this period but the benefits to the 'grassroots' was minimal (Mohan, 1996). Nevertheless, "Ghana has frequently been celebrated as the best case of the rise of neoliberalism in Africa and is, accordingly, regarded as the World Bank's 'star pupil'" (Obeng-Odoom, 2012: 85). Obeng-Odoom's (2012: 85) review of the four main development plans that have shaped the direction of the country from the 1990s "shows that policy makers have continued to extol the virtues of a market-oriented approach to urban economic development, particularly job creation, poverty reduction, and equitable economic development." He goes on to conclude that despite this rhetoric, "on the one hand, the increasing prominence of the private sector in the urban economy has impacted positively on capital formation and job creation. On the other hand, urban and national inequality levels have dramatically increased." Moreover, as we shall see in terms of tourism, "the Ghanaian case has shown that, even though neoliberal theory advocates a market economy, in practice the state is intricately involved in economic development. That is, the neoliberal emphasis on markets and the private sector does not necessarily flow through into policy practice and outcomes" (Obeng-Odoom, 2012: 109). We can see this tension at work in Ghana's tourism policy which has supported neoliberal ideologies through its dependence upon institutions such as USAID.

Ghana's neoliberal tourism policy was published in 2006 following extensive consultation and using assistance from the Dutch development agency SNV. Its vision was to become the leading African tourism destination by 2015. Moreover, the objectives of the tourism policy were firmly linked to the government's Poverty Reduction Strategy, which aimed "at the creation of the appropriate environment for a private sector-led development" (MoT/DR, 2006: 8) – for a critical perspective see Crawford, and Abdulai (2009). The policy outlines the following 'development goals':

To develop a selective number of high quality tourism products that would build on Ghana's *inherent attractions* and cater for specific *niche* markets.

To achieve a high level of customer satisfaction, by the proper *linking* of attraction sites that will deliver a complete and satisfying experience.

To *professionalize* the entire tourism industry in order to be able to provide high quality facilities and services.

To ensure that as many opportunities as possible are created for the involvement in, and benefiting from, tourism by local entrepreneurs and communities in terms of employment, income generation, training and awareness, and access to better social infrastructure.

To ensure that the tourism industry is financed, managed and administered as effectively and efficiently as possible.

> To channel efforts towards the following themes: tourism services, basic infrastructure, product development, marketing, training and investment. (Mot/ DR, 2006: 9, emphasis in the original).

Clearly, these development goals fit clearly with the neoliberal ideology of developing market niches, developing entrepreneurship and sound (in capitalist terms) financial management. Indeed, the whole language is neoliberal in character. As David Harvey (2007: 35) has written "[t]he corporatization, commodification, and privatization of hitherto public assets have been signal features of the neoliberal project."

Tourism development in Ghana had been largely dominated by the public sector until Government relinquished its majority interests in many commercial enterprises during the early 1990s. Since then, "the private sector has been expected to lead the tourism industry to greater heights" (MoR/DR, 2006: 11). This has, to some extent, been realized as the growth rate of arrivals has increased. However, it is acknowledged by the Ministry of Tourism that "the private sector has not been able to take full control of the sector" (MoT/DR, 2006: 11). Hence, in Ghana, tourism has been developed from a neoliberal perspective using state intervention to promote market forces. We will see this enacted below in terms of the development of the heritage tourism sector in the Ashanti Kingdom of Ghana. However, firstly, we outline use of the sociologist David Wank's concept of 'institutional commodification' to highlight how the state in Ghana engages with neoliberal ideologies to maintain wider neoliberal political interests.

Institutional Commodification

Out with the many discussions of commodification in the tourism literature, David Wank (1999) has developed the concept of 'institutional commodification' through his ethnographic study of business and politics in China by drawing upon neoliberal critiques. This concept has hitherto not been picked up by tourism scholars; hence, we introduce it here in some detail before utilizing it later in our analysis of the neoliberal institutional commodification of souvenir production in the Ashanti Kingdom of Ghana. Institutional commodification can be seen as a method of enactment of the policy discourses of neoliberalism.

In his seminal work, Wank (1999: 23) argues that China's development of a market economy challenged the 'fundamental Western beliefs on the link between markets and politics'. Conventional accounts of this transition, he argues, would either take a political economy approach or a cultural change approach to argue that this transition was the result of new formations of political power or the development of new social networks. Instead, he puts forward the concept of 'institutional commodification' to explain the development of private businesses in an emerging market economy that is pervaded by both bureaucratic power, where the state has a large monopoly over resources and popular values and traditions –

something we would argue also applies to Ghana and other African developing economies under neoliberalism. Thus, he argues that in so doing:

> The vast range of public resources accumulated by the state and administered by the bureaucracy have become commodified, as they are now the object of price calculations and profit seeking in commercial transactions. Commodities cannot, of course, go to market themselves [in this situation]; it follows that commodification is the transformation of institutionalized social relations of control over these vast resources, either through cadres' position of office or through clientelist ties by citizens to office holders (Wank, 1999: 29).

He goes on to examine how commercial operators will draw upon pre-existing affiliations, such as personal ties and diffuse social relations, with state agents to secure access to various resources. Institutional commodification, then, is a reconfiguration of the relationship between the state and the market, which may encourage a degree of co-operation in an emerging neoliberal market economy situation. He goes on to argue that:

> In its emphasis on strategic social action, the institutional commodification approach shares with the political economy approach a concern for interests and power but broadens these concepts considerably. Patron-client ties reflect not only the profit-maximizing interests of the exchange partners but also the institutional obligations and identities that inhere in personalized patron-client ties. … Entrepreneurs are also interested in forging and maintaining personal ties, enhancing and discharging obligations, and manipulating mutual recognition of relative identities to enhance expectations. Power is embodied not only in the monetary gains derived from trade but also in position in networks. (Wank, 1999: 31)

The concept of institutional commodification thus emphasizes how social knowledge, diffused through the population, enables people to form neoliberal expectations that constrain rationality while maintaining traditional practices, assets and resources in a changing global context. We now discuss how this can be seen to be played out in the context of Ghana's heritage tourism industry through the institutional commodification of its informal economy of souvenir production.

Institutional Commodification in Ghana's Heritage Tourism Industry

This discussion examines the various souvenirs produced and sold in the Ashanti Kingdom whilst taking into consideration issues of commodification and authenticity based upon observations made during the fieldwork at the various craft production villages in the region as well as the interviews conducted with the various stakeholders (Offeh, 2010). We develop the concept of the neoliberal 'institutional commodification' of cultural heritage through an examination, in particular, of the international and national governmental support for the production and sale of craft souvenirs in the Ashanti region.

The souvenirs produced in the Ashanti villages are mainly traditional style woodcarvings such as replicas of the ceremonial stools (seats) and traditional style textiles such as the 'kente' cloth. Local people in these villages see the production of souvenirs as their main source of livelihood and as a result, about 90 per cent of the total population of these villages are engaged in these activities including young men and children (Offeh, 2010). These young men and children engage themselves in the production process after school and/or during the weekends. One parent in the village noted that:

> Most of these children are financing their education through the weaving of kente in this town. One has to help the parent to finish a full piece of kente cloth so that some financial gains can be derived to support the household and to pay for tuition fees of the children. This sounds like child labour but it is not. We also learned it from our grandfathers (Interview with a Kente weaver, 5 June 2008).

All of the souvenirs produced are regarded as traditional style objects targeted at the international tourist market. However, the reliance on the souvenir production as a means of earning a living led to discussions over the authenticity of the souvenirs being produced in the Ashanti Kingdom due to both the growth of international tourist demand as well as the neoliberal processes of institutional commodification.

While the demand from tourists initially stimulated mass production of these local crafts, the government has intervened with the help of international agencies to further the mass production process. Although from a neoliberal development perspective, it could be argued that there is a positive influence in terms of the mass production of souvenirs found in the financial gains and the employment it creates for the local communities, from a more critical perspective (Bianchi, 2009) there remains a contested conflict over the authenticity of these products (for a related comparison see the work of Martin (2010) on Papua New Guinea).

The market place – driven by government interests remains in control. For instance, one veteran 'kente' weaver noted that their attention had been shifted from quality to quantity and stated that:

> We have been using certain types of cotton, which previously could be thrown away for the sake of quality. I want to say that as weavers, we have compromized with the quality of cotton being used and I can see that it is gradually affecting the image of our trade. The truth is that if I use poor quality thread for my work it will keep on tearing thereby slowing the whole production process down. Once the thread tears, it has to be joined before I could proceed and at the end of the day, it affects the beauty of the product. I don't want to say this but let me tell you that if a piece of kente is poorly done an Ashanti man who knows the difference can easily identify it but to the tourist that is not possible. All that the

tourists who come here are interested in is whether the cloth is handmade or not – but we have our own secrets. (Interview with a kente weaver at Bonwire, July 12, 2008)

In contrast, a manager at the Ghana Tourist Board noted in this context that:

I don't think anybody is thinking about authenticity of our crafts to ensure they are made to depict what they are supposed to depict according to our cultural heritage. Now authenticity is a huge problem because modernization is having a huge impact on everybody in Ghana. Go to the streets of Kumasi and Accra and see the way we dress, it has changed completely. (Interviewed, June 14, 2008)

The carving and textile souvenir production caught the attention of the Ghanaian government and funding agencies such as the United States Agency for International Development (USAID) due to the fact that the industry has led to the employment of many school leavers. Artisans who are involved in the production of souvenirs receive technical and financial support via the USAID programme and the National Board for Small Scale Industries and other non-governmental organizations. It was discovered that the National Board for Small Scale Industries have supported many small-scale enterprises through training in the quality control processes and standardized finishing of their souvenirs (Offeh, 2010).

Indeed, most villages are now using machinery that enables them to produce in larger quantities compared to what a traditional artisan could make. Since the modern production techniques and mass production have been placed at the centre of souvenir production in the Ashanti Kingdom, it can be argued that economic motives are now overriding the authenticity of Ashanti cultural heritage through the process of institutional commodification by setting up quasi non-governmental associations. For example, the Ghana Tourism Board confirmed how coordinated these government institutions are at ensuring mass production of these cultural heritage objects, supported by USAID:

We have associations like craft associations at Ahwiaa, kente weavers association at Bonwire and Ntonso. Sometimes GTB [Ghana Tourist Board] organize workshops for them. For example, about two years ago an American NGO came to teach artisans at Ahwiaa on marketing and finishing of their products. The group from America taught them and showed them the colours that Americans prefer their souvenirs finished in. These are some of the things the Americans shared with the artisans. We have this collaboration with them but it could have been more frequent. (Interview with a manager at the Ghana Tourist Board, June 28, 2008)

Moreover, a souvenir shop owner revealed that the USAID sent a handicraft consultant to show them the best ways to keep their production lines running during the rainy season to overcome shortages in supply. As a result, they were taken through the process of wood drying to ensure continuous production to meet the demand of tourists. However, a wood carver at Ahwiaa Village who had been carving for the past 76 years contested this production process and argued that:

> As far as I know, every woodwork should be left in the sun to dry. We have solely depended on the sun to dry our woods and it has been like that from generation to generation. I don't honestly see the reason why I have to put the wood in the oven. Look! Most of the souvenirs dried in the oven end up having many cracks and once this happens they have to go to the market and buy filler or sealant to conceal all the cracks. I see that to be different from what was handed over to some of us. If the wood has, cracks simply throw it away and you don't need to introduce anything foreign to make it look nice. If I conceal cracks and polish a doll with something modern, the doll loses its 'Ashantiness'. (Interview with wood carver, 5 July 2008)

In terms of sales outlets, at an institutional level it was found that once the various groups and associations have produced souvenirs, they are now being treated like any other commodity controlled by the government such as cocoa or gold. For example, a souvenir shop owner noted that:

> A project officer was here last week and gave us a list of potential companies, which may be interested in our products, and I hope this will help us break through the international market (Interview with a souvenir shop owner, June 21, 2009).

Conclusions

This chapter has thus identified and discussed the role of the state in speeding up processes of commodification through the use of a neoliberal tourism policy discourse. Specifically, it has examined the role played by both international development agencies and the national state apparatus through the technical support offered to heritage tourism practitioners to accelerate the production and sale of souvenirs in the Ashanti Kingdom of Ghana. In contrast to the traditional methods hitherto known to the local people, these agencies have succeeded in sensitizing them to the use of mass production methods. While this may have led to a loss of cultural authenticity, local artisans have supported the employment generated as a result whilst seeking to 'maintain their secrets' (Offeh, 2010).

Since the souvenirs from the Ashanti Kingdom are being treated like any other commodity, the artisans have formed associations (with the support of the state) and they receive training with regards to mass production quality standards. Significantly, individuals who are not members of such associations do not have the same opportunity of selling their souvenirs at the government controlled centres such as the regional cultural centres and/ or the national art centres. Furthermore, international organizations play a prominent role in identifying prospective customers and/or companies in the West for the local artisans. Hence, neoliberalism as a discourse for the promotion of particular types of tourism development and particularly the impact that this has had in terms of what has been termed 'institutional commodification' has been significant in Ghana and can be linked to wider global processes where the state intervenes to support neoliberal practices.

References

Amuquandoh, F.E. (2010). Lay concepts of tourism in Bosomtwe Basin, Ghana. *Annals of Tourism Research*, 37(1), 34–51.

Bianchi, R. (2009). The 'critical turn' in tourism studies: A radical critique. *Tourism Geographies*, 11(4), 484–504.

Brenner, N. and Theodore, N. (2002). Cities and the geographies of 'actually existing neoliberalism'. *Antipode* 34(3), 349–79.

Bruner, E. (1996). Tourism in Ghana: The representation of slavery and return of the Black Diaspora. *American Anthropologist*, 98(2), 290–304.

Chalfin, B. (2008). Cars, the customs service, and sumptuary rule in neoliberal Ghana. *Comparative Studies in Society and History*, 50(2), 424–53.

Crawford, G. and Abdulai, A. (2009). The World Bank and Ghana's Poverty Reduction Strategies: Strengthening the state or consolidating neoliberalism? *Labour, Capital and Society*, 40(1/2), 82–99.

Harvey, D. (2007). Neoliberalism as creative destruction. *The Annals of the American Academy of Political and Social Science*, 610(1), 21–44.

Jessop, B. (2002). Liberalism, neoliberalism, and urban governance: A state-theoretical perspective. *Antipode*, 34(3), 452–72.

Lockie, S. and Higgins, V. (2007). Roll-out neoliberalism and hybrid practices of regulation in Australian agri-environmental governance. *Journal of Rural Studies*, 23(1), 1–11.

Martin, K. (2010). Living pasts: Contested tourism authenticities. *Annals of Tourism Research*, 37(2), 537–54.

Mohan, G. (1996). Neoliberalism and decentralised development planning in Ghana. *Third World Planning Review*, 18(4), 433–54.

MoT/DR. (2006). *National Tourism Policy.* Accra: Government of Ghana.

Obeng-Odoom, F. (2012). Neoliberalism and the urban economy in Ghana: Urban employment, inequality, and poverty. *Growth and Change*, 43(1), 85–109.

Offeh, F. (2010). *Post-Colonial Heritage Tourism Development in Ghana: The Case of The Ashanti Kingdom (Region).* PhD thesis. University of Sunderland.

Peck, J. (2004). Geography and public policy: Constructions of neoliberalism. *Progress in Human Geography*, 28(3), 392–405.

Raco, M. (2005). Sustainable development, rolled-out neoliberalism and sustainable communities. *Antipode*, 37(2), 324–47.

Teye, V. and Timothy, D. (2004). The varied colours of slave heritage in West Africa. *Space and Culture*, 7(2), 145–55.

Teye, V. Sarakaya, E. and Sönmez, S.K. (2002). Residents' attitudes towards tourism development. *Annals of Tourism Research*, 29(3), 668–88.

Wank, D. (1999). *Commodifying Communism: Business, Trust and Politics in a Chinese City*. Cambridge: Cambridge University Press.

Chapter 10

Decommodifying Grassroots Struggle Against a Neoliberal Tourism Agenda: Imagining a Local, Just and Sustainable Ecotourism

Stephen L. Wearing and Michael Wearing

Nature Travels is the UK specialist for responsible travel to Sweden. We work together with small-scale, locally owned partner companies in Sweden to offer a wide range of ecotourism experiences, from wilderness canoeing to dog sledding tours to log cabin holidays. All are active members of the Swedish Ecotourism Society, an organisation committed to minimising the impact of tourism on the natural environment, and 17 are independently certified by a body comprising the Swedish Ecotourism Society, the Swedish Society for Nature Conservation and Visit Sweden ... (Nature Travels Web page accessed 4 April 2011 at http://naturetravels.wordpress.com)

It is not surprising that an advanced welfare state such as Sweden has significantly decommodified social policies and also demonstrates some of the community-based ideals and best local practices of an ethical and socially just ecotourism. The areas covered by Swedish certification include animal welfare, waste and resource management, use of local goods and services and use of fuel-efficient and sustainable transport alternatives. There are also limitations on the capacities of local economies and communities to resist, challenge and in some cases robustly respond to the imperatives of neoliberalism. Alternative ecotourism development is not the same as alternative social development because the tourist/client is dependent on highly unregulated market forces to sustain tourism (Salole, 2007). The impact of market principles on small-scale tour operators and hosts cannot be ignored in the drive for profits. Nonetheless, global capitalism has a way of delivering paradoxical movements to the modes of profit making, competition amongst economic interest and production that reflect the neoliberal agenda. Our arguments here suggest that there is some dynamic for a countermovement from local operators and hosts to such economic globalization in order to drive forward decommodified agendas in ecotourism.

This chapter will conceptualize a socio-political project that seeks to deliver social justice for grassroots communities involved in ecotourism and challenge the ideology and practice of neo-liberalism in various local contexts and local economies. Neoliberalism re-intensifies the older liberal projects of *individualism* – citizens as supposedly free from government intervention – and *marketization* – markets are the best way to enable individual autonomy and efficient economic outcomes – usually in the strategic form of privatization and free trade. It is important to remember that neoliberal governance provides external controls managed by powerful stakeholders that commonly justify their mission in these broad principles. The processes for governing are then commonly created as internal tasks for government programs and market-based companies in measures such as greater economic efficiency, lower award wages and individual work contracts. These are measures that embrace market or quasi market 'blind faith' in the capacity of markets to set prices and determine the quality of the product, amongst other supposed outcomes that match economy, efficiency and effectiveness against each other. These are the fundamentals of neoliberalism that work their ideological norms as the natural economic order into many and varied market systems today.

Neoliberal Hegemony in a Global World

The relations between capital and labour in the West are such that labour is outsourced and capital 'takes flight' to find cheaper labour in the Third World. The nature of the loads given to Third World countries from 1982 onwards by commercial banks and multilevel agencies has locked these countries into a global economic system that requires market liberation and an opening up to global capital to survive and enable such countries to repay these levels of debt (Robinson, 2004). What is at stake here is how this political economy impacts on the South's emerging sites of ecotourism and 'who benefits' from these relations. All of these 'hard' neoliberal agendas create the necessary environment for the commodification of social relations to increase the grip of international capital – read the global ruling class centred in the USA and transnational companies – and work to expand the reach of globalization into communities and individual lives.

   Such global dominance remains ever-present whether perceived as exploitative or beneficial to these communities. We also note the recent literature that points to the complex issues of indigenous and grassroots tourism across rich and poor countries (Butler and Hinch, 2007, Connell and Rugendyke, 2008). The importance for an eco-politics of 'grassroot struggle' and social justice is in opposing neoliberal development, negotiating new socio-political spaces in local communities and finding a balance between equitable resource distribution, conservation values and sustainable ecotourism. We argue in conclusion that socially just ecotourism is sustainable tourism for 'grassroots communities'.

   The theoretical and historical significance of neoliberal ideology is difficult to gauge and often underestimated in ecotourism studies. It is important to make analytical and practical distinctions between social and economic policies and programs that support neoliberal ideology and those that do not. There can be a tendency to overgeneralize and over-determine the power of neoliberalism. This general definition is useful to see the reach of the ideology and its practice: 'it is not difficult to recognize the beast when it trespasses into new territories, tramples upon the poor, undermines rights and entitlements, and defeats resistance, through a combination of domestic political, economic, legal, ideological and media pressures, backed up by international blackmail and military force if necessary' (Saad-Filho and Johnston, 2005: 2).

We add to the argument by suggesting that human agency as actions which free people from commodified ways of living i.e. as decommodifying the social – takes a less deterministic view of the current crisis. In some cases of ecotourism and related activism, rights and entitlements are asserted, resistance stands steady and political and social spaces are created for people to challenge economic globalization and neoliberalism. This reiterates the importance of global civil society such as NGOs and other powerful actors in helping to challenge, humanize and support activism and protest amongst the poorest communities involved in ecotourism.

Below we consider both Peru and Vietnam as good examples of this even though they have not escaped the hegemony of global free market ideology. The rise of multinational companies, and some have argued multinational states (Robinson, 2004), has escalated and driven economic liberalization and exploitation of the South. Below we will outlines some examples of grassroots struggles in host and indigenous communities over the appropriate use of nature and natural resources and how these struggles can lead to detrimental impacts on, as well as some positive benefits for, these communities. Part of this framework is to explore what has been done in communities and through working with partners to overcome strong market forces and rhetoric that is ever ready to exploit local and host communities involved in ecotourism.

The following will provide some case examples of ecotourism and grassroots struggles mainly in the South that also resonate with eco-activism and struggle in the North. These will broadly illustrate some of the resistance and struggle that communities, and more broadly various social classes such as the middle and working classes and the non-working poor, make in response to neoliberal policies on tourism.

'What do Rich Countries Do?' – *Sweden*

This can be illustrated by recent developments in Sweden, as indicated above, which has developed ecotours in relation to its wilderness, natural beauty and isolation. Nonetheless, there are tensions between the government, the business elite and actors in civil society such as green groups and environmentalists. The Government's recent call for culling and hunting the wolf in January 2011 brought about condemnation from activists, ecotour companies and the European Union.

In modern universalist welfare states such as Sweden where most citizens have strong welfare entitlements there are also minorities groupings who live both socio-spatially and politically at the periphery of society (see Ryan and Aicken Eds, 2005). The example of the Sami and tourism across Northern Europe gives illustrates both the constraints on indigenous communities and the potential for ecotour development. There are cultural norms and legal impediments for the Sami in Sweden to more fully embrace tourism as an income source (Müller and Huuva, 2009). Being on the periphery of Swedish society lends some uncertainty to market forces so that tourism develops either as a small scale independent venture or with input and assistance from international or national tour operators and other actors.

Ecotourism: A Way Forward?

This section provides examples of how we can conceptualize a process that enables engagement that may then deliver social justice 'from below' enabled by state intervention and therefore a fairer economic share for grassroots communities involved in ecotourism. In doing so, this challenges neoliberal ideologies that dominate corporate tourism interests and power relations in local contexts and economies. Ecotourism by its nature suggests a symbolic or mutual relationship where the tourist is not given central priority but becomes an equal part of the system. This is not apparent in much of the tourism that occurs in developing countries and many developed countries, nor does it appear likely to occur in the future within current operating practices. Further, the tendency to ignore or exploit local culture to enhance the tourist experience has given rise to conflict environmentally and culturally. Tourists have been conditioned to accept a structured experience often packaged by large operators with little understanding of local natural and cultural resources.

The tourist development framework created can often relegate the people and their natural and cultural resources to a stage show or the backdrop for the tourism experience. This ignores the opportunity for cultural exchange, and forgoes understanding of the rich natural and cultural heritage that can be part of the tourist experience. Overcoming this problem takes us back to the underlying difficulties inherent in development issues and tourism which can be addressed with the use of a community development process that engages a wider spectrum of stakeholders in the process and is sensitive to host community cultural issues (Campbell, 1999). By its nature, this process allows for a more diverse spectrum of opportunities to be explored and in context to issues that may require detailed engagement at the local level. Wearing and MacDonald (2002) explore this in Papua New Guinea offering some insights into what the process revealed, the type of engagement regarded as meaningful and the outcomes from the process. A number of examples are now reviewed. They suggest that the relationship between intermediaries and rural and isolated communities can be seen as a process involving many actions and participants' fields of knowledge – a continuous process where different social values meet and new meanings are created (Wearing, 1998).

The changing position and focus of some in the tourism industry has created, in some circumstances, a movement away from the predominance of western industrialized society's ownership and control of tourism operations in rural and isolated areas. However, the models of operations that have been presented to rural and isolated area communities has led to a paradoxical problem; because rural and isolated area communities have fewer alternative models of operation than those of the dominant western models – tour operators then tend to treat their own communities as "other" to be exploited as part of the drive for profit. However, due to changing discourses on the role of rural and isolated area communities and the increased availability of economic access, there are expanding opportunities for these communities to explore tourism as a business. These explorations will not simply materialize without a strategy of local engagement, awareness of cultural and resource capacity and a strategy to operationalize business or micro business opportunities.

Other examples of this engagement through ecotourism can be seen in several cases such as the one outlined by Leksakundilok and Hirsch (2008) about engaging with host communities in developing ecotourism in Thailand. The research found that outcomes are improved for both the host communities and visitors due to the involvement of the community in the process of establishing ecotourism activities. King and Steward (1996: 293) suggest that to protect both people and their places, native people's claim to control should be legitimized by conservation and government authorities. This is particularly important for indigenous people's role in technical management of the protected area, as park authorities can learn a great deal from traditional land management practices.

The evolution of ecotourism has seen many failures and successes but demonstrates that ecotourism moves beyond just a merging of conservation with capitalism. It has demonstrated that it is able to embrace concern for the economic and social welfare of indigenous people, and at times, appears to portray ecotourism as a mechanism to allow the engagement of grassroots communities to protect their cultures (Farrell and Runyan, 1991). In this sense, ecotourism has been presented as different from other kinds of tourism in that it claims to be controlled development that builds engagement and relationships between the tourism industry and other stakeholders such as those involved in protected areas and indigenous people.

Traditional Owners as 'Winners and Losers' in Australia and Papua New Guinea

Examples of how this engagement can be formulated can be found in the development of indigenous tourism businesses in Australia. In analysing the development of remote touirsm facitlites in three case studies, Beyer, Anda, Elber,

Revell and Spring (2005) find that engaging in consultation with indigenous stakeholders led to the success of the projects. Additionally, the development of criteria to engage with other stakeholders was able to guide the "developer" in establishing a successful partnership with local indigenous cultural interests in a process that ensured cultural integrity and respect and understanding of the colonization of 'Aboriginal Australia'. This research suggests the engagement of indigenous cultural interests in the development process must be genuine and transparent and embrace the knowledge that cultural tourism is the only commercial use of land that can be done only by indigenous people. Finally, the authors maintain that wherever possible the "developer" should be formed from the local and or regional Indigenous community, in whole or in part, which tells us about new ways of doing cultural tourism (Beyer et al., 2005: 20). It is interesting to note that in other areas of indigenous tourism, businesses measures of success are higher when there is prominent engagement with indigenous stakeholders (Tremblay and Wegner, 2009). Ali (2009) demonstrated this in the case of the Brambuk Visitor/Cultural Centre which was a culmination of nearly a decade of consultation between a committee of five Aboriginal communities from the western district and various tourism and government agencies. The Aboriginal (Koori) communities who were partners in this project included the Kirrae, the Whurang, the Goolum, the Gunditjmara and the Kerrup-Jmara, located in South West Victoria and the Wimmera Regions. The outcome of the study showed satisfaction within the communities with their inclusion in and representation by the ecotourism industry. Tourists were usually satisfied with the visit and the level of enjoyment experienced from visits was very high (Ali, 2009: 26).

Aboriginal traditional owners and their representative local community organizations should be encouraged to take a more pro-active role in facilitating the development of their own tourism enterprises (Palmer, 2001: i). Palmer's research has suggested that if Aboriginal communities and landowners wish to increase their direct involvement in the safari hunting and sports fishing industries the initial years of a business operation should be undertaken through a cooperative arrangement with an existing operator. In most instances, a joint venture approach, with operators who have pre-existing market experience is likely to be more commercially viable than if Aboriginal traditional owners are running operations directly themselves.

These examples suggest that through engagement and enablement we can find alternatives to the existing predominant models of doing tourism. A central concern in this process is the engagement of the "other" which moves beyond current neoliberal management models. Although there are many potential pitfalls in this approach, it provides new directions for the future. Tourism management is driven by neoliberal economic imperatives where yield dominates the discourse (Dwyer et al., 2006). Academics and governments recognize the importance of incorporating more than just the economic into the management of tourism. The triple bottom line suggests that economic imperatives must be balanced with environmental and social sustainability.

This balance can be demonstrated in both remote Aboriginal communities (Fennel and Dowling, 2003) and with village tribal negotiations over ecotourist endeavours in Papua New Guinea (PNG). PNG villages and tribes along the Kokoda trail have been subject to coercion, bribery and corruption by mining companies to allow traditional lands to be surveyed for minerals and mining. There are large resources at stake for the companies involved and there has been protest against and support from the communities for the economic benefits reaped by these companies. It is clear that such practices with little community consultation risk over-development in the middle to long term at a rapid and poorly planned pace and the destruction of the environment of highland communities in PNG (Wearing, Wearing and MacDonald, 2010).

These indigenous communities can follow the community-based paradigms for ecotourism developed in partnership with communities developed from case studies of the design and practice used in African countries and elsewhere. Salole (2007), for example, shows how a venture tourism project in rural Namibia was reasonably successful with the input of and profit sharing amongst small communities. This project in the North West of Namibia allows tourist to experience the isolated beauty of the area and the natural environment but had few resources to develop an ecotourist site. The final product was a tourist lodge with particular features suited to the predominantly farming communities of the area. A partnership with an experienced photography safari tour operator (developed itself by guides from a small bird tour to a larger safaris operation), government assistance in establishing new legislation and policy and four local tribal groups saw the venture establish a lodge for tourist. A contract was signed with the issue of local employment seen as being of mutual advantage and which included provisions such as local recruitment of all staff, 10 per cent of net revenue paid to the community, financial transparency and an option for the community to purchase the assets after ten years.

'A Buck Each Way' Eco or Nature Tourism – *Australia and New Zealand*

As if to hedge its bets both ways, Australia and New Zealand represent countries in the OECD who seem to struggle with the decommodification of ecotourism given these countries close ties between their respective national governments and hard and softer neoliberalism. Maori and Australian Aboriginal communities are taking control of their tourist destinations tied to sacred sites such as Uluru (Whittakar, 1994, Hollingshead, 2007, Sharpley, 2009). Colton and Harris (2007) also provide some excellent examples of community development with indigenous communities in Canada and space does not permit us to detail the important processes in such development work (see also Timothy, 2002). The basic assumptions behind community practice in this work is that it engages and provides an organized eco-activist agenda for ecotourism to flourish in more decommodified or less 'profit hungry' ways. The outcome is oriented towards both community participation and control of social and economic benefits in local markets.

If we look at what is occurring around ecotourism and Aboriginal culture and identity most notably in the Northern Territory of Australia, there is often a complicated nexus between welfare and tourism at the peripheries of these societies as low incomes are bound up with semi-traditional communities and lifestyle. It seems these places of tourist sites are also targets of "welfare reform" and their populations seen as welfare dependent with associated White racist or classist stereotypes. For example, regional Australian Aboriginal communities are commonly depicted in the media as being dependent on welfare benefits for their existence and are immersed in a series of other social issues including alcoholism (Hollingshead, 2007). Less visible in the Australian media are positive images of Aboriginal communities as proprietors, custodians and owners of key tourist and heritage areas such as Kakadu National Park or Uluru. Yet, with these views and the engagement of communities that have been traditionally "othered" we see the growth of tourism in a more equitable manner through initiatives such as joint management where a diversity of natural and cultural encounters provide the tourist with a wide-ranging and engaged experience and where the interest of the host communities is sustained.

Joint management has been successfully brokered where Aboriginal landowners and Parks Australia work together and decide what should be done to manage a national park with and on behalf of traditional owners and for other interests. Joint management is about working together to enhance and protect Aboriginal rights and interests while looking after the natural and cultural values of Kakadu National Park, and providing opportunities for visitors to experience and appreciate these values safely (Wearing and Huyskens, 2001). The joint management of Kakadu is an example of integrated nature conservation and community development albeit with some issues in practice. In Australia joint management is achieved through the appointment of a management board that has a majority of indigenous people nominated by traditional owners if the reserve is wholly or mostly on indigenous people's land. The board of management makes policy and strategic management decisions about park management and tourism.

It is however important to note that processes that attempt to empower indigenous stakeholders may not achieve this. Banerjee (2000) finds this with the Jabiluka/Kakadu World Heritage Site where the communities had no final power of veto on the process. This has also been seen in the joint management regimes in place in Australia where it was recognized that they are essentially Western cultural models of management with an inherent Anglo-Australian cultural bias (Wearing and Huyskens, 2001) and as De Lacy and Lawson (1997: 176) find some Anangu (indigenous people of Uluru) are highly critical of the 99 year lease at Uluru-Kata Tjuta National Park, as they see it as a "denial of their ability to determine for themselves appropriate land use options".

In affluent countries such as Australia and New Zealand cultural sites such as museums also offer ways for the White ethnocentric cultural gaze to be disseminated. Cultural representations have had to be re-appropriated and broken down into a decolonized, spiritual and secular authenticity (Said, 1989). First Museums and now places which are sacred and important to Aboriginal and Maori communities require long term processes of change and integration (Wjttaker, 1994, Laenul, 1996).

Therefore as ecotourism often involves interaction with the indigenous cultures visited it should encourage cross-cultural communication (Richardson, 1993), with many reasoning that is has the potential to enhance understanding about environmental values and open the possibility of supporting community economies (Wearing and Neil, 2009). However one needs to be wary as ecotourism has the potential for destructive intrusion for indigenous people and their community life leading to an invasion of privacy (Buultjens and Fuller, 2007). Ecotourism is seen as the meeting of two worlds yet Johnston (2005) believes that this can result in either exploitation or healing. Indeed, ecotourism appears on the surface to possess numerous positive elements for indigenous cultures however it has been argued that it can in fact be more damaging than other approaches because it targets indigenous people's culture and ancestral land directly and, even with the intention of protecting them, could result in the selling of sacred lands, knowledge and ceremonial sites (Johnston, 2005).

Johnston (2005) describes ecotourism as the force that erodes culture, lures people away from their traditional responsibilities and inflates prices. It has also been suggested that ecotourism is a 'highly oversold concept that profits off indigenous cultures behind a mask of good' (Johnson, 2005: 15) and can be seen as a contributing factor to rights violations and used as a vehicle to penetrate vulnerable areas (Johnston, 2005). Moreover, there is great unease around the control of tourism in sacred locations and that the indigenous community within Australia has little influence over land use and rights. De Lacy and Lawson (1997 cited in Wearing and Huyskens, 2001) have noted that communities such as the Anangu (the traditional people of Uluru) possess ownership of the land however tourism is a segment that they are unable to control. It is becoming increasingly apparent to them that they are being forced to contribute to the commodification of their culture and that this sacrifice may not lead to a guarantee that visitors will learn to respect their culture. Additionally, there is increased unease and tension revolving around the 99 year lease of the National Park in Uluru for this action is perceived by the indigenous community as a lack of confidence in their ability to determine appropriate land use options (De Lacy and Lawson 1997 cited in Wearing and Huyskens, 2001).

Ecotourism was to some extent introduced as an alternative to the constant leaking of money from host communities to foreign ownership (Richardson, 1993); however it is apparent that it has the potential to generate similar problems for 'much is promised and little gained' (Wearing and Harris, 1999: 2). Indigenous people have expressed their concern about the performance of the tourism industry, how it disregards their interests and rights and profits from their knowledge and heritage (Wearing and Neil, 2009). This is reflected in the cases where traditional cultures are used to promote destinations in ways that leads to trivialized and exploitative acts for those involved (Wearing and Neil, 2009). Particularly, some of those who wish to embrace ecotourism have found themselves in a position where they have little control over decision making processes, receive inadequate responses from the government, bring in few positive financial, social and employment benefits and experience extensive impact on community cohesion and structure (Wearing and Neil, 2009). Furthermore, there is a lack of appropriate information for local communities in order to grow in the industry and make important decisions (Johnston, 2005).

This demonstrates that those who want to be involved in the industry face the risk of being swept up in the 'backwash of the industry's impacts with opportunities foreclosed' (Johnston, 2006: 13). A common argument for encouraging indigenous communities to get involved in ecotourism is that there will be increased employment opportunities. However, this can be restricted and unrewarding for some especially in remote areas where locals can lack formal qualifications and resources which make it difficult to compete with outsiders (Wearing and Neil, 2009). This therefore demonstrates that although ecotourism attempts to open up opportunities for the indigenous community by creating an industry that will encourage tourists to respect their culture and their land there are numerous negative consequences that have the potential to affect indigenous people.

However there have been cases where ecotourism provides the opportunity for employment for indigenous people in remote parts of Australia where there are minimal economic opportunities (Wearing and Neil, 2009). In particular, the Anangu tribe of the Northern Territory have developed a business based around ecotourism that includes demonstrations of tracking skills, guided walks and food processing techniques. The most important part of this venture is that the board of managers is comprised of the Anangu, the traditional owners of the country (Howitt, 2001 cited in Wearing and Neil, 2009). This is a clear example of indigenous people embracing ecotourism and encouraging others to understand parts of their traditional way of life without sacrificing their culture in the process. Another example can be found in the Pajinka Wilderness Lodge which was initially an upmarket destination that did not hire any indigenous people. Eventually the local indigenous community bought back the land and now run and operate the lodge (Richardson, 1993). They now hire people from the Injinoo community creating increased employment within the area. These examples represent a form of joint management which has been described as a cross-cultural approach to the use and management of land within protected areas (Wearing and Huyskens, 2001). In further detail, it emphasizes the point that it provides a significant opportunity for indigenous people within Australia to remain on their land and have political and cultural power over decisions affecting their lives and the land (Craig, 1993 cited in Wearing and Huyskens, 2001). As mentioned, there is a significant difference in how indigenous people and Western society view the idea of nature and conservation. Therefore, this form of management attempts to combine the interests, values and concerns of both. The application of such models to present ecotourism practices within Australia and other parts of the world opens up the possibility that ecotourism can promote traditional culture in such a way that does not lead to its destruction.

After discussing the varying affects ecotourism has on indigenous cultures it is apparent that there needs to be an application of a consistent new model in order to prevent negative impacts ensuing. Considering that ecotourism attempts to step in as an alternative to mass tourism it needs to be ensured that it does not become another commodified product where benefits are exported and natural resources abused (Wearing and Harris, 1999). A fundamental strategy could be the adoption of consultation, open lines of communication and widely distributed information. Communication and consultation should not be underestimated for they have the ability to bring people with common goals together and can empower others in remote areas. In addition, if the same information is spread across all areas it gives people the opportunity to start on the same footing and grow in the areas that appeal to their culture and community the most. Lastly, education and training needs to be made available to indigenous business owners (Wearing and Neil, 2009). Education is crucial as the industry can only develop and improve the quality of life for individuals and cultures if it is acknowledged as possessing a significant role in the process. This could include providing knowledge on the industry, teaching business, technical and management skills and creating a system of locally owned and managed ecotourism developments (Wearing and Harris, 1999). However, in order for this to be effective it is important to avoid adopting Western education methods an thus moving in the same pattern as before and ignoring the fact that indigenous people have their own methods of teaching that could be more appropriate, as modelled by Freire's conscietization approach (Freire, 1970, 1971, 1997, Giroux, 1992, Wearing and Harris, 1999).

'Even in the Poorest Societies' – *Peru and Vietnam*

Both Peru and Vietnam are two of the world's poorest countries and yet these very poor communities have managed to struggle against some of the tyranny of inequality and the influence of the globalized project of neoliberalism. As a developing nation of the South, Peru has undergone some extreme exposure to the global market and neoliberal forces. As one of the poorest countries their local communities have not necessarily benefitted from the increased levels of tourism or focus on protecting the environment in ecotourism alone (Torres, 2008).

Understanding the long history of struggle for rural Peruvian peasants is important in understanding the short-term response to neoliberalism. Olsen (2008) seems to suggest that local rural communities in the South have not responded to the rise of neoliberalism in Peru in the last 20 years directly but have encouraged economic and democratic participation in keeping with the needs of the system and market. In the 1970s and 1980s, these same communities and their leaders had adopted strategies of local price setting, radical land reform and redistribution in line with support from the local Catholic Church.

Today it is unclear whether the protests and resistance to injustice and inequality in these communities can match the flexibility of neoliberalism and the difficulties in recognizing the impact on poor people's lives of key neoliberal fundamentals such as privatization. Against this backdrop, Peru has an abundance of natural wonders and destinations that make it attractive for tourists wanting to experience the real South America. Peru also has a population that can be exposed to a more critical consciousness about the environment and their standards of living. The work of authors such as Paulo Freire (1970, 1997) and Henry Giroux (1992, 2012) on dialogic and cultural action could begin to build political and economic awareness as a 'critical consciousness' in school education and in local communities. It is clear that some areas of Peru are being highly commercialized by tourist consumption, especially the well-travelled nature and ecotour sites such as Machu Picchu and the National Parks associated with these sites. Commercialized interests in the forests and tourism have created an unstable and possibly unsustainable tourist market (Wearing, MacDonald and Wearing, 2011).

Though the issues are different in Vietnam, there is an ongoing movement that links national culture to ecotour programs and operators. Vietnam has fallen somewhere between a development state model and a competitive model that emulates neoliberal thinking (Evans and Hai, 2005). There has been a contradictory effort to reconcile market reforms with market socialism in this country, which to a certain degree has opened up local economies for nature-based and in certain cases alternative ecotourist ventures. Vietnam over the last 30 years has become one of the fastest growing economies starting from a low base averaging 9 per cent GDP growth between 1986–1997. This, along with the natural beauty of Vietnam, has provided a good basis for the development of ecotourism and more broadly nature-based tourism.

In recent years, there have been several examples of ecotourism development especially in relation to the number of national parks increasing from 3 to 30 since 1986. Nonetheless there has also been a vast amount of environmental damage notably during the US-Vietnam war when forested land decreased from 43.7 per cent to 26.1 per cent between 1943 and 1994, increasing to round 36 per cent by 2003 (Suntikul, Butler and Airey, 2010). Much of what is called ecotourism in Vietnam is mass nature-based tourism without the specific criteria of ecologically sustainable tourism. There is some progress in terms of linking ecotourism to the development of national parks and bringing in powerful international and well as government stakeholders.

Social Justice and 'Grassroot' Struggles for Ecotourism

The political theorist Nancy Fraser (2010: 16–18) has recently argued for a three dimensional view of social justice that underpins our views on ecotourism development as a local struggle. We have positioned this argument within the three parts as whole of 'local', 'just' and 'sustainable' ecotourism. Fraser's theory enhances our social justice agenda for both an economically and culturally appropriate ecotourism. Fraser argues that 'the general meaning of justice is parity of participation ... (that) ... requires social arrangements for all to participate as peers in social life'. Within this general view are three dimensions. First, social justice requires the dimension of *distribution/redistribution* because parity of participation by local and host communities is commonly impeded by local, national and international economic structures in both developed and developing countries. We have argued that in terms of ecotourist entrepreneurship this involves giving back considerable profits and resources including significant paid work to local indigenous and host communities. Second, social justice requires *recognition* of cultural identity that is contextualized and determined by and large 'by institutionalized hierarchies of cultural value'. Public, political and economic recognition of local and host communities acts against suppression and denial of cultural and social identity and therefore on behalf of their economic, social and human rights. Suppression of cultural and social identity could also be a second hand and somewhat invisible effect in terms of non-recognition or misrecognition of unequal distribution. Importantly, neither the first nor the second dimension can work effectively without the other so that social justice strategies are dependent on both the economic and cultural outcomes for communities. This is crucially important in ecotourist enterprises in that local indigenous and host communities require their cultural status and identity as well as their economic, social and human rights to be respected when implemented in the frames of tourist practice.

These two dimensions will set together part of the decommodified frame for local communities to take control of such enterprises in cooperation with other sympathetic stakeholders. Finally, and Fraser indicates most importantly, the third dimension of social justice is '*political*' in that distribution and recognition are 'contested and power-laden'. This dimension has a specific political meaning for state intervention in that the state constitutes its scope of jurisdiction and decision rules 'by which it structures contestation over distribution and recognition in society'. In terms of social justice and ecotourism this means the values, form and content of state regulation and enterprise need to be in cooperation and sympathy with those least powerful, most disadvantaged and potentially made 'worse off' from economic development and the supposed benefits of ecotourism. These powerless groups are usually the indigenous and host communities who are at the mercy of the marketization of ecotourism and living in circumstances of relative and absolute deprivation compared to others in their own country and the wider world.

The arguments on social justice clearly indicate a significant role for strong government intervention in redressing inequalities that can come about from marketized tourism and for international organizations such as the United Nations and NGOs to advocate for social justice as foundational to sustainable tourist development. Both identity recognition and capital redistribution are central to new political and economic spaces for host and indigenous communities in the face of global capitalism (Erikson, 2007, Fraser, 2010). This is particularly the case for indigenous communities who require as part of their political goals territorial autonomy and cultural self-determination: 'Indigenous struggles against globalized external dominance tend to differ from class-based struggles through their emphasis on local community, identity politics, land claims, and rights to a variety of traditional practices' (Erikson, 2007: 147).

How can ecotourism strengthen indigenous struggles? The concept of struggle is a key sociological insight for grassroots activism and social change because the outcome is never a zero sum. In modernity this has been more commonly related to the working class or more recently to host and indigenous communities who are looking to wrestle control and resources back from transnational companies often complicit with governments in over-developing natural environment and 'modernizing' such communities. Community-based alternative ecotourism ventures can provide one important local strategy and a site of struggle for strengthening the identity politics of indigenous people as a response to globalization. We will use the ideals of decommodified strategies and community-based ecotourism as our measure for more just practice, greater identity recognition and more equalizing agendas for local communities.

Conclusion

In short, we have sought to lay out an agenda for participatory justice and sustainable ecotourism with evidence from ecotour case studies in Sweden, Australia, Peru and Vietnam and based on Fraser's (2010) three-dimensional theory. These case studies of decommodifying ecotourism have illustrated some of the grounds for struggle and recognition that host and local communities need to challenge. Once this is done, governments in cooperative work with such communities and other stakeholders need to set in place agendas for alternative or what we call 'grassroots' ecotourist development. Largely because of their socio-economic and cultural vulnerabilities, local and host communities can be tied economically to large powerful stakeholders such as mining companies or international tour agents. This has certainly been evident in the experience of such development in Australia (see De Lacy and Lawson, 1997, Banerjee, 2000, Wearing and MacDonald, 2002, Buultjen and Fuller, 2007, Ali, 2009).

Governments, advocates, tourists and tour operators need to step in and work cooperatively to break some of these economic ties (Wearing and Wearing, 2006, Wearing, Wearing and McDonald, 2010, Sennet, 2012). A broad agenda for change based on social justice as a goal of ecotourism is needed. Part of this broad agenda is devolution and a 'giving back' of local control in order to work with these communities on grounded community-based ecotourism strategies and social and economic development. Such strategies require a range of measures including: 'voices and cultural action from below' in the development process to strengthen the political and economic power of such communities; clear social justice agendas for change that recognize and promote cultural and indigenous heritage and understand the politically contested nature of the recognition and distribution of the profits of ecotourism ventures; and finally there needs to be independent evaluation of the range of socio-economic and cultural outcomes for stakeholders based on a just and equitable distribution of resources and profits made from ecotourism.

References

Ali, S. (2009). *Benchmarking Visitor Satisfaction at Brambuk—the National Parks and Cultural Centre.* Griffith University, Co-operative Research Centre for Sustainable Tourism Brisbane.

Banerjee, S.B. (2000). Whose land is it anyway? National interest, indigenous stakeholders, and colonial discourses: The case of the Jabiluka uranium mine *Organisation and Environment*, 13(1), 3–38.

Beyer, D., Anda, M., Elber, B., Revell, G. and Spring, F. (2005). *Best Practice Model for Low-impact Nature Based Sustainable Tourism Facilities in Remote Areas.* CRC for Sustainable Tourism.

Butler, R. and T. Hinch (eds) (2007). *Tourism and Indigenous Peoples: Issues and Implications.* Amsterdam: Butterworth-Heinemann.

Buultjens. J. and Fuller, D. (2007). *Striving for Sustainability: Case Studies in Indigenous Tourism.* Lismore: Southern Cross University Press.

Campbell, L.M. (1999). Ecotourism in rural developing communities. *Annals of Tourism Research*, 26(3), 534–53.

Chang, D. (2005). Neoliberal restructuring of capital relations in East and South-East Asia. In A. Saad-Filho and D. Johnston (eds) *Neoliberalism: A Critical Reader.* London: Pluto Press, 251–8.

Colton, J. and Harris, S. (2007). Indigenous ecotourism' role in community development: The case of Lennox Island First Nation. In R. Butler and T. Hinch (eds) *Tourism and Indigenous Peoples: Issues and Implications.* Amsterdam: Butterworth-Heinemann, 220–46.

Connell, J and Rugendyke, B. (eds) (2008). *Tourism at the Grassroots: Villagers and Visitors in the Asia Pacific.* Hokoben: Routledge.

Connell, R. (2006). Chicago values: The neoliberal dream and Howard government politics. *Overland*, 183, 32–8.

Conolly, J. (2004). Ecotourism saves Madagascar's rainforest and boosts living standards for locals. *Boston Globe* 8/11/04.

De Lacy, T. and Lawson, B. (1997). The Uluru-Kakadu model: Joint Management of Aborginal owned National Parks in Australia. In S. Stevens (ed.) *Conservation through Cultural Survival: Indigenous Peoples and Protected Areas.* Washington DC: Island Press, 155–88.

Erikson, T.H. (2007). *Globalization: The Key Concepts.* Oxford: Berg.

Evans, M. and Hai, B.D. (2005). Embedding neoliberalism through statecraft: The case of market reform in Vietnam. In S. Solederberg and G. Menz (eds) *Internalizing Globalization*. Basingstoke: Palgrave Macmillan, 219–37.

Fraser, N. (2010). *Scales of Justice: Reimagining Political Space in a Globalizing World*. Cambridge: Polity Press.

Freire, P. (1970). *Pedagogy of the Oppressed*. New York: Continuum Books.

Feire, P. (1972). *Cultural Action for Freedom*. Harmondworth: Penguin Books.

Freire, P. (1997). *Pedagogy of the Heart*. New York: Continuum.

Giroux, H.A., DiLeo, J., McClennen, S. and Saltman, K. (eds) (2012). *Neoliberalism, Education, Terrorism: Contemporary Dialogues*. Boulder: Paradigm.

Giroux, H.A. (1992). *Border Crossings: Cultural Workers and the Politics of Schooling*. New York: Routledge.

Hall, C.M. and Tucker, H. (eds) (2004). *Tourism and Postcolonialism: Contested Discourses, Identities and Representations*. London and New York: Routledge.

Hirschman, A.O. (1984). *Getting Ahead Collectively: Grassroots Experience in Latin America*. New York State: Permagon Press.

Hollingshead, K. (2007). Indigenous Australia in the bittersweet world. In R. Butler and T. Hinch (eds) *Tourism and Indigenous Peoples: Issues and Implications*. Amsterdam: Butterworth-Heinemann.

Johnston, A.M. (2005). *Is the Scared for Sale? Tourism and Indigenous People*. London: Earthscan.

King, A.D. and Stewart W.P. (1996). Ecotourism and commodification: Protecting people and places. *Biodiversity and Conservation*, 5(3), 293–305.

Laenul, P. (Burgessm H, F.) (1996). 'Processes of Decolonisation' in M. Battiste (ed.) *Reclaiming Indigenous Voice and Vision*. Vancouver: UBC Press: 150–60.

Leksakundilok, A. and Hirsch, P. (2008). Community Based Ecotourism in Thailand. In J. Connell and B. Rugendyke (eds) *Tourism at the Grassroots: Villagers and Visitors in the Asia Pacific*. Hokoben: Routledge.

Müller, D.K. and Houva (2009). Limits to Sami tourism development: The case of Jokkmokk, Sweden. *Journal of Ecotourism*, 8(2), 115–27.

Olsen, E. (2008). Confounding neoliberalism: Priests, privatisation and social justice in the Peruvian Andes. In A. Smith, A. Steening and K. Willis. *Social Justice and Neoliberalism: Global Perspectives*. London: Zed Books, 39–60.

Palmer, L. (2002). *Indigenous Interests in Safari Hunting and Fishing Tourism in the Northern Territory*. CRC for Sustainable Tourism.

Pawliczek, M. and Mehta, H. (2008). Ecotourism in Madagascar. In A. Spenceley (ed.) *Responsible Tourism: Critical Issues for Conservation and Development*. London: Earthscan, 41–68.

Robinson, W.I. (2004). *A Theory of Global Capitalism*. Baltimore, MD: Johns Hopkins University Press.

Ryan, C. and Aicken, M. (eds) (2005). *Indigenous Tourism: The Commodificaiton and Management of Culture*. Amsterdam: Elsevier.

Saad-Filho, A and Johnston, D. (2005). Introduction. In A. Saad-Filho and D. Johnston (eds) *Neoliberalism: A Critical Reader*. London: Pluto Press, 1–6.

Salole, M. (2007). Merging two disparate worlds in rural Namibia: Joint venture tourism in Torra conservancy. In R. Butler and T. Hinch (eds) *Tourism and Indigenous Peoples: Issues and Implications.* Amsterdam: Butterworth-Heinemann, 205–19.

Sennet, R. (2012). *Together: The Rituals, Pleasures and Politics of Co-operation.* London: Penguin.

Sharpley, R. (2009). *Tourism Development and the Environment: Beyond Sustainability.* London, Earthscan.

Spenceley, A. (2008). Local Impacts of Community-based Tourism in Southern Africa. In A. Spenceley (ed.) *Responsible Tourism: Critical Issues for Conservation and Development.* London: Earthscan, 285–303.

Suntikul, W., Butler, R. and Airey, D. (2010). Implications of political change on national park operations: *Doi moi* and tourism in Vietnam national parks. *Journal of Ecotourism*, 9(3), 201–18.

Timothy, D.J. (2002). Tourism and community development issues. In R. Sharpley and D.J. Telfer (eds) *Tourism and Development, Concepts and Ideas.* Bristol: Channel View Publications, 149–64.

Torres, G.R. (2005). Neoliberalism under Cross fire in Peru: Implementing the Washington Consensus. In S. Solederberg and G. Menz (eds) *Internalizing Globalization.* Basingstoke: Palgrave Macmillan, 200–18.

Wearing, S. and Huyskens, M. (2001). Moving on from joint management policy regimes in Australian national parks. *Current Issues in Tourism*, 4(2), 182–209.

Wearing, S. and MacDonald, M. (2002). The development of community based tourism: Re-thinking the relationship between intermediaries and rural and isolated area communities. *Journal of Sustainable Tourism*, 10(2), 21–35.

Wearing, S.L. and Harris, M. (1999). An Approach to training for indigenous ecotourism development. *World Leisure and Recreation Journal*, 41(4), 9–17.

Wearing, S.L. and Neil, J. (2009). *Ecotourism: Impacts, Potentials and Possibilities.* Oxford: Butterworth-Heinemann.

Wearing, S.L., Wearing, M. and McDonald, M. (2010). Understanding local power and interactional processes in sustainable tourism: Exploring village–tour operator relations on the Kokoda Track, Papua New Guinea. *Journal of Sustainable Tourism*, 18(1), 61–76.

Wearing, S.L. and Wearing, M. (2006). Re-reading the 'subjugating tourist' in neoliberalism: Postcolonial otherness and the tourist experience. *Tourism Analysis*, 11(2), 145–62.

Wearing, S. and Wearing, M. (1999). Decommodifying ecotourism: Rethinking global–local interactions with host communities. *Society and Leisure (Losire et Societe)*, 22(1), 39–70.

Whittaker, E. (1994). Public discourse on sacredness: The transfer of Ayers Rock to Aboriginal ownership. *American Ethnologist* 21(2), 310–34.

Chapter 11

Conclusion: Tourism and Neoliberalism: States, the Economy and Society

Jan Mosedale

Each contribution in this volume deals with different aspects of neoliberalization in the context of tourism and raises several significant questions regarding the neoliberal projects, discourses and practices in particular as they shape the relationships between states, the economy and society. One key aspect of neoliberalization processes is the changing role of the state (Church et al., 2000). The restructuring of governance during both roll-back and roll-out phases of the neoliberalization process leads to new constellations of governance actors (Mosedale, 2014). As government institutions are shifting their activities from regulating economies to facilitating economic opportunities, new actors have entered the governance arena (e.g. in public-private partnerships) or pre-existing actors at sub-national scales are gaining more responsibility (e.g. local and regional governments). Various examples in this book demonstrate the shifting and diverse relations within complex institutional landscapes in increasingly neoliberalized societies. Analysing the revitalization of city-centres in the US as part of urban tourism developments, Ioannides and Petriadou (Chapter 2) highlight the creation of urban development corporations as new governance actors (public-private partnerships) with planning and development powers that allow the over-riding of zoning restrictions. Transitional city-centre areas are thus purposefully being gentrified and turned into neo-bohemian neighbourhoods that retain at least some of the original features (such as architecture and social fabric) with the added diversity of new residents as well as new, often creative, businesses and tourists.

Such neoliberal urban developments may also involve the hosting of mega-events. Hall and Wilson (Chapter 3) focus on the analysis of a re-vitalization strategy at a local scale using an example of constructing infrastructure for mega-events. Although state activity in providing opportunities for local engagement in sporting activities has been increasingly reduced (roll-back neoliberalization) and has often been transferred to private business, the state still invest considerably (by way of subsidies or actual investments in infrastructure) in large-scale, professional sporting events and infrastructure in order to facilitate private commercial benefit. Hall and Wilson (Chapter 3) have noted a shift in the motives for hosting mega-events from solving internal spatial issues such as to rejuvenate impoverished urban neighbourhoods towards hosting mega-events to increase regional and urban competitiveness and to provide opportunities for private business. Analyzing the construction of a multi-purpose stadium in Dunedin, New Zealand for the 2011 Rugby World Cup and subsequent events, they highlight this paradox of local state investment for private business as the benefits are accrued by private business, yet the state (essentially the taxpayers) remains burdened with public debt.

Neoliberal reregulation has also resulted in a rescaling of governance as regional and local governance networks have taken on added responsibilities and roles. In the case-study of the Hurunui District of New Zealand, Shone (Chapter 4) has highlighted the regional government's entrepreneurial role as owner/operator of Hanmer Springs Thermal Pools and Spa. In contrast to other neoliberal governance networks where private business has taken on government responsibilities (i.e. for the provision of social services such as sport), the local government has, in this case, reacted to restructuring of local–central relations by assuming an active rather than merely supporting role in tourism development. This combination of entrepreneurial and regulatory responsibilities has raised significant questions regarding the role of the state in tourism development, particularly in respect to its accountability to its entire constituency. Its entrepreneurial focus on Hanmer Springs creates a spatial asymmetry in funding and supporting tourism development in the region. This raises the question whether the regional state's role as entrepreneur in a wider environment of neoliberal governance is compatible with its responsibility for the wellbeing of all its population.

Neoliberal Variants

A number of contributions in this book illustrate that neoliberalism is not detached from local/regional/national contexts but, through particular neoliberal projects, is embedded within these contexts. Cahill (2011) argues that three mechanisms embed neoliberalism in society. First, it is embedded institutionally and most notably within state institutions. Although roll-back neoliberalism has resulted in a *laissez-faire* strategy of national governments (reduced state involvement), during the roll-out phase of neoliberalism states have had a vital role in neoliberalization by implementing, reproducing and extending the reach of neoliberalism. Second, neoliberalism has been embedded discursively as it has become the dominant political-economic discourse in many societies and as some political actors have actively stifled alternative discourses. Yet, the neoliberal discourse is itself highly differentiated, as the ideology of neoliberalism is adapted to correspond to local cultures and histories. Third, it is embedded within the political-economic relationships between the state, the economy and society. These relationships may be interpreted along structural inequalities such as class (see Hall, 2011), gender, labour, or other social inequalities.

Brenner and Theodore (2002), therefore, make the distinction between wider neoliberal ideology, the ideal type neoliberalism, and 'actually existing neoliberalism', determined by path-dependency and adapted to local contexts. A context-specific view that is supported by Barnett (2005: 8): " ... 'neoliberalism' arrives differently in different places, combining with other processes to produce distinctive manifestations of what, nevertheless, remain varieties of a single genus". Neoliberalization is therefore context-specific and the articulation of the neoliberal ideology and its practices depend on the " ... interactions between inherited regulatory landscapes and emergent neoliberal, market-oriented restructuring projects ... " (Brenner and Theodore, 2002: 351). For instance, Ioannides and Petriadou (Chapter 2) argue that the mixed results of this strategy (successes and failures) point to the context-specific aspects of neoliberal projects or contingent neoliberalism. These contingent contexts include path dependent institutional arrangements and specific local histories that coalesce to produce a combination of specific governance models, social fabric as well as cultural history for tourist consumption. This combination of a neoliberal project (the transformation of city-centres to further increase economic growth and urban development) with local culture and social fabric turn these neo-bohemia neighbourhoods into the antithesis of cloned inner-city developments and render urban neoliberalization processes much more 'opaque' (Ioannides and Petriadou Chapter 2). It is therefore important to analyse the interactions between path-dependency and neoliberal practices, institutions and discourses in order to understand the materialization of neoliberalism in a particular place.

Scherle and Pillmayer (Chapter 5), in their chapter on the special economic zone in Jordan, offer an analysis of the context-specific implementation of neoliberalization in a rentier economy, in which capital is accumulated due to the shortage of resources rather than due to production. The Hashemite Kingdom of Jordan attempted to boost tourism development in Aqaba by creating a special economic zone, which allows for the implementation of neoliberal policies in a particular confined space rather than across a nation state. Only in the special economic zone did the Kingdom deregulate its economy in order to attract foreign investment in order to create trickle down benefits for the population. Scherle and Pillmayer demonstrate the strategies employed to implement neoliberal policies in Aqaba and highlight the (re)construction of a new business culture within a wider rentier economic culture. The Special Economic Zone Aqaba was partly a spatial outcome of close relations between the US and Jordan, which expanded from geopolitical relations into adopting a 'neoliberal experiment', spatially confined and differentiated from the rentier economy in the rest of Jordan. Yet, this case study reveals the complex interplay between economic policies and business culture as many small and medium-sized enterprises still operate according to a rent capitalist system and distrust the neoliberal policies adopted to increase tourism development in the special economic zone of Aqaba.

In the context of India, Hannam and Reddy (Chapter 6) analyse ecotourism policies through a political economic and historical lens. During neoliberalization, the state retained some elements of the colonial British Indian State (in particular the public service apparatus) and combined it with a neoliberal economic policy in line with structural adjustments as encouraged by global institutions such as the International Monetary Fund and the World Bank. Following Hannam and Diekmann (2011), they posit that path dependency has led to a unique neoliberal relationship between the state, business and society. Yet, Hannam and Reddy are keen to point out that this neoliberalization served to reinforce the unequal distribution of capital and opportunities across Indian society according to class and caste. Tourism was a key sector for the neoliberalization process and economic growth in India since the 1990s. Subsequently, ecotourism has been identified as a growth sector for tourism development. In a bid to increase the professionalism of ecotourism operations, the state in consultation with private business created Ecotourism Guidelines to regulate ecotourism operations, particularly in protected areas. Hannam and Reddy (Chapter 6) contend that ecotourism in itself is a global strategy to accumulate capital from natural resources. Thus, it is a model that is externally driven by global preferences making it often difficult to incorporate local needs into the management of ecotourist nature.

In another contribution to examine the neoliberalization of nature, Nyahunzvi (Chapter 7) analyses the impacts of commercialization of tourist services in Kruger National Park, South Africa. Due to a shrinking budget of the state institution managing national parks in South Africa and a neoliberal discourse that the conservation of nature should pay for itself, most service provision in Kruger National Park were commercialized. Within this process, the benefits to the various stakeholders, including the local communities were highlighted as a discursive practice to gather support and legitimize the neoliberalization project. This discursive framing of neoliberalization in the context of national parks is comparable to the uncritical packaging of ecotourism within a community development context (see Campbell et al., 2008). Nyahunzvi posits that this dominant discourse marginalizes a more critical point of view focussing on the structural inequalities inherent in nature conservation in rural South Africa which (re)produce poverty as well as the loss of biodiversity. The commercialization of certain services within the context of nature conservation leads to the expansion of markets and thus increases the neoliberalization of nature via the development of nature-based or eco-tourism (see Duffy, 2015).

Neoliberal Discourses

As discussed in the introductory chapter and apparent in the contributions following the introduction, neoliberalism has no fixed definition and is not a neutral term. Instead, it is discursively (re)constructed in the policy arena, the media and through political, economic and social practices. Language is thus instrumental in creating, controlling and disseminating certain narratives and discursive positions and in (re)producing the structural inequalities of neoliberal projects. In their contribution on the neoliberal projects of mega events, Hall and Wilson (Chapter 3) assert that the construction of the multi-purpose stadium in Dunedin for the

Rugby World Cup 2011 was accompanied by a discourse of social solidarity and national identity and a discourse of trickle down benefits as 'public good'.

Discourses exist in different constellations that " … are in contrast, strife and alliance with other (master) discourses as part of sociocultural and ideological changes and the pursuit of vested interests" (Petersen, 2007: 228). Hence, as powers shift, discourses about the relationship between the state, the market and wider society change and may re-surface over time. Contributions in cultural (Jessop, 2004) and poststructuralist political economy (Gibson-Graham, 2006, Mosedale, 2011) call for critical discourse analyses to inform political economic analyses in order to examine the shifts in the relationships between discursive positions. As demonstrated by Jóhannesson and Huijbens (2010) in a case study of tourism discourse during the 2008 economic crisis in Iceland, sudden crises may be occasions during which shifts in discourse occur.

Minnaert (Chapter 8) examines the shifting discourse concerning social tourism as an increasingly popular neoliberal ideology proscribes self-reliant citizens: each person must accept individual responsibility for his/her situation and take all opportunities presented in free markets. According to this political project, redistributive measures to support disadvantaged groups or individuals are deemed to be contributing to a dependency culture and are therefore only granted to those individuals that 'deserve' help because they are actively trying to improve their situation. As neoliberal ideas on welfare support permeate society, Minnaert demonstrates the changing discourses and relates these to policies regarding social tourism. She highlights that the rationale for providing social tourism initiatives has changed from being redistributive (eliminating the factors of inequality and social exclusion) to business-focussed (regenerating tourism economies e.g., by countering seasonality or "unlock[ing] suppressed demand" of 'deserving' individuals which also tend to have a higher ability to pay). Certain segments of the UK press have framed the discourse of social tourism as rewarding dependence on state support for those 'with a plasma screen television of less than 42 inch'. This popular discourse has surely been part of the reason for governments to shift towards a neoliberal interpretation of social tourism that is now more about regeneration measures for declining destinations than redistributive measures for the underprivileged.

Neoliberal Practices

Practices are important elements of neoliberal projects and may represent the enactment of neoliberal discourse. Practices are social in nature, influenced by a multitude of factors (economic, social, cultural etc.) and represent agency and produce structures such as firms, institutions, public-private partnerships etc. (Mosedale, 2012). This view of practices as being 'composite phenomena' requires a contextual analysis (Jones, 2008), which may shed light on 'actually existing neoliberalism', i.e. context-specific adaptations of the neoliberal ideology, which uncovers the interplay between structure and agency in a particular locality.

> ... neoliberal spaces and subjectivities are not simply imposed from above, nor is "resistance" simply a bottom-up political response to macro-level structural processes. Rather, new governmental spaces and subjects are emerging out of multiple and contested discourses and practices. Seen from this point of view, neoliberalism is likely to have many varied effects, and be subject to re-embedding contests in diverse, locally specific ways (Larner and Craig, 2005: 421).

Neoliberal outcomes, then, are "products of individual and collective practices in space and time that lead (in part) to tangible ... [neoliberal] effects and outcomes" (Jones, 2008: 79). In their contribution to this volume, Offeh and Hannam (Chapter 9) posit that the practice of institutional commodification in the production of heritage tourism souvenirs in Ghana is a manifestation of neoliberal policy discourse. Institutional commodification involves the reconfiguration of state-society relations for commercial exploitation rather than for regulation (i.e. public good). The previous institutional arrangements are reshaped to roll-out neoliberalization. Tourism development in Ghana was largely controlled by the public sector until the early 1990s; subsequently neoliberal roll-out provided a basis for institutional commodification. In their case study of souvenir production in the Ashanti Kingdom of Ghana, Offeh and Hannam argue that Ghana fits the model of institutional commodification as proposed by Wank (1999) for the state-supported, entrepreneurial shift towards a market economy in China. In the case of souvenir production in the Ashante Kingdom of Ghana, Offeh and Hannam contend that an initial demand of heritage cloth by tourists has led to state involvement (in conjunction with international aid agencies) in order to encourage the mass production of these heritage souvenirs with implications on the quality of materials. These changing practices promoted by government and international NGOs are altering weaving practices (i.e. the use of machinery), the perceived authenticity of these working practices and subsequently the cultural identity of cloth weavers. The creation of associations and government-controlled cultural or art centres has increased the barriers to entry into the production of heritage souvenirs making it difficult for young people to gain entry to heritage souvenir production. This example demonstrates active state intervention (in contradiction to the neoliberal free market discourse) to support further marketization of heritage souvenir production and the importance of practices to the implementation of the wider neoliberal project. Yet social practices may also contest the dominant neoliberal discourse by either presenting post-neoliberal possibilities of new regimes of accumulation and matching modes of regulation or, at least, by carving out space for alternative practices within a largely neoliberal environment.

Alternative Imaginaries

Challenging the hegemonic discourse of neoliberal ideology and recognizing alternative discourses, as well as practices, is a first step towards creating alternative political-economic imaginaries. Not only does a discursive analysis identify the discourse of hegemonic policy projects by bringing to the fore the regulation and marginalization of other, alternative discourses, a critical discourse analysis provides space for these other discourses, their manifestation in practices and thus alternative imaginaries (Aitchison, 2001). Critical discourse analysis would greatly contribute to the political economy of tourism by enhancing our understanding of the discursive strategies used to reproduce political projects and would provide opportunities for discussing alternative projects.

Yet, although the characteristics of neoliberalism include an increasing marketization and commodification of social practices (see Mosedale Chapter 1), many social practices remain outside of profit-motivated capitalist transactions (Williams, 2005). These alternative ways of performing alternative or diverse economies (Mosedale, 2011, 2012) often incorporate a different set of values based on other moral foundations (Higgins-Desboilles, 2011, Butcher, 2005). These moral foundations, which do not focus on the accumulation of wealth as ultimate social goal and aspiration, need to be the basis for non-neoliberal imaginaries. However, such 'decentring' of neoliberalism (Leitner et al., 2007) requires an awareness of the complex relationships between imaginaries, political projects and institutions in local socio-cultural contexts.

In their contribution to the volume, Wearing and Wearing (Chapter 10) discuss the concept of decommodification in the context of ecotourism as a socio-political practice to counter the prevalence of neoliberal thought and as a strategy to counter the expansion of market relations to all kinds of social relations. They use examples from Sweden, Australia, New Zealand, Peru and Vietnam to demonstrate spaces of agency that allow, on the one hand, the contestation of neoliberal projects and, on the other hand, alternative (in this case decommodified) ways of developing and engaging in ecotourism. Such examples serve as reminders that there is space for different economic practices following different sets of values and socio-political ideologies. They further extend their discussion of decommodification to include social justice in the (re)distribution of capital, the recognition of cultural identities and their associated rights concerning their ways of life and the natural/cultural capital relationship in order to counter institutional commodification (see Offeh and Hannam, Chapter 9).

Another alternative imaginary is the concept of de-growth, which challenges the unsustainable, neoliberal agenda of continued growth, commercialization and marketization and offers an alternative steady-state economy. "Growth does not equal development" (Hall, 2010: 140) and the cost and benefits of tourism need to be carefully considered in relation to economic growth but also in terms of the impacts on resources (natural, cultural, social) that tourism depends on. Hall (2010) posits that following ready-state tourism, all associated costs should be taken into account and borne by the tourist. Such a strategy is likely to have a profound effect on local, regional and global tourist flows and consumption patterns (see Voll and Mosedale 2014 for the potential effects of increased oil prices on tourist mobility in the European Alps). A discussion of alternative imaginaries should therefore incorporate further studies on the possible outcomes of these alternatives as they are likely to be place-specific and affect actors to varying degrees. Critical political economy studies will continue to play an important role in challenging tourism policies, tourism development, discourses and practices.

This book aimed to offer an initial collection of contributions with a focus on neoliberalism and tourism. As such, it was not feasible to provide a detailed analysis of the various angles that could be explored within the neoliberal ideology and the complex projects that are constituted of and manifested in distinct political-economic relationships between institutional landscapes and sets of discourses and practices. That each author has taken a slightly different perspective on and definition of neoliberalism demonstrates the varied nature of the concept. Nevertheless, this book contributes to the study of neoliberalism and tourism in three ways: First, it has emphasized that the manifestation of neoliberalism is context-specific and that despite a set of guiding characteristics, there is no single neoliberal design. Instead, neoliberal strategies are affixed to pre-existing political-economic histories and institutional landscapes thus creating neoliberal variants, contingent neoliberalism or "actually existing neoliberalism" (Brenner and Theodore (2002). The different case studies in this edited collection (US, New Zealand, South Africa, India, Ghana, Jordan) and the conceptual contributions drawing on various examples provide readers with examples of different contextual neoliberalization processes with different relationships between governments, private business and wider society and hence diverse outcomes.

Second, some of the contributions have analysed how neoliberal discourses (in the case of social tourism, also played out in the popular press) may frame particular neoliberal projects and may provide opportunities for the implementation of neoliberal strategies and practices, while at the same time regulating and marginalizing non-neoliberal discourses and possibilities. This is one field of research in tourism studies that requires more in-depth analysis in order to understand how discourses are formed, reproduced and how alternative discourses are side-lined and rebuffed. Critical discourse analyses of neoliberal tourism developments, policies and practices would greatly contribute to the political economy of tourism by enhancing our understanding of the discursive strategies used to reproduce political projects. Such analyses of discourse, as highlighted by Gibson-Graham (2006), would, on the one hand, reveal neoliberal discursive strategies and practices and, on the other hand, highlight the diversity of neoliberal and counter-discourses thus offering space for alternative imaginaries.

Third, these alternative imaginaries need to be discussed and analysed in order to determine their suitability either as a counter-flanking mechanism or as a new combination of regime of accumulation and mode of regulation. Alternatives to neoliberalization need to become legitimate political options as some of the destructive outcomes of the neoliberalization process are highlighted. The questions remain in what way tourism actors (tourists, workers, entrepreneurs, businesses, institutions etc.) can engage in alternative practices, such as social innovation and entrepreneurship.

The contributing authors to this volume have highlighted various aspects of the neoliberalization process as it influences and involves tourism. In the face of increasing neoliberalization and constricting neoliberal discourses, it is imperative to undertake further studies of neoliberalism as a political-economic process in order to provide a comprehensive and detailed analysis of its effects on tourism in particular temporal and geographic contexts. The contributions to this book constitute a collection of chapters covering an array of different case studies and perspectives on neoliberalism and form a foundation for further investigation of the relationship between tourism and neoliberalism.

References

Aitchison, C. (2001). Theorizing other discourses of tourism, gender and culture: Can the subaltern speak (in tourism)? *Tourist Studies*, 1(2), 133–47.

Barnett, C. (2005). The consolations of 'neoliberalism'. *Geoforum*, 36(1), 7–12.

Brenner, N. and Theodore, N. (2002). Cities and the geographies of "actually existing neoliberalism". *Antipode*, 34(3), 349–79.

Butcher, J. (2005). *The Moralisation of Tourism: Sun, Sand ... and Saving the World?* London: Routledge.

Cahill, D. (2011). Beyond neoliberalism? Crisis and the prospects for progressive alternatives. *New Political Science*, 33(4), 479–92.

Church, A., Ball, R., Bull, C., and Tyler, D. (2000). Public policy engagement with British tourism: The national, local and the European Union. *Tourism Geographies*, 2(3), 312–36.

Duffy, R. (2008). Neoliberalising nature: Global networks and ecotourism development in Madagascar, *Journal of Sustainable Tourism*, 16(3), 327–44.

Duffy, R. (2015). Nature-based tourism and neoliberalism: Concealing contradictions. *Tourism Geographies*, 17(4), 529–43.

Gibson-Graham, J-K. (2006). *The End of Capitalism (as we knew it): A Feminist Critique of Political Economy*. Minneapolis: University of Minnesota Press.

Gray, N.J. and Campbell, L.M. (2007). A decommodified experience? Exploring aesthetic, economic and ethical values for volunteer ecotourism in Costa Rica. *Journal of Sustainable Tourism*, 15(5), 463–82.

Hall, C.M. (2011). Yes, Virginia: There is a tourism class: Why class still matters in tourism analysis. In J. Mosedale (ed.) *Political Economy of Tourism: A Critical Perspective*. Abingdon: Routledge, pp. 111–26.

Hannam, K. and Diekmann, A. (2011). *Tourism and India*. London: Routledge.

Higgins-Desbiolles, F. (2011). Resisting the hegemony of the market: Reclaiming the social capacities of tourism. In S. McCabe, L. Minnaert and A. Diekmann (eds) *Social Tourism in Europe: Theory and Practice*. Bristol: Channel View Publications, 53–68.

Jessop, B. (2004). Critical semiotic analysis and cultural political economy. *Critical Discourse Studies*, 1(2), 159–74.

Jóhannesson, G.T. and Huijbens, E.H. (2010). Tourism in times of crisis: Exploring the discourse of tourism development in Iceland. *Current Issues in Tourism*, 13(5), 419–34.

Jones, A. (2008). Beyond embeddedness: Economic practices and the invisible dimensions of transnational business activity. *Progress in Human Geography*, 32(1), 71–88.

Larner, W. and Craig, D. (2005). After neoliberalism? Community activism and local partnerships in Aotearoa New Zealand. *Antipode*, 37(3), 402–24.

Leitner, H., Sheppard, E.S., Sziarto, K. and Maringanti, A. (2007) Contesting urban futures: Decentering neoliberalism. In H. Leitner, J. Peck and E.S. Sheppard (2007). *Contesting Neoliberalism: Urban Frontiers*. New York and London: Guilford Press, 1–25.

Mosedale, J. (2011). Thinking outside the box: Alternative political economies in tourism. In J. Mosedale (ed.) *Political Economy of Tourism: A Critical Perspective*. Abingdon: Routledge, pp. 93–108.

Mosedale, J. (2012). Diverse economies and alternative economic practices in tourism. In N. Morgan, I. Ateljevic and A. Pritchard (eds) *The Critical Turn in Tourism Studies: Creating an Academy of Hope*. London and New York: Routledge. pp. 194–207.

Mosedale, J. (2014) Political economy of tourism: Regulation theory, institutions and governance networks. In C.M. Hall, A.A. Lew and A.M. Williams (eds) *The Wiley-Blackwell Companion to Tourism*. Oxford: Wiley-Blackwell, 55–65.

Petersen, L.K. (2007). Changing public discourse on the environment: Danish media coverage of the Rio and Johannesburg UN summits. *Environmental Politics*, 16(2), 206–30.

Voll, F. and Mosedale, J. (2014) Postfossiler Tourismus: Realität oder Utopie in der Regionalpolitik der Alpenstaaten? In R. Egger and K. Luger (eds) *Tourismus und mobile Freizeit: Lebensformen, Trends, Herausforderungen*. BoD, 351–65.

Williams, C.C. (2005). *A Commodified World? Mapping the Limits of Capitalism*. Zed Books.

Index

Printed in the United States
by Baker & Taylor Publisher Services